EUROPEAN STRATEGY IN THE 21ST CENTURY

This book argues that Europe, through the European Union (EU), should act as a great power in the 21st century.

The course of world politics is determined by the interaction between great powers. Those powers are the US, the established power; Russia, the declining power; China, the rising power; and the EU, the power that doesn't know whether it wants to be a power. If the EU does not just want to undergo the policies of the other powers it will have to become one itself, but it should differ in its strategy. In this book, Sven Biscop seeks to demonstrate that the EU has the means to pursue a distinctive great power strategy, a middle way between dreamy idealism and unprincipled pragmatism, and can play a crucial stabilising role in this increasingly unstable world.

Written by a leading scholar, this book will be of much interest to students of European security, EU policy, strategic studies, and international relations.

Sven Biscop is a Professor at Ghent University, Belgium, and the Director of the Europe in the World Programme at the Egmont – Royal Institute for International Relations in Brussels. He is a Senior Research Associate at the People's University of China in Beijing and an Honorary Fellow of the European Security and Defence College (ESDC).

ROUTLEDGE STUDIES IN EUROPEAN SECURITY AND STRATEGY

The aim of this series is to bring together the key experts on European security from the academic and policy worlds, and assess the state of play of the EU as an international security actor. The series explores the EU, and its member states, security policy and practices in a changing global and regional context. While the focus is on the politico-military dimension, security is put in the context of the holistic approach advocated by the EU.

Series editors:
Sven Biscop
Egmont Royal Institute for International Relations, Belgium
and
Richard Whitman
University of Kent, UK

European Union Military Operations
A Collective Action Perspective
Niklas I.M. Nováky

The EU, Strategy and Security Policy
Regional and strategic challenges
Edited by Laura Chappell, Jocelyn Mawdsley and Petar Petrov

Europeanisation and the Transformation of EU Security Policy
Post-Cold War Developments in the Common Security and Defence Policy
Petros Violakis

EU-Japan Security Cooperation
Trends and Prospects
Edited by Emil Kirchner and Han Dorussen

European Strategy in the 21st Century
New Future for Old Power
Sven Biscop

For more information about this series, please visit: https://www.routledge.com/Routledge-Studies-in-European-Security-and-Strategy/book-series/SESS

EUROPEAN STRATEGY IN THE 21ST CENTURY

New Future for Old Power

Sven Biscop

LONDON AND NEW YORK

First published 2019
by Routledge
2 Park Square, Milton Park, Abingdon, Oxon OX14 4RN

and by Routledge
52 Vanderbilt Avenue, New York, NY 10017

Routledge is an imprint of the Taylor & Francis Group, an informa business

© 2019 Sven Biscop

The right of Sven Biscop to be identified as author of this work has been asserted by him in accordance with sections 77 and 78 of the Copyright, Designs and Patents Act 1988.

All rights reserved. No part of this book may be reprinted or reproduced or utilised in any form or by any electronic, mechanical, or other means, now known or hereafter invented, including photocopying and recording, or in any information storage or retrieval system, without permission in writing from the publishers.

Trademark notice: Product or corporate names may be trademarks or registered trademarks, and are used only for identification and explanation without intent to infringe.

British Library Cataloguing in Publication Data
A catalogue record for this book is available from the British Library

Library of Congress Cataloging-in-Publication Data
Names: Biscop, Sven, author.
Title: European strategy in the 21st
century : new future for old power / Sven Biscop.
Description: Abingdon, Oxon ; New York, NY : Routledge, 2019. |
Series: Routledge studies in European security and strategy |
Includes bibliographical references and index.
Identifiers: LCCN 2018036535 (print) | LCCN 2018047895 (ebook) |
ISBN 9780429764004 (Web PDF) | ISBN 9780429763991 (ePub) |
ISBN 9780429763984 (Mobi) | ISBN 9781138384712 (hardback) |
ISBN 9781138384729 (pbk.) | ISBN 9780429427442 (e-book)
Subjects: LCSH: European Union countries–Politics and government–21st century. | European Union countries–Foreign relations–21st century. | Security, International–European Union countries.
Classification: LCC JN30 (ebook) | LCC JN30 .B58 2019 (print) |
DDC 355/.03354–dc23LC record available at https://lccn.loc.gov/2018036535

ISBN: 978-1-138-38471-2 (hbk)
ISBN: 978-1-138-38472-9 (pbk)
ISBN: 978-0-429-42744-2 (ebk)

Typeset in Bembo
by Taylor & Francis Books

To my mentor and friend, Rik Coolsaet

CONTENTS

Acknowledgements	*viii*
List of abbreviations	*x*

	Introduction	1
1	Values and geopolitics: Europe is who and where it is	5
2	Strategy: what can Europe do, what does Europe want?	21
3	Europe and the (other) great powers	37
4	Europe and its neighbours	67
5	Europe, military power, and NATO	82
6	European defence and maybe even a European army	112
7	Brexit, strategy, and the EU: Britain takes leave	126
8	Conclusion: which Europe are we doing this for?	138

Index   *147*

ACKNOWLEDGEMENTS

If we as academics produce a text on a topic that cannot be understood by the politician, diplomat or official who actually works on the issue, it's probably not a good text. "Life is short, and those who will not take the trouble to write clearly cannot properly expect to be read" (Trevor-Roper, 2014, p. 139). This is what at the start of every academic year I tell the students who are considering writing their master's thesis under my supervision. I say that because it is my firm conviction that political science cannot be "l'art pour l'art": art for art's sake. I too long for "an era when social science was not yet hampered by impenetrable theories and methods or obscure postmodernist critique but instead sought to unveil the patterns of history and contemporary events in ways that would provide usable insights for policy" (Green, 2017, p. 170). For me, the point of political science is indeed to say something useful for the people that are engaged in politics: politicians, officials, and citizens. I hope that this is what I have managed with this book.

It is an enormous pleasure and a great honour to be able to dedicate this book to my mentor and friend, Rik Coolsaet. It is Rik, now emeritus professor at Ghent University, who taught me how a researcher can usefully contribute to the political debate. It is Rik, who at Ghent University in 2002 sat on the jury for the defence of my PhD, who subsequently hired me at the Egmont–Royal Institute for International Relations in Brussels, the think tank associated with the Belgian Ministry of Foreign Affairs. In January 2009 I succeeded him there as director of the Europe in the World programme. In October 2016, also in succession of Rik, I became a part-time professor at Ghent University. Trying to do only half of what he did for the university and for the public debate is already a major challenge. Having Rik for a mentor is worth a lot. Having him for a friend is priceless. Thank you, Rik.

Rik has directly contributed to this book as well. Many of my ideas have matured by discussing them, notably with Rik, and with three other close friends: Brigadier-General (Ret.) Jo Coelmont, a senior associate fellow at Egmont (who read the first draft of the original Dutch-language version of this book), Prof. Dr. Alexander Mattelaer, director of the Europe programme at Egmont and professor at the Vrije Universiteit Brussel (VUB), and Prof. Dr. Luis Simón, director of the Brussels office of the "Spanish Egmont", Real Instituto Elcano, and also a professor at the VUB. With them I can have conversations that I can have with nobody else. We work together so closely, effectively thinking together, that I dare no longer say which idea originated with whom. In any case, never trust a professor who claims to have thought it all up by himself. I also want to thank all other academic colleagues, in Belgium and abroad, therefore, as well as all Belgian, European, and other diplomats, officials, and military officers who were willing to share their insights with me. More often than not over a good glass or a good meal – as Talleyrand said, "Les bons diners font des bons dépêches" (de Waresquiel, 2006).

I want to thank my two employers, the Egmont Institute and Ghent University, for having given me the opportunity to turn my passion for strategy, in the broadest sense of the term, into my profession. I'd also like to thank them for allowing me the flexibility to organise my own work, so that I could dedicate time to writing this book. Professors can whine and moan as well as anybody else, but in the end we are very privileged, because our job gives us the chance to think and write about whatever we want. For that reason the Belgian Foreign Ministry has earned my gratitude as well, for purposely subsidising an independent think tank like Egmont.

Finally, I thank my sweet husband, Aberu. As the whole world is focussing more and more on Asia, in 2012 he left Asia (more specifically, Taipei, the capital of Taiwan), to move to Belgium and marry me. (I am proud, by the way, that after the Netherlands, Belgium was the second country in the world where a man and a man or a woman and a woman can get married – occasionally, Belgium works better than one thinks.) Aberu's first visit to Belgium had amounted to two and a half weeks of rain in August 2011, and still when I proposed he said yes – that must be true love. More than Aberu realises, he contributes to my academic work. He continuously surprises me with his views on world politics, views I hadn't thought of myself. With Mandarin as his native and Japanese as his second language, he follows many news channels that I cannot access, which makes me realise time and again how one-sided the European view can be. At home in Brussels, we speak English, and since arriving in Belgium he has also learned French. But he couldn't read the first, Dutch-language edition of this book, which is why I translated it into English. And to conquer the world market, perhaps. But only as an afterthought, of course.

References

Emmanuel de Waresquiel, *Talleyrand. Le prince immobile*. Paris, Fayard, 2006.
Michael J. Green, *By More than Providence – Grand Strategy and American Power in the Asia Pacific since 1783*. New York, Columbia University Press, 2017.
Hugh Trevor-Roper, *One Hundred Letters. Edited by Richard Davenport-Hines & Adam Sisman*. Oxford, Oxford University Press, 2014.

LIST OF ABBREVIATIONS

A2/AD	Anti-Access/Area Denial
ACT	Allied Command Transformation
AIIB	Asian Infrastructure Investment Bank
APEC	Asia-Pacific Economic Cooperation
AWACS	Airborne Warning and Control System
BRI	Belt and Road Initiative
BRICS	Brazil, Russia, India, China and South-Africa
CBSD	Capacity-Building for Security and Development
CCP	Chinese Communist Party
CETA	Comprehensive Economic and Trade Agreement
CFSP	Common Foreign and Security Policy
CIA	Central Intelligence Agency
CJEF	Combined Joint Expeditionary Force
CSDP	Common Security and Defence Policy
EAEU	Eurasian Economic Union
EaP	Eastern Partnership
EATC	European Air Transport Command
ECSC	European Coal and Steel Community
ECU	European Currency Unit
EDA	European Defence Agency
EDC	European Defence Community
EDF	European Defence Fund
EEAS	European External Action Service
EEC	European Economic Community
ENP	European Neighbourhood Policy
ESDC	European Security and Defence College
EU	European Union
EUGS	European Union Global Strategy

EUMS	European Union Military Staff
EUTM	European Union Training Mission
FAC	Foreign Affairs Council
FBI	Federal Bureau of Investigation
FCAS	Future Combat Air System
FPS	Federal Public Service
FTA	Free Trade Agreement
GCC	Gulf Cooperation Council
GDP	Gross Domestic Product
GNP	Gross National Product
ICBM	Intercontinental Ballistic Missile
IS	Islamic State
ISTAR	Intelligence, Surveillance, Target Acquisition, and Reconnaissance
JEF	Joint Expeditionary Force
LGBT	Lesbian, Gay, Bisexual, and Transgender
MEP	Member of the European Parliament
MINUSMA	United Nations Multidimensional Integrated Stabilization Mission in Mali
MIT	Massachusetts Institute of Technology
MP	Member of Parliament
MPCC	Military Planning and Conduct Capacity
NAFTA	North American Free Trade Agreement
NATO	North Atlantic Treaty Organisation
NDPP	NATO Defence Planning Process
NGO	Non-Governmental Organisation
OBOR	One Belt, One Road
PESCO	Permanent Structured Cooperation
PRC	People's Republic of China
R2P	Responsibility to Protect
Ret.	Retired
SACEUR	Supreme Allied Commander Europe
SHAPE	Supreme Headquarters Allied Powers Europe
THAAD	Terminal High Altitude Area Defense
TPP	Trans-Pacific Partnership
UGent	Universiteit Gent
UK	United Kingdom
UKIP	United Kingdom Independence Party
UN	United Nations
UNCLOS	United Nations Convention on the Law of the Sea
UNIFIL	United Nations Interim Force in Lebanon
US	United States
USSR	Union of Socialist Soviet Republics
VUB	Vrije Universiteit Brussel

INTRODUCTION

International politics is not about charity, a Chinese diplomat once told me. Or rather, two Chinese diplomats, for such is the case with many authoritarian regimes; Chinese diplomats are not allowed to invite someone for lunch just by themselves – they might just say something that goes against the party line.[1] The Chinese colleague was talking about Chinese investment overseas. Beijing is not simply showing off its benevolence: its investment is very targeted, in view of clearly defined interests. Not just its economic interests, but its overall strategic interests, including the political and security as well as the economic dimension – obviously.

And yet at this stage many European readers will have started to frown, because we in Europe have managed to convince ourselves that we no longer do this kind of thing. In bygone days, yes, when Britain and France still had empires and even my own country, Belgium, had a colony. In those days we too played power politics and pursued our interests without any inhibitions. But since the states of Europe united themselves in the European Union (EU), we pretend that its Common Foreign and Security Policy (CFSP) serves only to make the world a better place, as if the Union were nothing but a huge NGO. In our domestic politics we find it self-evident that all kinds of interest groups do just that: promote their interests. But in foreign policy we have almost begun to consider interests a dirty word. Many times have I sat in debates when someone criticised Europeans for intervening somewhere because that was in their interest. Would you rather that we intervene – and spend tax payers' money and put our diplomats' and military's lives at risk – when it is against our interest, was my usual reply.

Of course foreign, security and defence policy is about interests, just like any other policy. That is neither good nor bad – it is the essence of what policy is. Evidently, there are good and bad ways of *pursuing* those interests. One country will secure its interests by cooperating with its neighbours, another by invading them and grabbing their territory. But that it is about interests is self-evident to everyone – except to us in Europe.

True, foreign policy is not determined by interests alone – values play a part as well. The first rule of making policy is: know thyself. For whom am I writing policy? The answer to that question lies in Europe's values, which determine the model of society that we have built. For that society, that "European way of life" (to put it in American terms) to continue to exist, a number of conditions have to be fulfilled. Those are our vital interests, in the political, economic and security sphere, which guarantee the very survival of our system. The next step is to look at the world around Europe and to assess whether any events or developments may threaten those vital interests. Choices then have to be made: which are the priority problems that require a response first, in a reactive as well as in a preventive manner. Good policy does not only aim to solve, but also to prevent problems. For every priority, objectives have to be formulated (what do we want to achieve), instruments chosen (how do we want to do that) and means allocated (what are we willing to spend to that end). Here values come in again: not all objectives and instruments are legitimate, only those that are consistent with our values.

This is what one can call the grand strategy of a state, or of a group of states like the EU. A foreign, security and defence policy integrating all instruments, from aid and trade to diplomacy and defence, in order to safeguard one's vital interests. Whereas our values determine which kind of grand strategy is acceptable and which is not, our interests decide what our strategy needs to address in the first place.

Once adopted, it takes power to implement strategy: the political, economic, and military power to entice, to convince, and, if necessary, to coerce others to act according to our interests. Again many Europeans will be frowning now. Because we forget all the time that what is in our interest, can at the same time be in the interest of others. Interests may, but do not have to be mutually exclusive. A smart strategist will seek to create win-win situations, so that he can protect his interests without creating tensions, and without the need to use his power coercively. That is why soft power is so important: the attractiveness of our model of society, which will predispose others to look at us, and our strategy, in a benign way. Sometimes, however, coercion will be inevitable, by threatening or using hard economic power (sanctions and embargoes) or, exceptionally, military force, if there is no other way to guarantee our vital interests.

Has Europe, the old power, forgotten what power is? That question is the starting point of this book. Europeans are no longer used to looking at the world through the strategic process that I have just outlined. We no longer systematically think about strategy, about what our objectives should be, and about how we can use our power to achieve them. Even when lecturing for diplomats and officers from EU Member States and institutions, as I regularly do,[2] I often get the question: is strategy really necessary? The answer must be: "the need for strategy never sleeps!" (Gray, 2016, p. 29). Europe still has enormous power potential: the EU is the world's biggest economy, it has the most egalitarian society, and except for the

US it spends the most on defence. But we have forgotten the importance of power, so we don't behave as a power. That holds true for most European states, and certainly for the EU as such. The EU is the political centre of gravity of Europe, but it carries little weight in the world. Others don't see Europe as a power and therefore don't treat it as one.

That is not without risk, for many other states do know what power is, and don't hesitate to use it, including their military power, to pursue their interests. That certainly applies to the great powers, i.e. the powers with global reach: the US, China, and Russia. But it holds true for many regional powers as well, such as Iran, Saudi Arabia and Turkey. That does not mean that they are always successful, but it does mean that they know very well what it is that they want. Furthermore, the balance of power is shifting. From the bipolar Cold War, when there were just two super powers, followed by a brief unipolar period in which the US seemed to be the only remaining super power, we have now clearly arrived in a multipolar age, in which various great powers are at the same time competing and cooperating, in varying constellations, according to the issue at hand. Such a world order inevitably carries a great risk of conflict. The declining great power (Russia), the fast rising great power (China), and the great power that sees its position threatened by that rise (the US) might all opt for a drastic course of action. Not to mention the conflict potential between regional powers (such as Iran and Saudi Arabia, who are contesting dominance of the Gulf region). "Where there is actual or potential conflict, when interests collide and forms of resolution are required", then strategy really comes into play (Freedman, 2013, p. xi).

If the states of Europe do not just want to undergo all of this, but want to actively shape the world, in order notably to play a stabilising role, then they can only do so together, as the EU or at least as a core group within it. For several years now, the EU has not exactly been in good shape, but no single European state today can hope to influence world politics in any significant way. That is why in this book I will mostly talk about the EU, as the only way in which Europe too can be a great power. However, the EU should not do so at the price of abandoning our unique egalitarian model of society, and not by each and every means. Europe should not aspire to become a great power just like the others. Europe can play a distinctive part in the world, which respects the values on which our own society is based and promotes them in the rest of the world. But only if it learns again how to use its power, which it still has. To quote former President of the European Commission Jacques Delors: the biggest intellectual mistake of our time is that we have begun to mistake our humanitarian aid for our foreign policy.[3]

Notes

1 On my first visit to China after I drafted these lines, a Chinese academic actually made the exact same joke about the North Koreans, which goes to show that everything is relative.
2 Mostly in the framework of the European Security and Defence College (ESDC), an EU agency that organises courses on EU foreign and defence policy for diplomats, military officers and officials.

3 Delors was referring in specific to Europe's incapacity to end the civil war in former Yugoslavia in the early 1990s (Servent, 2017, p. 226).

References

Lawrence Freedman, *Strategy*. Oxford, Oxford University Press, 2013.
Colin S. Gray, *Strategy and Politics*. Abingdon, Routledge, 2016.
Pierre Servent, *Les présidents et la guerre: Une enquête inédite au cœur de la défense*. Paris, Perrin, 2017.

1

VALUES AND GEOPOLITICS

Europe is who and where it is

Knowing how to do something is not the same as knowing what one is doing. The former is tactics; the latter is strategy. Unfortunately, perfect tactical implementation will not produce results if the strategy is wrong. The way the EU stumbled into the Ukraine crisis perfectly illustrates the difference between the two concepts.

Ukraine: how not to do things

Once the EU had decided on a far-reaching trade agreement with Ukraine, the big machinery of the European Commission got into gear to manage the complex technical negotiations. Everything was done perfectly according to the manual, for the officials of the Directorate-General for Trade are professionals who know their brief inside out. The question should probably have been asked whether Ukraine was ready, given the state of its political and economic development, to conclude such a deal, which requires adopting an enormous amount of existing EU rules and regulations. But once the Commission got started, not a single mistake was made. Except for the one catastrophic mistake to wage these negotiations as if they were taking place in a strategic and geopolitical void, as if it were a mere technical matter, that could easily be left to the technicians. In reality this was an eminently political issue.

Russia did not see the trade negotiations as a technical matter at all, but as a geopolitical challenge on the part of the EU. In Russian eyes, the EU, using its economic power, was engineering the encroachment of "the West" into yet another former Soviet republic, after successive waves of enlargement had already brought the EU and NATO very close to the Russian border. For Russian president Vladimir Putin therefore this could never be a win-win situation. His strategic view meant (and means) that he is engaged in a zero-sum game with the

West: whatever the EU or NATO wins, Russia loses. For Putin's objective is to create a sphere of influence in the countries of the former Soviet Union. A sphere of influence implies exclusivity: it means that in that region Putin wants Russia to be the only power. Whether it wanted to or not (and it was probably the latter, as the EU had simply not thought about the geopolitical context), Brussels had thus entered into a geopolitical competition with Moscow. For which, obviously, it did not have a strategy.

The next part of the story is well known. Russia began to exert enormous pressure on Ukrainian president Viktor Yanukovych, who in November 2013 gave in and suspended the negotiations with the EU. That directly led to an escalation of the domestic political turmoil. Ukraine was a very divided country: if the western half rather looked to Brussels, the eastern half was mostly oriented on Moscow. One should never have forced the country to choose between those two orientations. Imagine what would be the result if someone would oblige my own bilingual country, Belgium, to either have relations with France or with the Netherlands, but not with both – of course that would lead to a crisis. Crisis is what we got in Ukraine, symbolised by the massive demonstrations on Maidan Square in Kiev, which in February 2014 caused the fall of the president, after which the opposition came into power.

Thereupon Russia, seeing all its influence in Ukraine disappear in a bang, overreacted. That same month Russian regular troops began to occupy the Crimean peninsula; on 18 March 2014 it was formally annexed to Russia. Also in March, separatist rebels in the east of Ukraine, in the Donbass region around the cities of Donetsk and Lugansk, launched an armed uprising against the central government in Kiev, with Russian military support in the form of arms and equipment and irregular forces (the so-called "little green men"). The EU (and the US) reacted by imposing sanctions. That was followed by Russian military posturing on its borders with the EU and NATO, whereupon NATO prepositioned additional forces in the Baltic States and Poland.

The situation in Ukraine has been completely blocked ever since. Relations between the EU and Russia have been frozen (though Europeans continue to consume Russian energy). The EU faces a moral dilemma. On the one hand, it has encouraged the Ukrainian opposition. For many Europeans politicians, the temptation to mingle with demonstrators waving EU flags before the eyes of the world media proved irresistible. It was encouraging, of course, to see that at least somebody could still muster enthusiasm for the EU – one would want to see more of that inside the EU itself. But when, as a consequence of us prodding Ukraine to seek closer relations with the EU, it got into trouble with Russia, our willingness to help Ukraine was limited. Nobody is going to start a war with Russia over Ukraine. Rightly so, but that has left Ukraine very disappointed with the West, from which it had expected a lot more military assistance than it got.

I have been able to see that for myself several times when speaking at an annual seminar at the National Defence University in Kiev, at the invitation of the EU, for an audience of a few hundred Ukrainian military officers. In any case, by telling there what I'm writing down here, I have not made myself very popular with those officers, who were already eying me suspiciously from under their huge peaked caps from the start. It is better for everybody, however, to be honest and dispel any false expectations.

Meanwhile there clearly is a lot of Ukraine fatigue in Brussels already. We are stuck with Ukraine now. Because of the Russian aggression, the country is now facing westward, hence it is our duty to put it on the right track. But in a huge country that is lagging behind in so many ways, that duty is proving to be a huge political and economic challenge. Reforms are proceeding very slowly indeed. One of the main problems is illustrated by the posters that are to be seen around Kiev airport: "Ukraine says no to corruption". Which means there must be a bit of a problem with corruption, or those posters would not be necessary.

The Russian strategy to create an exclusive sphere of influence in the countries of the former Soviet Union predates the Ukraine crisis. In 2008 already there was a war between Russia and Georgia, which was moving far too close to the West to Russia's taste. That war led to two territories, South Ossetia and Abkhazia, breaking away from Georgia; only Russia recognises them as independent states. That gives an idea of what might be the future of the Donbass. Tensions with Russia were probably inevitable therefore, except if the EU had reduced relations with all of its eastern neighbours to a minimum, to the benefit of Russia. That was never going to happen, if only because many of those countries are themselves seeking close relations with the EU. But if it hadn't been for the EU's precipitation towards Ukraine and its well-nigh unconscious, a-strategic use of its economic power, we might not have found ourselves in such a severe crisis with Russia. The comparison with those sleepwalking into World War One is not that far-fetched (Clark, 2012).

Strategic thinking is important – that must be the first conclusion from the Ukraine crisis. What other lessons can the EU learn from it? And what do those lessons mean for the EU's self-perception?

Blind for "the dark side of the force"

The first lesson is that it is dangerous to close one's eyes for the negative aspects of international politics – "the dark side of the force". That is what the EU has been doing in recent years, as if geopolitics didn't matter anymore and power politics no longer existed, and all the world's problems were going to be solved by cooperation between the great powers. The Russian–Georgian war was a first warning, but it was not enough to awake Europe from its slumber. The then-Georgian president, Mikheil Saakashvili, was not very popular in Brussels, and many felt that he had brought the war upon himself by his provocative policies. Although several East European Member States pleaded for a strong reaction against Russia, the EU very quickly returned to business as usual.

The Russian invasion of Ukraine has forced all EU Member States to open their eyes, however. And lo and behold: geopolitics still matters, and the great powers are still playing power politics. Since then several wars have started in the Middle East and the Gulf (in Syria, Iraq, and Yemen), which directly and indirectly involve the great powers and the regional powers. Each power supports its own allies in those wars, who are fighting each other (so-called "proxy wars"), but the powers have also intervened directly. The mounting tensions between China and its neighbours over the sovereignty over the islands and waters of the South and East China Seas are another example of a classic geopolitical issue that Europe cannot ignore.

That we did ignore geopolitics for so long is understandable, because relations among the EU Member States are of a completely different nature. The EU is in many ways a world in itself, the first "postmodern region", where states have abandoned geopolitical competition. The EU Member States constitute a "security community": having pooled their sovereignty, they can no longer imagine that they would settle their disputes by any other than peaceful means. How many armoured divisions you can mobilise does not in any way determine a president's or prime minister's influence in the European Council. Fortunately, or my own country, Belgium, would have very little say indeed, since we no longer have any tanks at all.

Alas, Europe is rather unique in its "postmodern" identity. Robert Cooper, a former British diplomat and afterward one of the leading officials of EU foreign policy, already wrote as much in 2003 (Cooper, 2003). That was the year in which the EU published the *European Security Strategy*, its first strategic concept (Solana, 2003). Drafted under the leadership of Dr Javier Solana, the first High Representative (the EU equivalent of a foreign minister), Cooper was one of the key co-authors of this document. The world beyond the EU however, Cooper said in his own book, is still very much living in the "modern" age, in which states compete with all means at their disposal in order to defend their interests in the geopolitical struggle. Part of the world is even stuck in "pre-modernity": "failed states" where the state has collapsed, or where there has never even been a well-functioning central authority. Here we find chaos and anarchy, and the law of the jungle. To remain blind for this, consciously or unconsciously, is to take a big risk, for then the drivers of international politics cannot be understood. Thus one will forever face unpleasant surprises, and cannot even assess the impact of one's own policies, as happened to the EU in Ukraine. Effective strategy then becomes all but impossible.

Yet all too often geopolitics is seen as an obsolete concept, a burnt notion from the last century, used only to justify shameless and aggressive power politics. One almost feels morally superior by ignoring geopolitics. But that is to the detriment of strategy. In reality, geopolitics is founded on an entirely objective and neutral fact: a state's geography. That inevitably influences the state's interests, so one had better taken it into account. Values don't come into it: Europe is where it is and one cannot change that. Similarly, the British can leave the EU, but not Europe, and therefore have to continue to take the geopolitics of Europe into account. This is not the return of geopolitics, as it is often said these days. Geopolitics has always mattered – Europeans just chose not to see it.

Because of its geopolitical position Europe must care far more than the US about the wars in Ukraine, Syria, Iraq, Libya, and Mali, which may directly threaten Europe's trade routes and energy supply. Moreover, many EU citizens have joined the Islamic State (IS) and other groups and militias in Syria and Iraq as foreign fighters (Coolsaet, 2015). Europe is at the same time the closest safe destination for many refugees trying to escape from violence and a main target for the many extremists that these wars generate. In addition, Europe must pay attention to the free worldwide access to the seas, air space, space, and cyber space (the global commons), which is vital to its prosperity.

Europe's strategic dependence

Analysing one's geopolitical position is an essential step in making strategy, for it determines to a great extent which threats and challenges are a priority and which are not. Skipping that step does not make one better than anyone else, from a moral point of view, but it does undermine the effectiveness of one's strategy. Which strategy one chooses can of course be judged from a moral standpoint. Some great powers attempt to improve their geopolitical position by dominating or even annexing neighbouring territories or waters. Such power politics are directly at odds with the values of the EU. Unfortunately Putin is not the only one who uses his military power to create buffer zones on his borders and to establish an exclusive sphere of influence. That is why the EU must urgently reintroduce geopolitical analysis – not to imitate actors such as Putin, but to understand them.

When the Cold War ended, we did seem to have arrived in an age in which such competition between the great powers had ended as well. The US was the only remaining superpower, Russia was absorbed by domestic change, and China was by far not yet the great power that it is today. Europe can be forgiven for assuming that cooperation had become the new paradigm of international politics. This period turned out to be nothing but a sunny interlude however, the exception in world history that proves the rule. In today's multipolar world the great powers still cooperate, for example, on climate change or on trade. But at the same time competition has greatly increased. Cooperation and competition coexist. The other great powers opt for the former or the latter according to their interests; values rarely play a part.

Another reason why Europe has forgotten how to think strategically is that during the long period of the Cold War, from the creation of NATO in 1949 to the fall of the Berlin Wall in 1989, it largely left strategy to the US. After a while, both sides of the Atlantic saw the advantages of such an arrangement. Americans wanted faithful yet pliable allies that met their NATO commitments for defence expenditure without demanding too much of a say in decision-making. Europeans, as long as they spent enough, were assured of an American security guarantee, including the nuclear umbrella, against the Soviet Union and its allies in the Warsaw Pact.

That did not mean that Europeans had no ideas of their own or that there were never any disputes with the US. The Harmel Report of 1967 is one of the best examples of Europeans making their mark in alliance decision-making. Under the leadership of the then Belgian foreign minister Pierre Harmel, military deterrence of the USSR was linked to détente in relations with the East, while the right of initiative of the smaller allies was confirmed. The year before president Charles de Gaulle had withdrawn France from NATO's integrated military command structure, one of the greatest disruptions in the history of the Alliance. France remained a member of NATO, but not until 2009, under president Nicolas Sarkozy, did it join the military structures again.

By and large, however, several decades of military dependence on the US led to a dependent mind-set in Europe. In many European states, strategy was limited to translating NATO strategy into national defence planning, without too much original thinking being required. Over time, many came to see American leadership as the natural way of things. No proper initiative seemed necessary, for the US cavalry would come and solve every crisis anyway. Two decades after the end of the Cold War that dependent, if not servile, mind-set still exists in many capitals. To this day many European decision-makers will look for an American decision, and regard Europe's role as a supporting rather than a truly autonomous part. If that is one's attitude, one does not feel the need to have a strategy.

A simple geopolitical analysis demonstrates that with the end of the Cold War, this attitude has become meaningless. With the demise of the Soviet Union the centrality of Europe in US grand strategy came to an end as well. The US still shares many interests with the EU, but it also has its own geopolitical concerns that are quite different from ours. For us in Europe our security is, of course, a vital interest, but for the US the security of Europe is essential – not vital. There is no automaticity therefore: in a multipolar world the US will not always take the initiative and come and solve our security problems for us.

The weakness of Europe's strong story

A second important lesson that the EU must draw from the Ukraine crisis is that its worldview is under pressure. EU foreign policy has always started from a rather idealist view of the world. That view produced the very optimistic 2003 *European Security Strategy* (Biscop, 2005). The first time that the EU attempted to formulate a comprehensive strategy for all dimensions of international politics (economic, political, and security) it did not arrive at a strategy against somebody else, but at a strategy in favour of a very positive agenda. Hence the strategy's subtitle: "A secure Europe in a better world". The objective, of course, was to keep Europe safe; the best way to do that was to make the world a better place. Wasn't that nice?

These two sentences from the European Security Strategy perfectly capture its philosophy: "The best protection for our security is a world of well-governed democratic states. Spreading good governance, supporting social and political reform, dealing with corruption and abuse of power, establishing the rule of law and protecting human rights are the best means of strengthening the international order". This is a very motivating agenda that can appeal to people outside the EU as well. Moreover, it is simply true that most of the security problems that Europe is confronted with today find their origin in states that are neither democratic nor very well governed. Authoritarian states that serve only the interests of the ruling regime and do not provide for the security, freedom, and prosperity of the great majority of their citizens are inherently unstable. It may take a long time, but the moment always comes when people no longer accept that situation. When that time arrives, the regime may implode, rapidly and relatively peacefully, like the Soviet Union in 1991 or Ben Ali's regime in Tunisia in 2011. Or it may explode, with a lot of violence, like in Libya and Syria. The revolution in Tunisia, which fortunately cost very few lives, heralded the beginning of the Arab Spring. But the hope for peaceful change in the region that it generated was blown away by the storm of violence that erupted in Libya and Syria. The Arab Spring turned out to be more like a Belgian spring: stormy and unpredictable.

But how does one create well-governed democratic states where there aren't any? Since 2003 we have found that, actually, we don't know. Democracy cannot be imposed. Afghanistan and Iraq can hardly be called well governed, in spite of the presence of huge Western forces for years on end. I, for one, am not considering moving to Kabul or Baghdad any time soon. At the same time, the Ukraine crisis has demonstrated that charity cannot create democracy either. In an age of increasing geopolitical tensions, the proverbial carrots (e.g. development aid, free-trade agreements, investment, visa-free travel to the EU) are insufficient to spread good governance and democracy. If there is no strong domestic basis of support, democracy cannot be engineered from the outside, certainly not by force of arms. But even where people do want to embrace democracy, financial and economic aid alone will not suffice. One has to stand ready to protect democratic forces from those, inside their own country as well as abroad, who want to derail their efforts or even eliminate them. If one is unable or unwilling to do that, one had better be careful in encouraging others along the democratic path. If foreign powers are resolved to fight for democracy in Ukraine only to the last Ukrainian, they better think twice before getting involved.

The lessons to be drawn from recent crises, in Ukraine and elsewhere, go even further. Not only is it difficult to export our worldview, but the European narrative itself is under pressure. One could summarise the 2003 strategy as: the more the rest of the world becomes like us, the better for everybody. The better for people in other countries, who will enjoy more good governance and democracy. And the better for us because, for a start, those people will then not be tempted to try and emigrate to Europe. But how credible is the European model today? Is Europe actually capable of providing its own citizens with the security, freedom and prosperity that they rightly expect? The credibility and effectiveness of the European model have been gravely undermined by the EU's slow response to two crises in which it has shown far too little solidarity: the financial crisis (especially the case of Greece) and the refugee and migration crisis.

Europe's intuitive reaction to the financial crisis was dubbed "austerity": introducing massive cuts in order to protect the budgetary balance and the banks.

Protecting citizens was only an afterthought. The southern Member States of the EU in particular were forced to reduce social security, which had the effect of aggravating the crisis as people's buying power diminished even further. The resulting impression was that the EU was first of all a banking union. Not just in Europe, but abroad as well, where governments were amazed at the lack of solidarity within the EU, and irritated at its cumbersome decision-making. The EU's slowness was a direct threat to others, for the longer it took the EU to solve its problems, the bigger the chance that their consequences would be even larger, for Europe as well as for the rest of the world.

The refugee and migration crisis showed that Europe was willing to show but little solidarity with people from other countries. The EU cannot but try to manage migration, for our model of society would not survive an uncontrolled intake of people. A debate is in order about whether Europe should not allow a lot more regular economic migration for the sake of its labour market, in view of its ageing population. But it does in any case have the moral and legal duty to help war refugees. Unfortunately there was little support for that inside Europe. According to UNHCR, 5.6 million registered Syrian refugees have found shelter in the neighbouring countries (mostly in Jordan, Lebanon, and Turkey), and only about 1 million in the whole of the EU. However one feels about this: it has become a lot more difficult now to point the finger at other countries for a lack of respect for human rights. The impact on EU foreign policy is undeniable therefore.

And then there is Brexit, of course. On 23 June 2016, 51.9 per cent of British voters opted for leaving the EU. Brexit too has severe consequences for the credibility of the European narrative and for EU foreign policy. For years to come, whatever the EU proposes, someone is bound to rise and say: how good can your offer really be, and why would we follow your lead, if even one your own biggest three Member States apparently thinks so badly of it all that it quits the Union? The EU's loss of prestige is enormous.

Furthermore, there are competing narratives out there that deny the universality of the values on which the "well-governed democratic states" of Europe are founded. There is the narrative of IS, which proposes universal values of its own, based on its very particular interpretation of Islam. Then there is the Russian narrative, which precisely does not pretend to universality but, in an authoritarian and populist fashion, flames nationalism and the belief in the necessity of a strong state (Snyder, 2018). Such a nation state is entitled to its place under the sun, which the strong leader is there to ensure. Putin consciously opposes very specific aspects of European society, such as the recognition of gay rights, which are denied in Russia and presented as evidence of the "decadence" of the West. The Russian Lesbian, Gay, Bisexual and Transgender (LGBT) community has thus become the victim of the president's geopolitical aspirations. Non-Russian minorities are constantly being scapegoated as well, so as to divert attention from the country's serious economic difficulties.

Under President Xi Jinping, the Chinese narrative as well is leaning more and more towards authoritarian nationalism. In China, propaganda is everywhere.

Television is full of images of fighter jets and aircraft carriers (except on the single English-language channel, which imperturbably lauds the natural beauty and cultural refinement of China). Every toy shop stores piles of models of the aircraft carrier that China has bought unfinished from Ukraine and then converted, and every travel agency offers daytrips to go and visit this former Soviet ship in the port of Tianjin. The difference is that China, contrary to Russia, is a rising power and that it attempts to redistribute some of its growing prosperity in order to keep the lid on social tensions and maintain the power of the Chinese Communist Party (CCP). Donald Trump has a very different view again, according to which the state should play as little a part in society as possible. Those who are entrepreneurial make it, and those who don't only have themselves to blame, or one can blame the nasty foreigners who destroy American jobs. Under the heading of "America First", Trump also represents a populist nationalism, which even has some authoritarian traits. Of the four great powers (among which I still count the EU), three are thus going the way of nationalism. One would grow pessimistic for less.

Moreover, it doesn't end there, as Europe itself is certainly not immune to nationalism and populism. These alternatives to the European narrative have their supporters in Europe as well. Thousands of European citizens felt sufficiently alienated from our society to follow the siren call of IS and take up arms, looking for redemption or just for adventure. How empty, hopeless or scary must life be, or how impressionable or vulnerable the young men and women, before they abandon a peaceful existence in Europe to join a war in Syria? Or explode themselves in their European home. This means that a lot of people no longer feel at home in Europe at all. The European narrative does not convince or simply does not reach them.

There are many more right-wing populists who ape Putin and Trump. Just like in the 1930s they seek to fence off their countries from Europe and the world; some, like Trump, even literally want to build a wall along their borders. From Putin they even take the homophobia and xenophobia, under the guise of defending traditional values. In reality they limit the rights and freedoms of citizens, even when they present their policies as regaining sovereignty from "Brussels" and the EU bureaucracy. The "pure" national past that they hold up as their ideal is nothing but a mirage, of course. In Hungary and Poland right-wing populist governments are in power and actively undermine EU foreign policy. In the UK, they are not in the government, but without right-wing populists such as Nigel Farrage and UKIP we would not be facing Brexit. In many other EU Member States similar parties play an equally negative role in politics. This applies to left-wing populists as well. From a different vantage point, they too deny reality and pretend that their countries can move on alone, without the EU.

Populists are intellectually unfair. Saying whatever it takes to please the voter is the essence of populism, in combination with the bypassing of regular political channels in order to have the "popular will" voiced directly. That is what makes a democracy, in which the other parties do play by the rules, so vulnerable. And the EU is feeling vulnerable for sure.

Implicit pragmatism

Fortunately European leaders are not immune to reason. After the Ukraine crisis, nobody could pretend any longer that the EU did not need a new strategy. That strategy would have to be a lot more pragmatic and pay a lot more attention to defending Europe's vital interests. The third lesson of the Ukraine crisis therefore was that the 2003 strategy ought to be replaced by a new document, because no strategy can remain valid for more than a decade – the world evolves much too fast. The Arab Spring and the resulting wars in the Middle East and North Africa played a big part in this growing awareness as well. The dream of 2003, to build a ring of friends around Europe, sadly turned out to be an illusion. Last but certainly not least, the steep rise of China was important in convincing EU Member States that a strategic update was now really necessary. In 2003 everybody expected that China would rise, but nobody had predicted that it would rise as fast as it did. There is not a single issue in world politics today in which China does not play a part.

In June 2015, the European Council (the Heads of State and Government of the EU Member States) tasked the current High Representative, the Italian Federica Mogherini, with the writing of a new strategy. Mogherini made it clear from the start that a different, more pragmatic approach was necessary. "We need a strategy to protect proactively our interests, keeping in mind that promoting our values is an integral part of our interests", is how she put it at a conference that launched the consultation process on the future strategy in October 2015 (Mogherini, 2015). *Interests* clearly no longer was a dirty word.

It is important to know, however, that on the ground the EU has been pursuing a much more pragmatic approach than would appear from its idealist rhetoric for a long time already. But because this pragmatism always remained implicit and the EU formally held on to its idealist narrative, EU prestige has been severely undermined.

The idealist 2003 strategy was implemented mostly via bilateral partnerships. Those operated on the principle of "positive conditionality": a partner country undertook to reform itself and to introduce more good governance and democracy. In return for that the EU promised development aid, investment, access to the European market, and visa-free travel to Europe. The more a country reformed itself, the more it was rewarded by the EU – or that was the theory. If the reform effort faltered, a country would not lose the benefits already received, but it would not be offered any additional advantages. "Negative conditionality" or sanctions were but very rarely applied, though in principle they were provided for in case of grave human rights violations. Many of the bilateral partnerships were anchored in a multilateral framework. On our eastern flank, the EU created the Eastern Partnership with six countries; in our southern periphery, the Union for the Mediterranean with 11 countries; together they constitute the scope of the European Neighbourhood Policy (ENP).[1] There is a separate policy framework for the Balkan countries. Furthermore the bilateral relations with ten great powers and regional powers have been upgraded to so-called strategic partnerships.[2]

In Europe this approach has worked, more or less, especially when EU membership was on offer as the ultimate reward for successful reform. With just a few exceptions the EU has had much less success where geopolitically it mattered most (apart from the European continent itself): in its southern periphery and in its relations with the strategic partners. These different outcomes of the same policy indicate a crucial difference in the perception of the values that the EU is trying to promote, and of the way in which it operates.

In Europe, conditionality as a way of promoting well-governed democratic states is accepted more widely by the EU's partners, certainly if there is the prospect of accession to the EU. The reason is that a large part of public opinion in these countries sees close relations with the EU as a return to the normal state of affairs. Before World War Two many of these countries were democracies, or transitioning towards democracy, and they played their part in European politics. Geographically, historically, and culturally they are a part of Europe. During the Cold War they were artificially cut off from Western Europe by the Iron Curtain. For a dissident campaigning for human rights and against the communist regime in a country such as Poland, Western society was a source of inspiration. Most East European countries have now joined the EU. Without exaggerating, this enlargement can be called one of the most important strategic decisions since the end of World War Two, second only to the start of the European integration process itself. Enlargement has ensured that all Member States of the EU enjoy durable peace and stability. Back when the Berlin Wall fell, in 1989, that was far from evident.

Now the question is how far to the east this positive appreciation of the EU and its values applies. In Ukraine, as already mentioned, and certainly also in Moldova, a large share of the population supports the European aspiration. Belarus is more difficult to assess, but the opposition against the authoritarian regime of President Aleksandr Lukashenko certainly shares the values of the EU. What about the Caucasus? Is the Caucasus part of Europe in the first place? Georgia definitely sees it that way, but the EU itself remains rather uncertain about how close a relationship it can develop with the country. Armenia and Azerbaijan have a much more vague relation with the idea of Europe, which is mirrored in the vagueness of European strategy for the region.

Outside Europe, however, and particularly in its southern neighbours, conditionality is seen as a return to the past rather than a return to normality. The past is one of colonialism and imperialism, in which the European states pursued their interests without any regard for the local population. The majority of public opinion in these countries therefore does not see the EU as a model at all. Rather it opposes any interference by outside powers, and by Western powers in particular. The president is a dictator, but he is our dictator and it is our decision whether and how to get rid of him – that often is the prevailing attitude. In such a context it is very difficult to gain influence, even when one comes with the best intentions. During my first visit to Egypt, long before the Arab Spring, I had the chance of meeting people of the opposition movement Kefayah ("Enough"). For the benefit of foreign visitors they had summarised their demands in English on a single page, under the heading (in a big font): make an end to American and Zionist aggression. Under that heading, in normal type, were listed all the demands that can be found in EU documents too: human rights, democracy, etc. But in order to appeal to public opinion, it had to be sold under the label of anti-Americanism and anti-Zionism. These people welcomed EU support, on the condition that it was not too visible, for otherwise the regime could easily portray them as puppets of the West and undermine their credibility with the public.

An approach that works in postmodern Europe and the countries that want to join that approach does not necessarily work in the rest of the world. In practice the EU began to deviate from its rhetoric, and on the ground that explicit idealism often turned into implicit pragmatism. That is both cause and effect of the lack of success of "positive conditionality".

Gaps in European strategy

The result of this "pragmatism in practice" is that several large gaps have emerged in European strategy.

First of all, a gap has emerged between the eagerness with which the EU continues to promote its narrative outside its borders and the apparent weakness of the EU itself. To the outside world, the EU keeps repeating that peace and stability are possible only where there are well-governed democratic states. But as already stated, the perception of many people outside Europe is that EU is having great difficulties in maintaining good governance and democracy itself. The impression is that the EU has only barely resisted the pressure of successive crises, such as the financial crisis and the refugee issue. Authoritarian regimes eagerly point out to their publics what they dub the failure of democratic decision-making in order to justify their own system. Every European scholar visiting China, for example, has been confronted with a strong sense of Schadenfreude.

Often the weakness of the EU is strongly exaggerated. External observers easily underestimate the difficulties of undoing the deep integration that Europe has built, and the strength of the ties between the Member States that this integration has created. According to many predictions, the Schengen Agreement, for example, the abolishment of internal borders among the participating Member States, should have been cancelled a long time ago. But not only would the end of Schengen come at an enormous economic price, it could also not be justified to European citizens who are used to travelling freely around the EU. Of course, the negative perception does contain a grain of truth. Denying that would show neither much realism, nor much strategic insight. What is clear is that the European narrative will not appeal to the rest of the world if Europe itself does not remain faithful to it.

Second, there is an even wider gap between the idealist European rhetoric and the actual substance of many bilateral partnerships. Again our southern neighbours offer the clearest example. Instead of applying "positive conditionality", the EU has in reality supported any regime, quite regardless of good governance and democracy, that wanted to cooperate with it in stopping migration towards Europe and in fighting terrorism. The less savoury details of how that was achieved, Brussels did not need to know. If a country possessing energy resources was willing to supply the EU, that naturally also greatly commended it in the eyes of Europe.

Then came the Arab Spring. It started in Tunisia on 17 December 2010, when fruit salesman Mohamed Bouazizi, protesting how the authorities treated him, lit himself on fire. Nearly everybody, myself included, has forgotten the brave man's name, but he deserves to be remembered, for the ensuing protest totally unexpectedly produced a genuine revolution. Less than a month later, on 14 January 2011, President Zine El Abidine Ben Ali stood down and escaped to Saudi Arabia. This revolution happened in spite of, not thanks to, the EU. For the EU was cooperating very closely with the regime. Therefore its initial reaction was very hesitant. The French Minister of Foreign Affairs, Michèle Alliot-Marie, even proposed to assist Ben Ali with French security forces – a statement that did cost her her job. Sadly, the Arab Spring also ended in Tunisia, the only country that has started the transition to democracy. In Egypt, following an intermezzo in which the Muslim Brotherhood won the elections and governed the country, in 2014 the army came back in power. The only difference is that one general, Hosni Mubarak, has been replaced by another, Abdul Fatah al-Sisi. In Libya and Syria the Arab Spring led to bloody civil wars that are still ongoing.

So not much has changed – including EU policy. The rhetoric has been somewhat adapted. After the Arab Spring, the slogan became "More for more": countries that introduced more reforms would get more support. That policy basically amounted to more of the same, and in practice it was as inconsistently applied as before the Arab Spring. Indeed, in order to prevent even more countries from sliding into civil war, the EU quietly opted to support rulers that seemed to be able to bring some stability, such as Egypt's al-Sisi, even though the military regime is now even more repressive than under Mubarak. That naturally reinforced the perception that the EU does not really care about democracy and human rights, that its rhetoric is but that: rhetoric, masking its self-interest. At the same time, many in Europe began to feel that EU policy actually did not pay enough attention to EU interests, something that would greatly influence the strategic debate.

All of this points to a third gap, between two European objectives that can be mutually exclusive: creating well-governed democratic states and promoting peace and stability. It comes as no surprise perhaps that former US Secretary of State Henry Kissinger has worded this dilemma better than anybody (Kissinger, 2015, p. 125). Should the West feel obliged to support every popular uprising against a non-democratic regime, even if until then it worked with that regime to maintain the regional or even the global order? Kissinger refers to the example of Saudi Arabia: is the government of a country an ally only as long as there are no domestic demonstrations against it? For until this day Saudi Arabia officially is an ally of Europe too, as an active member of the anti-IS coalition. Kissinger's position is more nuanced than many of his critics would expect. Supporting every potential revolution without taking into account the possible consequences for regional and global security can be catastrophic, but blocking a potentially democratic future can equally have very bad consequences.

Faced with this dilemma, the EU has made different choices in different cases. In Tunisia and afterward in Egypt, the EU (just like the US) initially was most reticent. Only after it had become absolutely certain that Ben Ali and Mubarak had lost power did the West voice its support for the revolution. But in Egypt the West then quickly switched its support to the counter-revolution and al-Sisi, who appeared to offer more guarantees of stability. In Libya, Europe and the US decided to intervene militarily when in 2011 President Muammar Khadafy, fearing he was about to lose power also, tried to suppress the opposition by force of arms. Through their intervention, they sealed Khadafy's fate. Its main motivation was to demonstrate that the West was "on the good side of history" and to correct the bad impression that the initial hesitance towards the Arab Spring had created.

When the same scenario occurred in Syria, where the opposition against President Bashar al-Assad undoubtedly also counted on Western military support, the West at first decided not to intervene. For whereas Khadafy did not have a single real friend, Assad had powerful allies in Russia and Iran. Only when in 2014 the fast rise of IS made Syria and Iraq into a single theatre of war did US President Barack Obama take the initiative to forge a coalition that began air strikes against IS – but not against Assad. These different choices show that European rhetoric on human rights and democracy hides an approach that in reality is much more nuanced, but also much less consistent than EU discourse.

Finally, there are huge gaps in the way the EU applies "positive conditionality" from one country to another. Few governments will enter into a partnership the objective of which is their own demise. But in a non-democratic state, that is what creating a well-governed democratic state amounts to: regime change. In some cases the EU applies "positive conditionality" very strictly, for example, in countries that are relatively weak and rely on external support, such as Ukraine, or in countries where few European interests are directly at stake, such as Myanmar. But the EU has a lot less leverage to promote change in countries that are rich in resources and therefore do not need its assistance, such as the Gulf states. Or countries whose cooperation the EU requires in the security field, such as Algeria, without which the Maghreb cannot be stabilised. When it comes to the great powers, such as China, the EU has hardly any leverage at all.

That does not mean that the EU never dares to make courageous decisions: witness the already mentioned sanctions against Russia after its invasion of Ukraine. True, the energy sector is mostly excluded from the sanctions, except for technology transfer, which Russia needs in order to exploit new resources; its absence will be felt in the long term. Europe continues to import Russian energy, because halting Russian supply would cause a lot of difficulties for Europe itself. But also because the aim is not to push the Russian economy into the abyss – that would cause even more instability than Putin's adventurism. Against Iran too severe economic sanctions were in force until the 2015 agreement about the country's nuclear capacity. In both cases the sanctions were motivated by concerns about security rather than about good governance and democracy. The same holds true for the rising doubts in several European countries about our close relations with (and arms exports to) Saudi Arabia. We have not suddenly become more concerned with the human rights situation in the country, but have begun to realise that its policies (for example, its financial support for an arch conservative version of Islam in our society) have direct negative consequences for our security.

Overall, however, the perception is that conditionality is really only ever applied to weaker countries. It should be noted that in the case of Ukraine it is fully justified, and necessary for our security, for the EU to exert strong pressure in order to ensure that Ukraine truly reforms – and that our money is well spent. But the great powers are more or less immune to this approach, because economic considerations will nearly always prevail. Once again it is clear that the EU narrative about equal treatment of citizens hides its own unequal treatment of different countries.

The conclusion of this analysis of recent strategy is not that the EU is cynically hiding behind its rhetoric, and in reality is pursuing its interests regardless of the values that it advocates. The European belief in its idealist agenda and the promotion of its values is sincere. But the pragmatic implementation of this agenda on the ground is a reality too. Because this pragmatism has remained implicit, it has produced inconsistency. That should push us to question ourselves. The objective: a new strategy.

Notes

1 The Eastern Partnership includes our immediate neighbours, Belarus, Ukraine and Moldova, and the countries of the Southern Caucasus, Georgia, Armenia and Azerbaijan. The southern neighbours that are members of the Union for the Mediterranean are: Turkey, Syria (though it has suspended its membership since 1 December 2011), Lebanon, Jordan, Israel, Palestine, Egypt, Tunisia, Algeria, Morocco, and Mauritania; Libya has observer status.
2 They are the US, Canada, Japan, South Korea, and Mexico, and the five BRICS countries: Brazil, Russia, India, China and South Africa. In 2017 Australia became a "strategic relation" of the EU. The difference between a strategic relation and a strategic partner would take a separate book to explain.

References

Sven Biscop, *The European Security Strategy: A Global Agenda for Positive Power*. Abingdon, Ashgate, 2005.
Christopher Clark, *The Sleepwalkers: How Europe Went to War in 1914*. London, Allen Lane, 2012.
Rik Coolsaet, *What Drives Europeans to Syria, and to IS? Insights from the Belgian Case*. Egmont Paper No. 75. Brussels, Egmont, 2015.
Robert Cooper, *The Breaking of Nations: Order and Chaos in the Twenty-First Century*. London, Atlantic Books, 2003.
Henry Kissinger, *World Order*. New York, Penguin, 2015.

Federica Mogherini, *Remarks by the High Representative/Vice-President at the EUISS Annual Conference*. 9 October 2015.

Timothy Snyder, *The Road to Unfreedom: Russia, Europe, America*. New York, Tim Duggan Books, 2018.

Javier Solana, *A Secure Europe in a Better World: European Security Strategy*. Brussels, EU, December 2003.

2
STRATEGY
What can Europe do, what does Europe want?

When crafting a new strategy, one has to be willing to ask oneself the difficult questions – and to accept that there might not always be an easy answer. The starting point is clear enough: the 2003 EU strategy, which sought to promote a universal model of well-governed democratic states, was too idealistic to be practicable. In order to arrive at a better strategy, the EU must ask itself three questions. First, are the values on which our society (and the 2003 strategy) is based truly universal? Second, if the answer is positive, is it in our interest to continue to try and promote these values in the rest of the world? Third, if the answer is positive again, what exactly should we be promoting, and in what way, and with what objectives?

Values?

The answer to the first question cannot be but a resounding yes. To believe in the values on which our own democratic states are founded inherently implies a belief in their universality, because the opposite ipso facto amounts to a violation of these values. To pretend, for example, that human rights do not equally apply to all humans is to deny the very idea of human rights. Then we shouldn't be speaking of human rights but of Western, European or even just Belgian rights. It is evident as well that if the rule of law does not apply equally to all citizens, there simply is no rule of law. And as long as democracy does not include all citizens in all states, and all states in all international organisations, decision-making cannot be perfectly democratic.

Not all governments recognise the universality of these values, but that does not affect their universal validity. It is only to be expected that those who benefit from the absence of democracy and the rule of law will do their best to find arguments (other than their self-interest) to uphold their position. Hence the thesis is that human rights would be culturally determined and therefore would not apply equally in all cultures. Another often-heard argument is that when the United Nations adopted the Universal Declaration of Human Rights, the majority of states existing today were not yet independent and therefore had no say.

Much more important than the fact that not all governments accept and respect these values is that across the globe the large majority of citizens share the same universal aspirations. We all want our governments to (1) guarantee our physical integrity and protect our security; (2) give us a say in political decision-making and to apply the law equally to all of us; and (3) ensure that we each get a fair share of the prosperity that our country produces. Citizens in other countries may not always formulate these aspirations the way we do. Sometimes they even see Europe as an obstacle rather than as an ally in achieving them – not entirely without reason, as the case of Tunisia has demonstrated. But from the brave Tunisians who started the Arab Spring to the anonymous Chinese who protest against the excesses of their government, from the refugees who are trying to escape from war by making their way to Europe to we in Europe ourselves: ultimately we all want the same from our states. In the end we act on the same aspirations: they are the reason we demonstrate, protest, vote and sometimes fight. Herein lies the true universality of these values.

Promoting values?

Does the EU serve its interests by actively trying to convince other governments to heed their citizens' aspirations – or does that harm our interests? That is the second essential question to be answered.

The most controversial value that the EU is trying to promote is democracy. Many of the states with which the EU maintains diplomatic relations are not democracies. For them, democratisation amounts to regime change – to a revolution. Hence putting democracy front and centre of our diplomacy means that we inherently antagonise many governments just as we are reaching out to them. Once again Kissinger perfectly captures this dilemma. The conviction that our values are universal values implies that we do not consider governments that do not respect them as fully legitimate. We act as if "a significant portion of the world lives under a kind of unsatisfactory, probationary agreement, and will one day be redeemed". Until then, our relations with these states cannot but have an "adversarial element" to them (Kissinger, 2015, pp. 235–236).

Making democratisation our foreign policy objective thus implies high transaction costs, for it automatically leads to friction with every non-democratic government (and there are many). The objective of democratisation often hinders our diplomacy. The result of our advocacy is less clear, alas – there are but very few examples of successful democratisation. Not even where the EU has committed the most, in its neighbouring countries, does it have much to show for its efforts. The lesson from past experience is rather that democracy just cannot be introduced from the outside, certainly not by force of arms, but has to grow organically, inside a country.

Promoting human rights is often controversial as well. The EU maintains a critical human rights dialogue with all countries with which it maintains diplomatic relations, in order to point out problematic issues. Oftentimes that happens behind closed doors, but that can be the best way of having an impact. Regimes usually want to avoid losing face and will see a public condemnation as a provocation, but can be found willing to compromise as long as the case is not made public. In principle, economic considerations do not intervene here. In practice, however, EU Member States often hesitate to be too critical if important economic interests are at stake. Or they leave it to the EU ambassador to address human rights so that the national ambassador can engage in trade promotion without being "hindered" by other considerations. At the same time, powerful countries, with which the EU has a relationship of mutual dependency (for example, because of the size of their market, or because of energy supplies), don't hesitate to simply blackmail the EU. A typical example is China putting a European country before the choice: either cancel a visit by the Dalai Lama, or cancel a planned trade delegation. Even though the Chinese know fully well that Europeans will only discuss the human rights situation in Tibet and not independence (and rightly so). The outcome usually is the same: for "health reasons", the Dalai Lama "postpones" his visit.[1]

Clinging to democratisation and respect for human rights as preconditions for cooperation can disadvantage Europe. Other powers, in particular China, do not impose such "inconvenient" conditions and are therefore more attractive partners for regimes who disregard human rights. Certainly in Africa this has cost Europe a lot of influence, though it should be said that when the West was dominant and the Chinese presence in Africa was still in the future, we definitely did not always treat our African partners very nicely ourselves. That makes it rather difficult today to point the finger at China.

From a purely pragmatic point of view, one could conclude from this analysis that for our foreign policy it would be a lot easier to simply abandon all talk about democracy and human rights. For the EU that is not an option, however.

First of all, one cannot be half-democratic. As long as we pretend to be a union of democratic states, our foreign policy must uphold the same values that we want to see respected at home. One cannot imagine that for the sake of expediency the EU would no longer take into account human rights and the rule of law when it issues new telecom regulations, just to speed things up a bit. Ignoring our own values in our foreign policy is equally absurd. Precisely because these are universal values, the EU must at all times avoid the impression that it only respects them internally and does not cares when no Europeans are concerned. Do unto others as you would have them do unto you. The EU must stay consistent with itself. These values determine who we are and should therefore determine how we act.

No single actor can long maintain a policy that is at odds with its fundamental values. Gradually, internal support will crumble and a reversal of policy will become inevitable. The reason why we feel ill at ease cooperating with repressive regimes is because that does not tally with our values. The same applies for waging wars at the expense of the local civilian population. The times of the Vietnam

War, when to save villages from communism they were bombed with their inhabitants in them, are long past. In fact, even back then the American people eventually no longer accepted that for the sake of defending its values, those very same values were being violated abroad. This holds true for domestic security policy as well. When terrorists challenge our identity as an open society, the answer cannot be to abandon our identity and create a police state. Exaggerated security measures quickly run into protest, and so they should.

Continuing to respect values in our foreign policy is a matter of principle, but the principle is tied up with our interests. Not respecting our values would do great damage to our legitimacy and credibility, and would thus immediately affect the success of our foreign policy. Moreover, it is also not in our interest to engage in cooperation with authoritarian states without maintaining a critical distance. As stated in the previous chapter, such regimes are inherently instable, and engender the very problems that we are confronted with in our foreign policy. No population will accept suppression forever. Either an authoritarian state will eventually implode, when it has lost all domestic credibility, even with those who are part of the system, or the result will be bloodshed, when the people, seeing no other way to vent their anger, take up arms. We cannot control who will lead that fight: those seeking to establish democracy, or those merely seeking to replace one dictatorship with another (a secular with a religious dictatorship, for example). Neither can one predict whether once a power transition is achieved in a country, it will end there, or other countries will be affected as well.

Pending the implosion or explosion of an authoritarian system, economic development usually falters. Such regimes are entirely self-serving. Profits are diverted to line the pockets of the regime and its cronies (hence "crony capitalism") instead of invested in the country. Indeed, those who profit from the system always put their money in offshore accounts or invest in real estate in the fancy neighbourhoods of Europe and the US, because they know very well that the system is not trustworthy. Repression and poverty naturally stimulate emigration. One cannot blame people for seeking their luck elsewhere. Finally, authoritarian regimes very often purposely flame nationalism and hatred of specific neighbours or of domestic minorities in order to channel discontent and to divert attention away from the country's real problems. Dictatorship and an assertive or even aggressive foreign policy often go hand in hand, which demonstrably creates international tensions.

The final reason that the EU cannot just drop its values is that this would amount to a slap in the face for all those brave human rights activists in dictatorships around the world who defend those very same values, often at great risk to themselves. They deserve at least our moral support.

The answer to the second question, whether we should continue to promote universal values, is nuanced. On the one hand, the EU has clearly been overoptimistic. Where there are no well-governed democratic states it is beyond our power to create them. Where, therefore, there are authoritarian states, promoting democracy and human rights comes at a price and creates tensions. And where the absence of good governance and democracy has led to conflict and war, the EU has not always been as responsive as it could and should have been. On the other hand, both morality and interest dictate that we cannot just abandon the value-based agenda altogether. Pure idealism did not work, and in reality was often closer to an unspoken pragmatism. Pure pragmatism is not an alternative. A middle road is necessary, therefore, to answer the third question: what exactly should we be promoting?

The pragmatic middle way: equality

If the EU can neither ignore human rights nor overemphasise democracy, the solution is perhaps to broaden the narrative. This leads us back to the very first question to ask oneself when writing a strategy: for whom am I writing it?

What distinguishes the EU and its Member States? Not only that we are democratic states that respect human rights and the rule of law but also, and perhaps especially, that our societies are founded on the idea of equality among all citizens. And, very importantly, that the state should actively intervene to create equality where it would otherwise not spontaneously come into existence. This is the welfare state or the Rhineland Model, the true heart of Europe, in every meaning of the word. At the end of his magisterial history of Europe since World War Two, the British historian Tony Judt becomes a bit philosophical (and who wouldn't, having written over 700 pages) and asks himself: what is Europe, actually? His answer: "a sense . . . of the balance of social rights, civic solidarity and collective responsibility . . . a social consensus . . . regarded by many citizens as formally binding" (Judt, 2005). It is this social contract that binds citizens to their states and to the EU, or turns them away from them if they feel that it is being violated.

This egalitarian aspiration distinguishes Europe from nearly every other country in the world. Even from the US: although clearly we share most values, American society has a markedly different idea of the role of the state. Being distinctive is not an end in itself: North Korea is even more distinctive, but that doesn't make it a model to be followed. Europe, however, distinguishes itself in a positive way; hence, it has a positive story to tell the rest of the world. The welfare state works, and that's worth pointing out. It must be pointed out, in fact, for it is one of the, if not the most, important sources of soft power for the EU. And as stated in the Introduction: when one possesses soft power, one can hope to tempt rather than to force others into following a certain path.

Where else would our soft power come from? Not from our trade and our market, which are either regarded as self-evident (by the industrialised countries) or as far too assertive (by the developing countries). From our culture, yes, but that is insufficient to incite others to follow a specific course of action. Our "way of life" does have that power. This applies in China, for example, where both the regime and the public greatly appreciate certain key aspects of the European model of society. One aspect is not only our social security system, but also the way the

EU's structural funds redistribute prosperity from rich to poor regions inside the Union, which inspires the Chinese, who are looking for ways of maintaining domestic harmony.

Since 2006 I teach every year at the People's University of China in Beijing.[2] Over the years I have seen my Chinese students grow more self-confident. They know that China has become a great power. Europe's foreign and security policy, in contrast, often appears to them as weak and naive. But they also have the feeling that European governments care much more sincerely about the wellbeing of their citizens than their own government does about theirs, notably on such everyday issues as food safety and air quality. Social security, which is much more comprehensive in Europe, is a case in point too. I always surprise my students with the same statement: in this regard Belgium is much more communist than the PRC.

Equality is a motivating concept. But in China, as in other countries, a justified pride in the country's achievements implies that an all too paternalistic approach on the part of the EU would quickly antagonise everybody. We will not be able to promote equality by preaching about it (even though, in view of my surname, I do like to pontificate). We can do it by cooperating with other countries on concrete projects that bring more equality. Other countries can probably achieve similar results as we in did in Europe, but in a different manner. If an existing system is perceived as legitimate by the majority of the population in a country, then who are we to say that they should do things differently? The aim is not to promote European-style institutions and regulations, therefore. It's not the manner in which a country achieves equality, but the notion that equality should be the purpose that the EU should promote: the egalitarian aspiration.

Equality, just like power, has a security, economic and political dimension. Equal security means that the armed forces and the security services of the state equally protect all citizens rather than, as in a dictatorship, protecting the state against its own citizens. Equal prosperity means that every citizen is entitled to a fair share of the prosperity that his or her country (and in our case, union of countries) produces in order to participate fully and in a dignified manner in society; that requires redistribution. Political equality means equality before the law, equal protection of everybody's human rights, and equal participation in decision-making, hence democratic elections; together this constitutes freedom. The reason authoritarian states are inherently unstable is because they offer their citizens neither equal security nor equal prosperity nor equal freedom. Inequality equals instability.

Exporting equality

Equality is a multidimensional concept, and that offers a great advantage: flexibility. Europe does not have to work on every dimension of equality simultaneously with every partner, but can adopt a sequential approach.

Equal participation in political decision-making (i.e. democratisation) clearly is a long-term objective. That much experience has taught us. By first focussing on other dimensions of equality in its relations with non-democratic regimes, the EU can avoid having its diplomacy perceived as a moral condemnation from the start. Otherwise every relationship with a non-democratic state is condemned right away to mutual suspicion, and hence to ineffectiveness. The EU will always fear being too closely associated with an authoritarian regime if cooperation goes too far. The regime in turn will always fear that if it allows the EU to come too close, eventually the Union will undermine it. A broader focus on equality in all of its dimensions, on the other hand, allows for more flexibility and thus for more reciprocity. The EU can cooperate with a country on a project that increases equality in one dimension without the obligation to work on all other dimensions as well. It is up to the EU and the other country to assess where win-win situations can emerge. In this approach to cooperation, the other country has more options itself, so that cooperation on equality can also be a cooperation between equals.

Democratisation no longer is a compulsory part of relations with the EU then. The countries that want to cooperate on democratisation, for example, because they are in the midst of a transition to democracy, can of course ask the EU for expertise and support. But countries that don't want to can cooperate with the EU in other areas without their political system being put in question by Brussels. The EU can thus simply be honest with itself and toward others. Would it be nice if Egypt were a democracy? Yes, of course. Is the EU going to turn Egypt into a democracy? No, so let us not fool ourselves and pretend that we can. Only the Egyptians can democratise Egypt.

An area in which the EU can cooperate with most countries without any objections is social and economic equality: development aid, trade, but most of all, investing in projects that create durable employment with exemplary labour conditions. Authoritarian regimes too need economic development, but to attract foreign investors they must create the right conditions, at the very least in special economic zones if not in the country as a whole. If until now Europe has invested much less in North Africa than in Asia, for example, that is mostly because investors feared they would never earn their investment back. Investors, be they public or private, need to make a profit and will avoid excessive risk.

Attracting investors implies respecting the rule of law, for example, as foreign partners will demand contracts to be upheld, and disputes to be settled by an independent court, without having to pay any bribes. This directly contributes to the rule of law and the fight against corruption in the state as a whole. Foreign investors will require trained personnel, and healthy personnel that are adequately housed, so that their work does not suffer from their living conditions. And of course they will want the security of their personnel to be guaranteed. In such a way European investment can create an upward spiral, from which gradually an ever greater part of society will benefit. This is on the condition, of course, that European investors remain faithful to these principles and treat their employees abroad the same as their employees in Europe (whose labour conditions, depending on the sector, are sometimes far from ideal as well). In other words, the EU must take care that by cooperating it does not create new inequalities.

Why would an authoritarian regime be interested in any of this? Because economic development, undertaken in such a way, generates domestic stability, which the regime needs. Domestic stability, especially in our neighbours, directly benefits the EU. But the EU's long-term calculation is also that as social and economy equality increases, citizens will start demanding more political equality as well, so that gradually a dynamic for democratic reform will emerge organically. That is an expectation, not a certainty, and there are exceptions to this rule. China, for example, has successfully lifted millions of people out of poverty, while maintaining internal regime security. As of yet, there are many protests against arbitrary government decisions, but no general wave in favour of democratisation. Perhaps because people fear that another system would no longer be able to guarantee internal security and that change would lead to anarchy and chaos?

Nevertheless, promoting social and economic equality does seem to the best way of generating a desire for political equality over time. In a peaceful way, without creating any shocks, because when people are hopeful about their economic situation they will at first be hopeful about improving the political situation of their country too. If a regime responds with increased repression, it might yet come to an explosion – nobody can guarantee a peaceful transition.

Democratisation is a long-term objective, but the EU must critically monitor the human rights situation in any country with which it cooperates. Ultimately, democracy and human rights go hand in hand, but in the framework of a sequential approach to equality, human rights can and must be on the agenda from day one of any diplomatic relationship. Countries must clearly understand that the fact that they need not commit to democratic reforms in order to enter into close relations with the EU does not mean that the EU will no longer speak out about human rights (publicly or behind closed doors, whatever is most effective). We should not do that in the expectation to create change in the short term. But we must do it in order to remain true to our values and to preserve our legitimacy and credibility. In the past, too often those have been damaged because we did not maintain sufficient critical distance from all kinds of unsavoury regimes. By consistently standing up for human rights, the EU will at least stand on the good side of history when, one day, political reform does come to a country – contrary to what happened with the Arab Spring, when the local population saw the EU as a faithful ally of the regimes that they sought to depose.

Human rights is the red line, therefore, which the EU can never cross. That red line must be drawn at the right place though. The EU can cooperate with undemocratic regimes. The EU can even cooperate with regimes that violate human rights. It has no choice, or it will never be able to achieve its objectives in areas in which those regimes have power. No one can end the war in Syria, for example, without sitting at the table with Iran and Saudi Arabia. The same applies to the war in Ukraine and Russia. That feels uncomfortable, but the alternative, to say that Europe cannot talk or cooperate or even trade with any undemocratic regime, simply amounts to locking ourselves out of international politics. That is precisely the ignorance of the real world that we should leave behind us. Of course, the Saudi Arabian theocracy repulses us, but clamouring for an end to relations is too easy. There are too many dictatorships in the world. The EU cannot afford to go back to square one, to politics as charity, in which the EU, as if it were a huge NGO, may preserve its virginity but will never maintain its interests. Poor but pure cannot be our strategic objective.

What is the red line then? That the EU, by cooperating with a country, cannot in any way become party to human rights violations itself. The EU cannot fund activities that lead to human rights violations, cannot export weapons if they are put to use in wrongful ways, and cannot participate in military operations in which war crimes are committed.

There will always be a grey zone, however, especially when it comes to security cooperation. In the fight against terrorism, for example, European intelligence services cooperate closely with the intelligence services of our southern neighbours. Moroccan and Turkish intelligence also keep a close eye on Moroccan and Turkish communities in Europe, even though most people concerned are (also) citizens of an EU Member State. The same goes for the services of many other neighbours. We know that those services use methods that would be totally unacceptable in Europe. If I ever were a suspect, and could choose who would interrogate me, I would very quickly give myself up to Belgian intelligence, and not just because I think the catering would be more to my taste. Clearly, therefore, cooperating with such services directly undermines our discourse on human rights. The use of torture in the fight against terrorism probably provokes even more terrorism. But at the same time cooperation with our neighbours is crucial to prevent terrorism in Europe. Not an easy choice.

Accepting that there is no 100 per cent clean answer and still daring to make a choice that is in our best interest: that too is part and parcel of the more pragmatic approach to international politics, of the middle way. Avoiding choices and letting things be, is a choice too, by the way – but seldom the right one.

No equality without sovereignty

Developing a long-term approach to promote equality is hardly possible in a state with limited power to govern, because it is dominated by another state, or because it is engaged in war with armed groups on its territory or with another state (and the two often go together). A state that seeks to create equality must first of all be sovereign. That means making its own decisions, in full independence and without any external pressure, and maintaining full territorial integrity. If the EU seeks to promote equality, it should thus also help defend the sovereignty of the states that are willing to cooperate with it to that end.

I emphasise this because it is more important and less evident than it seems. Many other powers follow a very different strategy. Russia, for example, does not seek equal and sovereign partners at all. In what it considers to be its sphere of influence, it wants pliable protectorates, client states that align their foreign and security policies with Moscow and ensure that their economies serve Russia's needs. The EU should make it crystal clear that its approach is entirely different.

Think of our neighbours in the east. The EU objective is not that all of those countries would align with us. It is not as if there has been a secret meeting on the top floor of the Commission's Berlaymont Building in Brussels where the EU decided: Ukraine must be ours. To put it frankly: the EU does not need Ukraine. If Kiev, in all freedom, would have opted for closer relations with Moscow than with Brussels, that would not have been a problem for the EU. Somewhat cynically, perhaps, one might even say it would have made things a lot easier. We would not have had a crisis with Russia and we would not have needed to worry about the security of our energy supply from Russia via Ukraine. But if Ukraine itself chooses to (also) forge close relations with us, and accepts to adopt our values and a lot of our regulations to that end, we cannot accept that another country would block that choice.

For the EU, the one does not need to exclude the other. For Brussels, Ukraine can very well enter into close relations with Russia at the same time. Putin is the one who has turned this into a competition, by insisting on an exclusive sphere of influence. The EU objective should be that all states can make their own choices without anybody else making their choices for them. Not the Russians, not the Chinese, not the Americans – and not us either.

To put it very starkly: in certain cases, this objective may imply that the EU must militarily assist another state, if the destruction of its sovereignty and its appropriation by another state, or its dissolution, threatens vital European interests. In itself, the fact that a state is a dictatorship does not constitute a ground for military action, however, because that would cause an endless series of wars. Only in cases of the gravest human rights violations (war crimes, crimes against humanity, ethnic cleansing, genocide) can the Security Council (and it alone) order military intervention. This is the principle of the Responsibility to Protect (R2P): the notion that only in the case of these serious crimes, the international community must prioritise the protection of the civilian population over the sovereignty of the state concerned, if that state is unable or unwilling to defend its own people, or is itself the perpetrator. I will return to the cases in which the EU can consider the use of force in more detail in Chapter 5.

Realpolitik with European characteristics

Equality and sovereignty can be the core of a new EU Grand Strategy. Our fundamental purpose is to maintain our equality-based model of society (and to improve it, for in Europe too there is a lot of inequality yet). The best way of doing that in a peaceful and non-confrontational manner is by cooperating as equal partners with other countries, regardless of the political nature of their regime, on those dimensions of equality (security, economic, political) in which we and they both see a win-win situation. Without obliging others to commit to steps that they actually are not willing to take, and without obliging ourselves to pretend that we can achieve things that actually are unachievable. Our educated guess is that over time increased equality in those other dimensions will induce the citizens of the countries that we cooperate with to demand more political equality too. In the long term therefore, the objective remains the emergence of well-governed democratic states, for those do not wage war against each other and are internally stable. Pending that, our red line is that by cooperating with other countries we can never become party ourselves to human rights violations. Our commitment is that we are ready to help defend the sovereignty of those countries that are willing to go far in their cooperation with us, especially if precisely because of that choice they run into trouble.

Such a grand strategy remains true to the universal values upon which Europe itself is built, but in an honest and pragmatic way, without generating expectations that we cannot fulfil, and taking into account opportunities and limitations in the real world. It is a positive and resolute way too: in Europe we have built a model of society in which we can take pride, which we can promote in the rest of the world without shame. In the past we have done too much finger-pointing, but the EU should not overcompensate: one cannot base a grand strategy on humility. Adopting a humble stance when one is a great power will either be seen as false modesty, or as another example of European otherworldliness – and we will still not be taken seriously. Whether we like it or not, the EU is a great power, because of its political, economic, and military weight. The question is whether we are willing to act like one: to use all instruments of power in order to shape the world, instead of passively undergoing history. That does not mean that the EU should play classic power politics just like so many others. Equality and sovereignty can be the heart of a distinctive great power stance, which positively distinguishes the EU from the other great powers.

This type of grand strategy amounts to a return to *realpolitik*, in the original meaning of the term. Realpolitik has acquired a rather negative connotation. When we hear the word, we think of Bismarck, Kissinger, and (anachronistically) Machiavelli: the end justifies the means. The man who in 1853 coined the term was a German liberal, however (Bew, 2016). In the revolutionary year 1848, Ludwig von Rochau was involved with the attempt to introduce a liberal constitution in Germany. That attempt ended in failure, which induced von Rochau to reject liberal utopianism – but not the liberal democratic values as such. For him realpolitik meant the necessity of having a pragmatic strategy to bring those liberal values into practice. Put sharply: those who just dream about liberal values will never achieve them. Without a realistic strategy to gain power and to exercise it, the liberal dream will always remain just that: a dream. This is exactly what the EU should do: bring into practice all dimensions of equality in a pragmatic manner. Since today the notion of realpolitik is mostly used in a different meaning though, we could call this realpolitik with European characteristics.

The new strategy that Mogherini presented to the European Council in June 2016, following a one-year consultation process, goes in this direction (Mogherini, 2016). The *Global Strategy for the European Union's Foreign and Security Policy*, or

Global Strategy or EUGS for short, outlines the direction of EU external action for the next five to seven years.[3] The new strategy precisely tries to find the middle way between dreamy idealism and unprincipled power politics. It calls this middle way *principled pragmatism*.[4] Not exactly a catchy term, unfortunately, and indeed in Brussels it hasn't caught on. Thought was given to it though, for in an earlier version of the text it was "pragmatic idealism", but apparently someone objected to that. Nonetheless, "principled pragmatism" truly is the European realpolitik that the EU needs.

The centrality of a more realpolitik approach is reflected, first of all, in the fact that the *Global Strategy* for the first time ever defines the vital interests of the EU. As already mentioned, for a long time interests were simply not discussed in an EU context. The general feeling was that it might be an interesting academic exercise to try and list the common interests of the EU, but that in reality Member States would never be able to reach consensus on that. But now they have, and EU vital interests are written down black on white. The list is not surprising, but the opposite would be unexpected as in reality everybody actually had a pretty clear idea of what our shared interests are. We just had to formulate them.

First, the *Global Strategy* states that the EU will "guarantee the security of its citizens and territory". Second, it will "advance the prosperity of its people". Importantly, the *Global Strategy* explicitly adds that "prosperity must be shared". Understand: it's not only the aggregate prosperity of the EU as a whole that matters but also the prosperity of every individual citizen. Third, the EU will "foster the resilience of its democracies". Again there is an important addition: "Consistently living up to our values will determine our external credibility and influence". These three vital interests cover the three dimensions of what I have defined as *equality*. In order to be able to maintain these interests, the EU will, fourth, "promote a rules-based global order with multilateralism as its key principle and the United Nations at its core". Now that these four vital interests have been codified, every Member State that wants to take an initiative, or Mogherini and the EU institutions themselves, can forever refer to them.

Mogherini's priorities

Realpolitik also informs the five priorities that the *Global Strategy* then defines. Five areas in which in view of the threats and challenges around us, priority action is necessary in order to defend our vital interests.

The first priority is "the security of our union". Our territory, our borders and our citizens must be protected. There is an evident link between internal and external security. The 2003 strategy did not really address the former. Although it was adopted in the wake of "9/11", the terrorist attacks by al-Qaeda against the World Trade Center in New York and the Pentagon in Washington, the focus was on the world around the EU. In 2016 that was no longer possible. Citizens that worry about terrorism in Europe, about the refugee and migration crisis and, in the eastern Member States, about Russian assertiveness, expect a strategy that first of all guarantees their very own security, at home and in their own countries. Had the *Global Strategy* not put domestic security first, it would not have been taken seriously.

Priority number two is "state and societal resilience to our east and south". The EU cannot save the world, at least not in a day, and thus opts for a clear focus on its own periphery: "We will take responsibility foremost in Europe and its surrounding regions, while pursuing targeted engagement further afield". The importance of geopolitical analysis is obvious: if the regions surrounding us would be destabilised, the potential impact on our vital interests would be the largest. Our periphery should be understood broadly, however: according to the *Global Strategy*, it reaches until Central Asia in the east and Central Africa in the south. That is quite a large part of the world, which encompasses many more countries than the existing European Neighbourhood Policy (ENP). A part of the world, moreover, in which numerous wars are raging. The emphasis on the European periphery should not be mistaken for a lack of ambition, therefore. Quite the opposite: if the EU, together with its allies and partners, were to prove itself capable of solving the crises that stretch from Ukraine to Mali, it would truly have earned great power status.

In its new strategy, the EU effectively distances itself from the earlier policy of active democratisation. Where in our neighbouring countries an internal dynamic towards democratisation emerges, the EU will of course support it, because in a best case scenario their "success as prosperous, peaceful and stable democracies would reverberate across their respective regions". But the *Global Strategy* refers only to Tunisia and Georgia as successful examples. In many other neighbouring countries there is no trend toward democratisation. Many countries are not even aspiring to closer ties with the EU. Hence a new emphasis emerges: not on equality, but on the resilience of states and societies as an alternative for democratisation.

What is *resilience* exactly? "States are resilient when societies feel they are becoming better off and have hope in the future", says the *Global Strategy*. That is in tune with the egalitarian aspiration on which European society is founded. But the *Global Strategy* remains rather vague on what resilience means in practice, and offers various interpretations that complicate rather than complete the picture. Apparently resilience concerns "desertification, land degradation, and water and food scarcity", but also "the fight against terrorism, corruption and organised crime" and "the protection of human rights", as well as "development, migration, trade, investment, infrastructure, education, health, and research". How this very broad concept can be made operational, and how it is to lead to peace and stability, the *Global Strategy* doesn't say. Nor does it specify the means required or where these are to come from.

The third priority that the *Global Strategy* advances is "an integrated approach to conflict". The recognition of the stark reality outside the EU and the choice for realpolitik appear clearly from a much stronger awareness than before of the need to combine political and economic with military power. "For Europe, soft and hard power go hand in hand", Mogherini says in the foreword to the document. The 2003 *European Security Strategy* did already demonstrate geopolitical insight. "Even in an era of globalisation, geography is still important", it said at the time. In the *Global Strategy* the EU shows that in addition it has understood how other powers are engaged in geopolitical competition and do not hesitate to use blackmail and force to prevail. Hence the need for a clear military level of ambition for the EU: "Europeans must be able to protect Europe, respond to external crises, and assist in developing our partners' security and defence capacities, carrying out these tasks in cooperation with others". If necessary, the EU should be able to act on this level of ambition alone, or so it can be deduced from Mogherini's plea for "strategic autonomy" in her foreword. The *Global Strategy* does indeed say that "European security and defence efforts should enable the EU to act autonomously while also contributing to and undertaking actions in cooperation with NATO".

The fourth priority, "cooperative regional orders", can also be read as a recognition of the need for realpolitik. In various regions around the world an intense competition for spheres of influence and natural resources is ongoing between great and regional powers. The region in between the EU and Russia, the Middle East and the Gulf, and the East and South China Seas are all examples of contested regions. What is really needed in these parts of the world is a new regional order, which satisfies all powers concerned, so that a new balance of power can bring stability. This is a diplomatic challenge more than anything else, for which the EU is well placed.

The *Global Strategy* mentions, for example, that the EU will try to deepen dialogue between Iran and the states of the Gulf Cooperation Council (GCC), led by Saudi Arabia, who are competing for dominance of the Gulf region, including by intervening militarily on opposite sides in the wars in Syria, Iraq and Yemen. This is a good example of the diplomatic potential that the EU holds, as one of the few major actors that can maintain good relations with both Tehran and Riyadh. In the US, by contrast, relations with the "arch enemy" Iran have always remained controversial, in spite of the 2015 agreement about the country's nuclear programme, from which Donald Trump eventually withdrew (in May 2018). Most Europeans do not quite see how the "ally" Saudi Arabia is so much better than the "enemy" Iran: both countries violate human rights, implement the death penalty, and deploy their armed forces in the region without any regard for the civilian population. Politically, Iran actually is more open than Saudi Arabia, for there are presidential elections that, though they are steered, do allow for a certain degree of choice.

Finally, the fifth priority links back to the more idealistic agenda of 2003. Unbridled power politics lead to tensions and increase the chance of conflict. The only way to prevent conflict is to incite the great powers and other actors to cooperate as much as possible, through all kinds of international organisations, treaties, regimes and ad hoc groupings. That too is a task for a proactive European diplomacy. Under the heading of "global governance for the 21st century", the *Global Strategy* therefore states that "The EU will strive for a strong UN as the bedrock of the multilateral rules-based order, and develop globally coordinated responses with international and regional organisations, states and non-state actors". The 2003 strategy called this "effective multilateralism". The EU aim is not just to preserve the multilateral system, but to thoroughly reform it. Otherwise there is a risk that states that feel underrepresented could create their own organisations, which would be detrimental to the universal membership and the universally applicable rules of the various UN bodies. It would certainly not be in the interest of Europe, for if China and Russia set up institutions of their own, we will not have a seat at the table. It is important therefore to make room for everybody in the existing institutions.

Real and realistic

The *Global Strategy* defines a real yet realistic ambition for the EU as an international actor. Real, because if the EU wants to implement this agenda, it will have to up its game. This will require a much more active and creative foreign policy than the EU has waged up to now. But realistic, because the EU is capable of waging such a policy: it possesses or can acquire all the necessary means, if only it wants to. Realistic, also in the sense that this strategy is anchored in the real world, the harsh world outside the EU, which is driven by power politics, interests, and geopolitics. Ideals are necessary, for they indicate the overall direction. But you also need a concrete plan of action on how to follow that direction, step by step. That is "principled pragmatism" or "realpolitik with European characteristics".

The EU must play this role, for "a fragile world calls for a more confident and responsible European Union", as Mogherini says in her foreword. Success cannot be guaranteed, for the world really is fragile. The election of Donald Trump as President of the United States on 8 November 2016 has added an additional factor of uncertainty to the many existing tensions. The EU itself is fragile too, more than we thought. There's not only Brexit but also the success of explicitly anti-EU parties, both old and new.

Before the EU can bring its new realpolitik into practice, it will have to further clarify its strategic orientation and make some tough decisions. How autonomous does Europe really dare and want to be with regard to the US, and what does that mean in the long term for the role of NATO? Which sort of relationship do we want to maintain at the same time with the two other great powers, China and Russia? What does "principled pragmatism" mean exactly for relations with our neighbours? Is resilience a sufficient basis for a new start or should the EU rather advance the notion of equality? Does it make sense to talk about resilience or even equality if the EU cannot help protect the sovereignty of those neighbour states that are inclined to close cooperation, with military means if necessary? Does Europe have the required military means for such a role?

All these difficult questions are on the table. In today's global environment they can no longer be escaped. Further postponing the debate does not make any sense, therefore: the longer we wait to make our own decisions, the more we will be the object of the decisions of the other great powers. I, for one, certainly don't trust any of those to have the European interest at heart.

Notes

1 I have often thought that China always overreacts to this. The Dalai Lama visiting a European head of state or government is not big news. Few people in Europe will care – unless China makes it into an issue by protesting against it, prompting the public to expect that their government will assert its right to receive whomever it wants.
2 I warmly thank Emeritus Professor Gustaaf Geeraerts of the Vrije Universiteit Brussel, who introduced me there, and Professor Xinning Song, who has continued to invite me.
3 *Global* is to be understood in both geographical and functional terms: the strategy encompasses EU relations with the globe, in all of its dimensions, from trade and development to diplomacy and defence.
4 At the same time, "un pragmatisme à principes" is one of the definitions of Gaullism, the doctrine of Charles de Gaulle (Servent, 2017, p. 422). This is a coincidence, but it does bring to mind the trick played by the French when the name for the predecessor of the Euro was chosen. ECU supposedly stood for European Currency Unit, but it just so happened that it also was the name of an old French coin, the écu.

References

John Bew, *Realpolitik: A History*. Oxford, Oxford University Press, 2016.
Tony Judt, *Postwar: A History of Europe Since 1945*. London, Penguin, 2005.
Henry Kissinger, *World Order*. New York, Penguin, 2015.
Federica Mogherini, *Shared Vision, Common Action: A Stronger Europa. A Global Strategy for the European Union's Foreign and Security Policy*. Brussels, EU, June 2016.
Pierre Servent, *Les présidents et la guerre: Une enquête inédite au cœur de la défense*. Paris, Perrin, 2017.

3

EUROPE AND THE (OTHER) GREAT POWERS

Is Europe more concerned about the direction that US policy has taken than about the actions of the other two great powers, China and Russia? The election of Donald Trump came as a shock to Europeans (and to many Americans, of course). Many of the ideas that Trump announced during his campaign were directly at odds with the worldview and the interests of the EU. Many of his actions since being inaugurated as 45th president of the US (20 January 2017) have confirmed all of Europe's fears. The world got to see many more examples of Trump's black-and-white views, and of his radical turnabouts, than it cared for. The important thing to realise is that this goes way beyond Trump. He voices his views in an extreme way, but many of those views are shared by wide sectors of American society. Some of his policies even reflect a long-term structural change in America's role in the world. No matter who follows Trump in the White House, neither US policy nor transatlantic relations will return exactly to what it was like before Trump.

With friends like these . . .

There are many areas in which US policy under the Trump administration has begun to diverge from European policy. The most glaring illustration of Trump's warped view of the world is his idea of the global economy. Trump feels that the US has been tricked, not just by its adversaries, but even by its friends. According to him, the US is at the losing end of the global economy, and is put at a serious disadvantage by the existing multilateral free-trade agreements (FTAs). Those who took advantage from that, says Trump, are mostly China and Europe. Within Europe, Germany is his preferred scapegoat. During his first meeting with the Presidents of the European Council and the European Commission (May 2017), he actually singled out Germany as being "bad, very bad" (Teffer and Maurice,

2017). Trump's favoured remedy is protectionism: introducing tariffs in order to limit the competition from imports into the US, and renegotiating trade agreements in favour of the US.

Trump reckoned he could force through a new bilateral trade agreement with Germany. During their first meeting (March 2017), Chancellor Angela Merkel had to explain to the President that, unfortunately for his plans, that is legally impossible. Since the EU is a single market and a customs union, external trade is an EU competence; individual Member States simply can no longer conclude trade agreements even if they wanted to. Ironically, the press dubbed the Merkel-Trump meeting a meeting between the leader of the free world and the President of the US – the latter has forfeited the title that traditionally accrued to his predecessors (Rubin, 2017). The way Trump interpreted Merkel's lesson was probably not what Europeans had expected, however. He reportedly suggested French President Emmanuel Macron during his state visit to Washington (April 2018) to just leave the EU then and get a better bilateral deal with the US in reward. Macron's laconic reaction: "You can imagine my response" (Gray, 2018).

In spite of all the EU's efforts to convince him of the danger and foolishness of such a course, Trump announced punitive tariffs on steel and aluminium against the EU as a whole in March 2018. Only to immediately postpone their implementation, but then he suddenly announced their entry into force on 1 June. Europe is not the only victim: sanctions were introduced against Canada and China as well, and Trump also renegotiated the North American Free Trade Agreement (NAFTA) between the US, Canada and Mexico. Protectionism can lead to a general trade war, with dramatic consequences for the entire world. If the US continues along this road, it will lead to an inevitable breach with Europe.

Protectionism will certainly not revive the abandoned coal mines and factories in the US. If Trump really wants to get the US economy going again to the benefit of "Joe Six Pack", he should implement his investment plan, his only sensible campaign promise. Everybody who has travelled to the US can testify how the superpower is lagging behind in terms of infrastructure, not just compared to Europe, but in many ways even to China. But since more than half of US citizens do not have passports, they never travel abroad and probably don't realise that their dilapidated airports and crumbling bridges are not the best in the world. Or that the rest of the world has high-speed trains. That investment plan will likely never happen though. Trump started his administration by increasing the defence budget with 10 per cent per year (and, at close to $600 billion, it was huge already) and by implementing a major tax cut that mostly benefits the big incomes. Where would he find the money to invest in infrastructure? That suits the Republican Party nicely, for, with the exception of defence, they stand for an as-small-as-possible federal government anyway.

Europeans should not forget however that during the 2016 presidential campaign, even Trump's opponent, Hillary Clinton, was forced to distance herself from the Trans-Pacific Partnership (TPP) that President Barack Obama had negotiated, under pressure from the left wing of the Democratic Party. Free trade may be a vote-loser in the US for some time to come. Hopefully protectionism will not inflict too much damage before the US comes to its senses.

A second reason for concern in Europe is Trump's fraught relations with China. Even if Trump hadn't imposed tariffs on Europe, a trade war between the US and China would be a disaster for the global economy. But Trump is also increasing military pressure in Asia in order to maintain the US' dominant position in the Pacific. That, however, is the continuation of a strategy initiated by his predecessor, Obama. In 2012 Obama announced the "pivot to Asia": a shift of the focus of US Grand Strategy to Asia and especially to China. This is a structural change in American strategy. The reason is simple: seen from Washington, Russia no longer threatens America's position in the world. Russia is a declining power, with a unidimensional economy that is entirely dependent on the energy market and with a stagnating population.[1] It remains a nuclear power, of course, and even a power in decline can strike hard when it wants too; it might in fact be even more motivated to do so, in order to shore up its position. But Russia has not been able to challenge America's global predominance for a long time. The only great power that could catch up with or even overtake the US is China. At the 19th congress of the Chinese Communist Party (CCP), in October 2017, President Xi announced that by 2050 China aims to create a "world class military". This statement cannot but have reinforced the school of thought in America that considers China a potential future military threat to the US. In Europe, by contrast, we too observe how assertively China behaves toward its neighbours, but almost nobody thinks in terms of a potential Chinese military threat to Europe itself.

This different American assessment of Chinese power and China's possible intentions explains the "pivot". It does not really entail a major redeployment of military assets, although the US has reinforced its Pacific fleet vis-à-vis the Atlantic fleet, whereas in the past they used to be of equal size. But the American forces in Europe have been downsized several years ago already, from 250,000 at their peak to some 60,000 today. What remains, for the most part, are big logistic hubs rather than combat units, from which forces can be deployed and supplied anywhere in the world (including in Europe itself, if that were necessary). Only on the border with Russia has the US deployed new combat units again, starting in 2017, as part of the prepositioning of forces in Poland and the Baltic states by various NATO allies so as to signal to Russia that the Alliance stands ready to defend itself. This concerns thousands of troops – but not hundreds of thousands as in the days of the Cold War. The "pivot" means that the US has reordered its priorities. Washington looks at the world differently. Naturally, the US remains a global power with global interests, and if those interests are threatened it will intervene, including in Europe or the Middle East. But those regions are increasingly seen as distractions rather than objectives in their own right. What Washington wants to focus on if it can is China and Asia.

The question is: how will the US pursue its Asia strategy? In his first months in office, Trump emphasised the military dimension of the pivot, presumably in order to contain China. Relations with China got off to a bad start when Trump appeared to put the "One China Principle" in doubt, according to which states recognise only the People's Republic of China as a state and not Taiwan, which Beijing considers to be a province. In practice most states support the status quo and consider only peaceful change to be acceptable. Most do maintain diplomatic relations with Taiwan, which is a democratic and open society, but formally they have "trade offices" or the like in Taipei rather than embassies. Trump went much further and declared that if China were unwilling to revisit economic relations, he might just revisit the status of Taiwan. Against all precedent, he also accepted a phone call from Taiwanese President Tsai Ing-Wen (December 2016) to congratulate her on her election earlier that year. Subsequently, in a telephone conversation with Chinese President Xi Jinping, Trump confirmed that the US would not put into doubt the "One China Principle" after all, though he later declared that he said that because Xi had asked him to, which did not betray a lot of conviction. Since then, the US has been stepping up the military component of its relations with Taiwan.

Not surprisingly, the world held its breath when Xi visited Trump in his Florida resort, Mar-a-Lago, for their first meeting (April 2017). The hundred-day cooling-off period that was agreed and Trump's state visit to Beijing at the end of 2017 have since been overshadowed by the start of a US–China tariff war. Xi's visit itself was already clouded by Trump ordering a missile strike against a Syrian air force base (7 April 2017) as a retaliation for an apparent chemical weapons attack by Assad's forces (whereas until then the US had only targeted IS and not the government's armed forces). One can be certain that Xi was not amused – if there is one thing that Chinese decision-makers do not like, it is surprises. Trump seemed to get the taste of it on the other hand, for barely a week later, on 13 April, the Massive Ordnance Air Blast (MOAB, commonly known, in action movie style, as "the mother of all bombs") was deployed for the first time, against IS elements in Afghanistan.

In all likelihood, the missile strike on Syria during Xi's visit was meant to impress the Chinese President with a not very subtle message: we can do this in Asia too. That message was underlined shortly afterwards by the action in Afghanistan and by fleet movements in Asia. That may work in the short term. China knows that today it cannot compete militarily with the US. But in the long term it may actually have the opposite effect, and encourage China even more to build up its military power in order to be able to withstand similar American pressure in the future. Again, it is very clear that if the US would seek a confrontation with China, in the economic or even in the military sphere, it would not be in the interest of the EU to follow suit.

Ever since that first Trump–Xi meeting, a game of testing and teasing has been going on. One day Trump announces that a series of Chinese companies are no longer allowed to do business in the US, only to announce exceptions the next day, which then however are followed by the imposition of heavy fines quite regardless. And so it continues on many issues: volatility rather than strategy.

One crucial area in which this plays out is the North Korean nuclear issue. Trump began to threaten military action against North Korea, in order to force President Kim Jong-Un to abandon his nuclear weapon programme. That crisis reached a pitch when, after several missile tests earlier in 2017, on 4 July, Independence Day in the US, North Korea successfully tested its first intercontinental ballistic missile (ICBM), thus presumably putting the continental US within range of its nuclear weapons. Once again the world held its breath as Trump threatened North Korea with "fire and fury", and Kim Jong-Un responded with a threat to the US island of Guam. The problem is North Korea, of course, which ran a first nuclear test in 2006 already, and not the US. But from the US we would expect help in solving the problem, not in escalating the crisis by the use of incendiary rhetoric. The world saw a US President who seemed to act impulsively, without much consideration for the effect his words can have. In early August, the UN Security Council adopted strong sanctions against North Korea, with the support of China, the country's traditional ally, and Russia. Nevertheless, Trump repeatedly blamed China for its lack of assistance.

Chinese pressure did seem to have an impact this time, however, as Kim unexpectedly invited Trump to meet (though the real reasons for this volte-face are difficult to gauge). Trump, even more surprisingly, immediately accepted and the two met in Singapore on 12 June 2018. The only immediate outcome was that during his press conference afterward, Trump, seeming à l'improviste, announced a halt to US military manoeuvres in South Korea, in return only for a repetition of previous vague undertakings on the part of North Korea to abandon its nuclear weapons programme. Europeans continued to worry, therefore, about how Trump would react if it would become clear that there really was no deal. Very disconcerting for the US' European allies was how Trump treated his ally South Korea, which learned about the suspension of military exercises live at the press conference.

In the past China had certainly not done as much as it should have to steer North Korea into the right direction. But the US, if anybody, should understand that China does not fully control North Korea, for the relationship is very similar to that between the US itself and Israel: the ally you wish you never had. An ally that causes trouble more than anything else, but which, for reasons of domestic politics, one cannot abandon. US Middle East policy is a third area of contention with Europe. Trump visited Israel in May 2017. In spite of rhetoric about peace and a meeting with Palestinian President Mahmoud Abbas, it quickly became clear that Israeli Prime Minister Benjamin Netanyahu has nothing to fear from Trump. Quite the contrary, on 6 December 2017 Trump announced that the US would recognise Jerusalem as the capital of Israel, ignoring the rights of the Palestinians and the position of the international community and of the EU in particular. The US embassy in Jerusalem was opened by Trump's daughter Ivanka on 14 May 2018. As predicted, anger and riots throughout the region were the immediate consequence. So much for Trump's call to join "the noble quest for lasting peace" (Trump, 2017a).

If the objective of Trump's other main Middle East initiative, the missile strike against Assad's forces, was to force a breakthrough in the Syrian war, it quickly turned out that Assad need not fear anything either. The Russian military intervention has assured that Assad stays firmly in the saddle. Even a second missile strike (April 2018), together with France and the UK, in retaliation for another instance of the use of chemical weapons, could not change that basic fact. A permanent settlement of the war in Syria, and in Iraq, is impossible if it does not include Iran. It is a consequence of the 2003 US invasion and subsequent implosion of Iraq, which acted as a balancer towards Iran, that Iran has become an indispensable power in the Middle East. Yet for Trump and the Republicans, Iran remains part of the "axis of evil", in spite of the international agreement about its nuclear programme. The EU on the other hand quickly started normalising its relations with Iran. During a visit to Saudi Arabia in May 2017, Trump openly sided with Riyadh against Tehran. That is exactly what the EU realises one shouldn't do. Rather than choosing sides, the EU should assume an equidistant position in between Saudi Arabia and Iran, and seek a regional balance of power that is acceptable to both. In May 2018 Trump did what everyone feared and withdrew the US from the Iran nuclear deal. Since both President Macron and Chancellor Merkel had very publicly pleaded to maintain the deal during visits to Washington just before, this was nothing less than a slap in the face of America's European allies.

The only advantage of Trump's involvement in Syria, as seen from Europe, was that we no longer had to worry that Trump, seeking to demonstrate his statesmanship, would conclude a quick deal with President Vladimir Putin at the expense of European interests (notably in Ukraine) – a fourth issue on which the EU and the EU might diverge. During his campaign, Trump steered very close to Putin, and suspicions soon arose of collusion between the campaign and Russia. Trump's first National Security Advisor, General Michael Flynn, even had to step down, because he had lied about his Russian contacts, and a special investigation was started. The Russian reaction to the Syrian strike made it clear however that there would be no Trump–Putin honeymoon. That doesn't mean an agreement between the US and Russia is impossible, but it will, as always, be the result of long negotiations on concrete interests. It will not drop from the sky simply because that is what Donald Trump would like.

The US is not the cause of all of the world's troubles. Russia and China both do their part to cause worry in Europe. But Trump's extreme style, or rather the absence of style, cannot but captivate everyone's attention. The result is that many in Europe do indeed worry more about what the President of the US, our most important ally, is going to say or tweet next than about any other actor in world politics. Trump's confrontational way of doing foreign policy increases rather than reduces global tensions. The new *National Security Strategy* (NSS) that his administration published (December 2017) actually promises as much (Trump, 2017b). The keyword is competition, notably with China and Russia. "An America that successfully competes is the best way to prevent conflict", Trump's NSS states. And here I am thinking that competition creates conflict.

Unpredictability and unreason

Trump's first Brussels trip took place on Ascension Day 2017 (25 May), but he certainly did not ascend very high in the esteem of Europe. The whole world saw footage of a group photo being taken at NATO, where Trump unceremoniously shoved aside the Prime Minister of Montenegro, so that the Head of the House of Trump could take his rightful place in the first row, chin up and chest out, as shining and pompous as any Trump Tower. On that day Europeans got the picture of "America First": what it really means is "Trump First", and woe unto those who risk obscuring his place in the sun.

Under the Trump administration, one never knows what US policy will be. We in Europe don't, and arguably neither do many American officials. This unpredictability is very dangerous. The more the great powers are clear about their intentions, the more one can guide global politics along a stable course. Because of his enormous ego, great impulsiveness, and lack of any depth, Trump has been compared with the German Emperor Wilhelm II, who through his ill-considered alliances and provocations plunged his country into the First World War (Heisbourg, 2017). Wilhelm II quickly started steering the wrong course as soon as he had fired the architect of the empire, Chancellor Otto von Bismarck, and began to imagine himself as a master strategist. Sorcerer's apprentice Trump began without a Bismarck or a Kissinger to guide him at all.

The unpredictability of the Trump administration is due to not only the personality of the president but also to the fact that there are at least three factions inside his White House. They continuously contradict each other and it is never quite clear which one has most influence at which time.

First, there are the ideologues, led initially by White House Chief Strategist Steve Bannon, who later was fired from this post. Euphemistically dubbed "alt-right" in the US, this man and his acolytes should be called for what they are: the extreme right. Bannon got himself fired, but others remain, not in the least John Bolton, Trump's third National Security Advisor. Vice President Michael Pence too belongs to the far right of the political spectrum; witness his term as governor of Indiana, which was marked by an active limitation of the right to abortion and a confrontation with the LGBT community. If Trump were to be impeached, which many in Europe seem to be hoping for, in Pence we would definitely have a president with more sense of decorum, but in terms of policy he would be as far removed from the European mainstream as Trump himself.

Under the influence of the likes of Bannon, Bolton, and others, Trump is the first-ever American president who is opposed to the existence of the EU as such. Many of his predecessors were sceptical about the EU's ability to achieve results, especially in foreign and security policy – one can hardly blame them. But all of them realised that the stability of the European continent is an essential interest of the US – and that it is the EU that guarantees it. The US was one of the main initiators of the process of European integration, after the Second World War, by linking economic support under the Marshall Plan to European cooperation. In

2017, however, which saw the 70th anniversary of the Marshall Plan, Trump welcomed Brexit and expressed the hope that more countries would follow the British example and leave the EU. During a visit to Warsaw, in July 2017, he encouraged the Polish government in what he seemed to consider its brave resistance against the Brussels bureaucracy. In June 2018, Trump's newly appointed ambassador to Germany went so far as to say that he would try to empower conservatives (read: Trump allies) across Europe. The EU cannot just dismiss this: such an attitude at the highest level of our most important ally is very dangerous indeed.

Next to the ideologues, there are the professionals, starting with the generals: James Mattis as Secretary of Defence, Herbert McMaster as National Security Advisor (succeeding another general, Flynn, but replaced in turn by Bolton), and White House Chief of Staff John Kelly. When Trump entered office, Mattis especially was referred to by many as the voice of reason, the man who would guard the president from risky ventures. But can we be so sure of that after all the muscle flexing towards Syria, Afghanistan, and North Korea? It didn't seem very promising in the first place that a man nicknamed "Mad Dog" Mattis was presented as the most reasonable in the cabinet. These men may see themselves as restraining the president, but they do share many of his views, notably on Iran. Let us not forget that President George W. Bush was also surrounded by cabinet members and counsellors with loads of experience who advised him to invade Iraq and bring down the regime of Saddam Hussein, with the consequences that we all know. Trump's first Secretary of State, Rex Tillerson, former CEO of ExxonMobil, remained rather invisible at first, but then also joined the camp of the active professionals. As he gained more prominence, he also began to dismantle his own apparatus though, cutting the State Department budget by 30 per cent. As a close friend, herself a retired US diplomat, put it to me: soon between Tillerson and the lady who makes his coffee, there will be nobody left. Tillerson himself left the building, in fact, and was replaced by former CIA chief Mike Pompeo, whose worldview is closer to that of the ideologues.

And then there's family: in this White House the president's family members seem to have great influence on decision-making, especially daughter Ivanka and her husband Jared Kushner, both of whom have been officially appointed as advisors to the president. In combination with the quick turnover of senior cabinet members, this makes it very difficult for the EU and its Member States to find the right way of dealing with the Trump administration.

Pence, Mattis, and Tillerson were all dispatched to Europe before Trump's own first visit. All three told us Europeans what we wanted to hear: that the US continues to support the EU and NATO. But all of them immediately qualified these pronouncements. Tough economic decisions will have to be made, Pence told the EU, whatever that may mean exactly. If Europeans don't spend more on defence, the US may feel obliged to moderate its own contribution to the Alliance, Mattis told NATO. That was probably the first time the Trump administration showed itself moderate on any issue – until then it had all been pretty extreme. Trump himself confirmed this during his own visit, displaying his brutal style for the

European heads of state and government to see with their own eyes. But there are as many cases when a cabinet member says one thing and the president another. Whether a statement by the vice president or a cabinet member actually commits the president, no one can say. The president doesn't even feel bound by his own statements. What he says today, he contradicts on Twitter tomorrow. This too contributes to the unpredictability of the White House.

What further makes the US difficult to read is the absence of reason in Trump's decisions. Strategy is about making rational choices based on facts. The evidence from strategic history is clear: those who ignore the facts and allow religion, ideology, or emotions to determine strategy instead lose. The American invasion of Iraq in 2003 is a good example of a strategy that had nothing to do with reason and facts. The "neocons" wanted to bring down Saddam Hussein, and that was that. The facts were just adapted to fit that ideological choice. Surely Saddam would have had something to do with al-Qaeda and 9/11. If not, he was bound to be developing weapons of mass destruction. And when that turned out not to be the case either, it suddenly had been all about democratisation from the start. By then, the Middle East had sunk into chaos. Trump's decision to pull the US out of the nuclear deal with Iran is of the same kind. Of course, the Americans know that Iran actually upheld its part of the agreement. But that's not the point. The White House has made an ideological decision: Iran is the enemy. The fact that its strategy will only serve to increase instability in the region doesn't matter in the decision-making process. The same holds true for the tariffs on European (and Canadian) steel and aluminium that Trump introduced, "for reasons of national security". The fact that the American corporate sector itself has warned that with this strategy everybody will lose doesn't come into it. In the economic realm, we too, for ideological reasons, have been dubbed enemies.

The problem is that if a strategy doesn't have a rational basis in the first place, rational arguments have no effect. When the facts prove that a strategy doesn't work or even has the opposite effect from the one intended, leaders who are blinded by religion or ideology usually react not by changing their strategy, but by pushing it through even more radically, until total failure leaves them no other choice but to change course. Like Napoleon in Russia: win one more battle, conquer one more city, conquer Moscow, and the Russians must give in. Well, they didn't. To make another, more daring comparison: that's how one ends up alone in a bunker in Berlin, clueless, because the facts refused to align with your worldview. That's what makes it so difficult for the EU to react to Trump today. The US obviously is not our enemy. The EU must avoid escalation, for that will only make things worse. But not reacting at all isn't an option either. Trump would jump on that as evidence of the rightness of his view: see, they already give up, because they know they're wrong.

Yet it's not just the unpredictability that causes concern. A president who blames all ills on the outside world, who thinks that America doesn't need anybody and can simply do its own thing, who attacks the press as enemies of the people, who dubs all who disagree with him "bad Americans", and who puts members of his family in official positions: were it to happen in any other country than the US, we would say that these are the tell-tale signs of a dictatorship in the making. But because it does concern the US, we try to find evidence to the contrary. Americans worry about this themselves, however, even though the US is of course a vibrant democracy (Frum, 2017). There is strong resistance against decisions that violate the Constitution and basic ethical norms, especially by the courts. Apart from the late John McCain, senator and former presidential candidate, not much resistance is to be seen from within the Republican Party, however, which in fact has been usurped by Trump (who previously called himself a Democrat). A party that can only win the White House by allowing this takeover is badly placed to restrain the president afterward. Many American observers compare the political situation not just with the era of Wilhelm II, but with the 1920s and 1930s (Browning, 2017). Many of Trump's less-well-to-do voters could turn their backs on him though if he does not manage to create the jobs that he promised.

None of this means that the US will sink into authoritarianism – probably not – but it is a wake-up call for democrats everywhere, in America as in Europe. Democracy remains a daily struggle. Once we let down our guard, it will fast become clear how fragile our democracies really still are.

Beyond Trump

Trump fascinates us, but he frustrates us, too. Europe doesn't have ahold on Trump. Or, if truth be told, Europe doesn't have a hold on the US, no matter who the president is. We wait and submit but rarely have the chance to steer the US in a certain direction. Admittedly, there is a certain amusement value to "the Donald". We all enjoy being collectively shocked by his latest tweet. And then nothing happens, until he tweets something again, and we can comfortably express our outrage (and our sense of superiority) again. Mentally, however, too many European decision-makers remain dependent, even servile, toward the US. It is, of course, of crucial importance for the European interest what the US president does or doesn't do. But that doesn't mean that we should simply follow the US no matter what.

Europe can no longer afford that, not just because of Trump, but because of the fundamental truth that today we are living in a multipolar world. That has been the case for several years now – Trumps behaviour just makes it abundantly clear. Had Hillary Clinton won the presidency or were Pence to take over, this would still hold true. In a multipolar global order, American interests do not automatically coincide with ours, not like it was the case during the bipolar age of the Cold War. During that time, Europeans had to choose sides, between Washington and Moscow. Today there no longer are any sides. In a multipolar world several great powers simultaneously compete and cooperate, in ever-changing coalitions, depending on the issue. In such a world, nobody will defend our interests for us. Nobody will even necessarily take our interests into account or consult us as they pursue their own interests. On which of his many controversial steps has Trump asked anybody in Europe for an opinion?

Trump knows very well in which world order we are. When he says "America First", his campaign slogan, he is just rephrasing in his own brutal way what British Foreign Secretary Lord Palmerston already said in the 19th century – another multipolar age. "We have no eternal allies, and we have no perpetual enemies. Our interests are eternal and perpetual, and those interests it is our duty to follow". This famous dictum is as valid today as it ever was.

When Trump mentions his allies, it usually is to pressure them into paying more. That includes his allies in Asia, by the way, not just those in Europe. In the midst of exchanging threats with North Korea, in April 2017 Trump suddenly, and against the agreement made with Obama, proclaimed that South Korea would have to pay for the missile defence system that the US had promised (THAAD). The cost: $1 billion. At the same time Pence declared that the 2012 US–South Korea free-trade agreement needed to be revised, because it disadvantaged the US. All this from South Korea's main ally. Trump has adopted the same attitude toward his European allies in NATO: he wants to revise the trade relationship and he wants to see an increase in European defence spending. Countries that don't comply might just find themselves without American support when they get into trouble, or so Trump alluded.

Europeans must be fully aware that this goes very much beyond the person of Donald Trump. The generation that constitutes today's American establishment is much more diverse than before. No longer does the white east coast elite, with its European roots, call the shots all by itself. In the minds of many American decision-makers, Democrats and Republicans alike, there no longer is any automaticity. If Europe needs help, it will have to prove why it would be in the interest of the US to lend assistance. This certainly applies to both aisles of Congress.

This view is also strongly underpinned by academia and the think tanks. In 2014, MIT professor Barry Posen wrote that the basis of a new American grand strategy should be restraint (Posen, 2014). The US, says Posen, has ended up assuming nearly the entire burden of the defence of its allies. Has that made the US more secure? No, because it was secure already, having only Canada and Mexico as neighbours and an ocean on both sides. The main result is that US allies themselves make far too little effort. The solution: dissolve NATO, thus forcing the EU to mount its own autonomous European defence, and then a new alliance can be concluded with the EU as such. Mutatis mutandis, the same applies to US allies in Asia. A whole new school of "restrainers" has now emerged in US universities and think tanks. This is not some marginal view, therefore. It's only in Europe that many decision-makers still believe that the US cavalry will always come and save us – or try to convince themselves of that against better knowledge.

That does not mean that Europe should seek to put an end to our alliance with the US: quite the opposite. When NATO works and relations with the US in general are good, that is a great boon to the European interest. But *interest* is the key word here. The transatlantic alliance is one cornerstone of European grand strategy. But a building with just one cornerstone will collapse before long. In a multipolar world, the alliance with the US is still necessary but no longer sufficient to defend Europe's vital interests. In addition, the EU must use its autonomy to forge coalitions with the other great powers, and with other actors, flexibly and creatively, whenever that suits its purpose. A full alliance, including a collective defence guarantee, in principle can only be envisaged with other democracies, but partnership should be possible with everyone.[2] In a mature transatlantic alliance this flexibility ought to be possible, without it leading to a questioning of the fundamentals of the alliance. It doesn't matter, therefore, which of the world leaders of the moment we think is the most dangerous or the least disreputable: Trump, Putin, or Xi. The only, very pragmatic question that we must ask ourselves is with whom we can cooperate on which issue. None of them will hesitate to work with one of the others when their interests demand it. So why should we?

What Europe certainly shouldn't do is fixate on NATO only. But Europe is suffering from the "Maginot Complex". The symptoms: lack of self-confidence, incapacity to see the bigger picture, and a general state of lethargy. This syndrome was first diagnosed in France in the 1930s. Just like before World War Two, the French put all their trust in the Maginot Line, the defensive works running along its eastern frontier from the Swiss to the Belgian border. Similarly, many in Europe today put all their hopes in the alliance with the US and NATO – that is their "Maginot". There was much rejoicing when (on the occasion of NATO Secretary-General Jens Stoltenberg's visit to Washington on 12 April 2017) Trump declared that NATO isn't obsolete after all, in spite of his earlier declarations. Does that guarantee the security of Europe? France imagined itself safe behind its fortifications, but over time got so fixated upon the Maginot Line that it no longer saw how new developments limited its usefulness (e.g. panzer divisions, to name but one). That did not render the Maginot Line superfluous, but it did mean that it alone could no longer protect France. Today NATO certainly isn't useless – to the contrary. But if at the same time the confrontational behaviour of our most important ally in NATO leads to mounting global tensions, isn't it clear that NATO alone cannot defend the European interest? Just keeping the American president happy is not a strategy at all – that's mere ostrich policy. The EU will have to defend its interests itself, putting to use its diplomatic and economic instruments in order to stabilise world politics.

Europe has the instruments. Through its trade and diplomacy the EU can exert a positive influence on relations between the great powers. It doesn't have to deploy carrier groups to achieve that – which is for the best, since it doesn't have any. But does the EU dare to act autonomously? The June 2016 *Global Strategy* has in fact proved to be prescient. It charts a Realpolitik-based course that the EU can follow in a multipolar world – must follow, as Trump's election should have made abundantly clear. It would be very ironic if the EU now couldn't muster the courage to act upon its own strategy. Of course, it would be much easier to pretend that nothing has changed, as if it were sufficient to keep Trump happy (if such a thing is possible) and to act (and to pay) according to American wishes to safeguard our interests. If nothing has changed, nothing must be done. To start thinking for ourselves, however, demands courage.

A chance with China

Trump's policy has actually created quite a few chances that an active European diplomacy should put to good use. To start with, Trump has dealt us a "trump card" in our relations with China. Just like my own country, Belgium, but on a somewhat bigger scale, China has a very export-dependent economy. Its domestic market remains too small to support the economic growth that the country needs in order to continue to offer the prospect of improved living standards to its population. That in turn is what the CCP needs for its power and legitimacy not to be questioned. Behind the façade of confidence, which was notably on display at the 19th party congress, the regime is worried. Trump's revocation of multilateral trade deals in Asia creates opportunities for China to step into the void. But if he were to push protectionism too far and trigger a trade war, for China not just the economic but the political repercussions as well would be potentially huge. This is why to a certain extent China is more of a *demandeur* than usual. Usually it's the other way around, with European (and other) countries pushing each other out of the way in order to attract the most Chinese investment. Now that China needs the EU to help maintain the free-trade regime, Europe must use this opportunity to the fullest and try to arrive at a more balanced relationship with China.

In February 2017 already, very soon after this had become clear, the European Commissioner for Trade, Cecilia Malmström, issued a statement that can serve as an example of what active EU diplomacy should look like. Europe is ready to fight against protectionism alongside China, Malmström stated, but China will have to reform itself too. She referred in the first place to the ongoing negotiations on an EU–China bilateral investment treaty (Zalan, 2017). To this day, China remains very much closed to foreign investors and that has to change, otherwise an equitable investment treaty will be impossible. It is indeed ironic that China, the country of state capitalism, now presents itself as the champion of free trade. China talks the talk of free trade, but all too often does not act upon this. Various obstacles and mechanisms for control of foreign companies prevent a fair functioning of the market; in addition, there is enormous state support for Chinese companies. The EU must use the present opportunity and instrumentalise China's vulnerability to protectionism to incite it to introduce substantial reforms to the benefit of the European interest.

If China's market is too closed to foreign investors, Europe's, by the way, is too open. In Europe anybody can buy anything.[3] Ports, airports, electricity grids, high-speed rail, TV stations, even nuclear plants: there's almost no limit to what foreign actors (be they private actors or states masking as private actors) can acquire in Europe. In this way Europe hands foreign powers, in particular China and Russia, the opportunity on a silver platter to steer our decision-making when they choose to. Once a media outlet in an EU Member State is in foreign hands, will it still report the news or present "alternative facts"? When a port has a foreign owner, can it still be used without any problem to ship in military reinforcement and supplies when NATO is facing a crisis?

The EU is the only actor that does not impose limitations on foreign ownership of critical infrastructure. The main reason is that the European Commission remains dogmatically attached to absolute free trade. This too is an example of an all too naïve European policy – a pragmatic middle way is in order. Only in the course of 2016 did some Member States, Germany in particular, begin to show concern about this, mostly for economic reasons: the loss of valuable technologies and intellectual property. No EU Member State can introduce any limitation on its own, however – Chinese and other investors would just shift their attention to its neighbours. The EU did set up a Hybrid Fusion Cell, for Member States to report so-called hybrid threats, so that the EU can gain an overview of who is trying to undermine its sovereignty and that of its Member States. Yet what good will this do? No Member State is going to report an increased vulnerability to Brussels when it has just invited in the Chinese investors itself. Only binding EU-level legislation can solve the problem. A serious debate about this didn't start until February 2017, when Germany, France, and Italy addressed a letter on the issue to Commissioner Malmström. The commission subsequently announced it would introduce a degree of investment screening, though the focus is still on economic rather than security considerations. Nevertheless, in combination with the negotiation of the bilateral investment treaty with China, this would be a good opportunity to create more reciprocity between Brussels and Beijing.

Not just in the area of free trade, but on climate change as well the EU is now closer to China than to the US. But the EU should obviously not be blind for China's own problematic policies, notably its attempt to create a sphere of influence in the South China Sea. Not only does China lay claim to a number of islands on rather spurious grounds, to say the least. It has also created several artificial islands that serve as military bases. Moreover, it now considers the area around them as its territorial waters. The result would be that the entire South China Sea could only be sailed through with Chinese permission, contrary to international law, which clearly states that artificial islands do not generate such rights. The international community therefore does not accept China's claims, and the American, but also the British and French navy and air force regularly traverse the area in order to underline this. Yet China's neighbours, most of which are heavily economically dependent on China, are under severe pressure.

The EU must clearly state that in spite of the shared interest in maintaining free trade, China's assertive stance in the South China Sea will continue to act as a brake on relations. In a way, how exactly the claims of the various countries concerned are settled does not really make a difference to the EU. Who owns which rock or islet does not really concern us in Brussels – as long as all disputes are settled peacefully and in a way that does not hinder the freedom of navigation. The alternative, so China should understand, is that the US will continue to increase military pressure and the region will see an acceleration of the arms race that is already gripping it, as military expenditure in most countries of the region is on the rise. But to get that message across, the EU will have to take a much more resolute and united stance than has been the case hitherto.

An example of how not to do things was the weak EU reaction to the verdict in the arbitration procedure that the Philippines had started against China with the Permanent Court of Arbitration in The Hague in 2013. In 2016 the Court validated nearly all of the Philippines' claims, but China refused to accept the authority of the Court from the start. The EU was unable to agree anything but a meagre "acknowledgement" of the ruling. For the usual reason: there's always one Member State that happens to be in the midst of an important economic negotiation with China and doesn't want to rock the boat just now. And that thus prioritises the national over the collective European interest. Divide and rule: the EU divides itself and China rules. Or Russia, or the US, because the same happens in EU relations with all three of the great powers. One can hardly blame them for playing off one EU Member State against another if we make it so easy for them.

China naturally prefers to discuss its territorial disputes with each of its neighbours separately, in a purely bilateral setting, because that way it can bring a lot more leverage to bear. Beijing has consistently resisted all interference from an international organisation or another great power. The message that the EU should deliver to China is that Beijing cannot just follow those international bodies and rules that happen to suit its purpose. For the EU, multilateralism is a matter of principle, because whenever possible we prefer to pursue our interests by cooperating with others through a series of bilateral, regional, and global frameworks, rather than by trying to impose our ideas. At the same time such cooperation is a way of reducing tensions between the powers. That is why the *Global Strategy* refers to effective multilateralism as a vital EU interest. Europe must make it clear to the other powers that multilateralism *à la carte* cannot work. China needs the multilateral economic system, which enables global free trade. The point to be made is that international maritime law (UNCLOS) and the peaceful settlement of disputes are as much a part of the multilateral order as the free trade regime or a bilateral investment treaty.

Were China in the future to behave consistently as a responsible great power, cooperation with the EU could go a lot further. If the territorial claims in the South China Sea could be settled in a way that satisfies all parties and guarantees the freedom of navigation, then why could the EU not accept that in a certain region the Chinese navy carries the primary responsibility for maritime security in international waters? Until World War Two it was the British Royal Navy that patrolled the seas. Today the US Navy plays that role. But the US hardly always took the right decisions when it intervened militarily, officially in order to safeguard international peace and security. In a multipolar system one should not a priori exclude the emergence of a division of labour. Telling a rising power such as China that there will be no room for it can only serve to increase tensions. Whether the US, for whom military primacy is an objective as such, can accept this remains to be seen, but for the EU such power sharing should be possible.

Accepting a division of labour does not equate to recognising a sphere of influence. The idea is not that only the Chinese navy can sail in the international waters bordering on China. But in some future arrangement it may well be the case that in specific areas China assumes first line responsibility for the security of all nations' commercial shipping, with the participation of the European and American navies. Alternatively, the EU could take the lead in securing the Mediterranean and, with the US, the western part of the Indian Ocean, with Chinese participation. We're not there yet, but it should also be realised that China has nothing to gain from escalating the maritime disputes and risking an armed conflict, for that would be as disastrous for its economy as for ours. Yet as long as China does not abandon its assertive stance, the risk of incidents cannot be fully excluded.

China remains an authoritarian state – the 19th party congress has amply confirmed this.[4] Like all authoritarian states, Beijing too actively promotes nationalism in order to distract attention from the many domestic problems that actually concern citizens much more directly. That's not without risk, because once conjured up, emotions cannot always be easily controlled, not even by a repressive regime. Under Xi Jinping the regime is becoming more repressive again, not less. In time, that will be harmful for the Chinese economy. No country has ever succeeded in reaching the summit of technological and intellectual development without freedom of expression. Creativity and limitation are mutually exclusive. But even if China's economic growth continues to slacken, it will likely remain higher than growth in Europe for some time to come. And given the size of the country, that growth will remain of crucial importance for the global economy (Shambaugh, 2016). Whether China will catch up with or even overtake US power is far from certain, but is more than probable that it will remain a great power.

Realpolitik does not mean that Europe should rush into an alliance with China, replacing its alliance with the US. It cannot be the intention to become as dependent on (and servile towards) Beijing as we are vis-à-vis Washington today. "Principled pragmatism" does imply though that we can cooperate with China in any field, whenever that is in our interest, as long as by doing so we do not become party to human rights violations – that remains the red line. While cooperating, the EU must maintain a critical human rights dialogue with China, first and foremost in order to remain faithful to its own values. Of course, Europe is not going to change China's political system – that is not the objective. But by actively engaging with the human rights situation the EU can hope to alleviate any excesses. It will definitely serve as moral support for human rights activists in China who brave repression in order to stand up for their fellow citizens.

The absolute precondition that must be fulfilled before the EU explores the opportunity for more cooperation with China is unity. A self-assured and resolute Europe can engage in a new relationship with China. If a hesitant and divided Europe embarks upon this course, China will read it as weakness – which it will not hesitate to exploit.

Ambition in Asia

Europe trades with all of Asia, of course, hence the EU must have an Asia rather than just a China strategy. In this regard, too, Trump has at the same time created the need to act and the opportunity for the EU to do so. Trump withdrew the US from TPP, which ought to have been a regional free trade agreement between Australia, Brunei, Canada, Chile, Japan, Malaysia, Mexico, New Zealand, Peru, Singapore, Vietnam, and the US – so without China. That withdrawal does not make strategic sense, for it implies that Trump is downscaling the economic dimension of the American pivot to Asia just as he is increasing the military side. And as he learned during his tour of Asia and his participation in the APEC Summit in November 2017, there is but little enthusiasm for his proposal to negotiate new bilateral FTAs that would correct what he sees as the disadvantages that the US has suffered. For those Asian countries that try to maintain an equidistant position between China and the US, the economic anchorage that TPP would have offered is very important. With the economic foundation of the pivot gone, it will be even more difficult for these countries to avoid being sucked completely into the Chinese maelstrom. And China indeed did not waste any time stepping into the vacuum that Trump has created.

At a stroke, the FTAs that the EU has concluded or is envisaging (with South Korea, Japan, Singapore, Australia, and others) have become much more important. Not just economically, but in strategic terms, for these will be the only FTAs available with a Western global economic actor. An FTA with the EU can have significant political impact, as it can help a country maintain some distance from China and avoid total economic (and hence political) dependence. Beijing doesn't hesitate to use its immense economic power to try and steer the policies of other Asian countries.

The European approach is inclusive, though: the EU doesn't have a strategy against China, but for Asia. The economic encirclement of China should not be a European goal. Our aim is to work with China in the economic sphere and conclude FTAs with other Asian countries at the same time. In view of its current economic system, an FTA cannot now be envisaged with China itself, but the bilateral investment treaty can be a first step to gradually incite the regime not just to pose but also to act as a defender of free trade. Through this inclusive approach the EU can hope to play a stabilising role in Asia. A role that is probably acceptable to the states of the region precisely because in Asia the EU and its Member States are not significant military players.

There are a number of evident partners for such an EU strategy. First of all Australia, which is caught between its military alliance with the US and the increasing weight of China in its economy. Canberra thus has no interest whatsoever in increased tensions between China and the US, for that may force it to make a choice that can only turn out badly. Canada is a partner for an inclusive economic strategy too. Although the US is irreplaceable for the Canadian economy, Ottawa nevertheless is actively looking for ways of partly compensating a possible reduction of trade with the US. Canada has recently concluded a Comprehensive Economic and Trade Agreement (CETA) with the EU, and is looking into options in Asia. Japan ought to be an evident partner for the EU, but Prime Minister Shinzo Abe has opted for another course. He reckons that the best way to safeguard Japanese interests is to steer as close as possible to the US. That's why he was the first head of government to visit Trump, even before his inauguration. That said, in early July 2017 Japan did announce an agreement with the EU about a new FTA. Coming just before the start of the G20 meeting in Hamburg, this was a clear anti-protectionist message to the US.

Using its economic power in Asia to pursue its overall strategic interests is in the genes of the EU. An expensive term for this is *geoeconomics*: the use of economic instruments to achieve political, security, and economic objectives (Blackwill and Harris, 2016). That's the opposite of how the EU acted in Ukraine, where it pursued economic objectives without paying thought to the political and security implications. Although it is the essence of grand strategy that it comprises all instruments of power, political, economic, and military, the Ukraine example shows that in practice it is not always applied like that. The new *Global Strategy* does say a lot about trade, contrary to the 2003 strategy, but if it wants to adopt a geoeconomic approach the EU will have to purposely organise itself and effectively integrate trade policy into its overall foreign policy. Today the Commission's Directorate-General for Trade and the European External Action Service (EEA) are living in their own worlds. A geoeconomic strategy will not just fall from the sky.

Moreover, one of the latest big FTAs, CETA, very nearly turned into a disaster for the EU. Because of my own country, Belgium, alas. Or, better, because of the Walloon Region of Belgium, where regional premier Paul Magnette for reasons of domestic politics refused to agree with the signing of the treaty by the Belgian federal government. Eventually a compromise was reached, which allowed the Belgian government to sign, following which CETA was ratified in the European Parliament (in February 2017). But the parliaments of all Member States, and in Belgium of all the regions, have yet to ratify it too.[5] The CETA-saga has done great damage to Belgian interests, but it also meant an enormous loss of face for the EU as a whole. Outside Europe, the impression now is that one can negotiate with the EU for years (for that's how long FTAs take) only to be turned down in the end because one small region of one small country (for that's how people see things) is opposed. Just when geoeconomics is becoming more important than ever, the trustworthiness of the EU has been undermined.

Why was the whole charade necessary in the first place? CETA had become a symbol for those who oppose uncontrolled globalisation. That opposition is justified: the EU should indeed work to steer and control globalisation, and to mitigate its negative social, ecological and other consequences through strict regulation. That should follow from its own fundamental purpose: to defend and to deepen our own egalitarian model of society. But that's exactly what FTAs aim to do: to regulate globalisation.

That doesn't mean that all FTAs are beyond criticism. But the symbolic focus of criticism of CETA, the special arbitration tribunal, is often misunderstood. Such special courts, which include judges from both parties to the treaty (including judges from the corporate sector), have precisely been created at the demand of the

EU, because in some states with which we conclude treaties the local justice system cannot be trusted. Whom do you want to turn to under such circumstances: a national court that just does what the government, or the one who pays the highest bribe, tells it to, or a special arbitration tribunal? That said, in the case of CETA there is of course no reason not to trust the rule of law in Canada. Many, however, seem to be protesting not just the specifics of a particular FTA but also the principle of free trade as such. That is economic nonsense: the engine of the strong European economies, and thus the source of the welfare state, is exports. It's exactly to safeguard the prosperity of European citizens that one has to be in favour, and not against, balanced and comprehensive FTAs.

Perhaps the most important thing is that the EU, when designing an Asia strategy, should assume that in spite of the many tensions, it doesn't have to come to war. Contrary to what many in the US, and a very few in Europe, seem to think, war never is inevitable (Allison, 2017; Holslag 2015). There is no such thing as a law of history that means that a certain combination of established, rising, and declining powers necessarily leads to armed conflict. Those who think like this are propagating a dangerous view, for it might easily become a self-fulfilling prophecy. Those who really believe it, put on eye flaps: they no longer look for ways of reducing tension and preventing conflict, but are only interested in how to best position themselves to win the coming war.

If war really would break out between the US and China, the Americans don't really count on Europe, by the way. It is both striking and enlightening how the academic authors of a noted nonfiction work that primarily seeks to illustrate how such a war would be fought in this high-technological age, mention Europe just as an aside. After a Chinese surprise attack against the US, with which the book opens, a NATO meeting is called, at which the European allies quickly conclude: this is not what NATO was meant for – so we're staying neutral (Singer and Cole, 2015). And rightfully so: what interest could Europe possibly have in becoming involved in a great power war, if it is not directly attacked? Much more important is the question how great power war can be avoided. A war involving one of the great powers always has negative consequences for the overall political and economic stability. But a war between two or more of the great powers would destroy the world order. The importance of an active strategy of stabilisation is evident.

A Russian threat?

Russia is the third great power, after the US and China, but Europe's relations with it have been deadlocked by the Ukraine crisis.

Does Russia pose a military threat to Europe itself? Not really. Russian objectives concern the former Soviet republics: Moscow aims to incorporate these countries in an exclusive sphere of influence. In fact, this strategy has already largely failed. After Georgia, Putin, through his own over-reaction, has now also pushed Ukraine into the Western camp. In Central Asia, Chinese influence is increasing day by day, but Putin is in no position to voice any concerns, since he needs good relations with China in order to be able to signal to Europe that he doesn't care much about our economic sanctions.

Nonetheless Russia will continue to attempt to counter European influence, notably in the countries in between the EU and Russia. To that end, Putin will seek out and exploit every European weakness in order to undermine our resolve. But it is not a Russian objective to conquer EU territory. Not even in the Baltic, even though Estonia, Latvia, and Lithuania had been annexed by the Soviet Union. The aim is Ukraine; subverting the EU is only an instrument. In Russia, Ukraine, the heart of historic Russia, is almost seen as a domestic issue. That explains why Russia is willing to go so far and to pay a heavy price for it, but at the same time it means that its actions in Ukraine do not constitute a precedent for actions elsewhere, certainly not against any EU Member State. In fact, it is much more in Russia's interest to maintain ambiguity vis-à-vis the EU: probing just enough to unbalance us, without going so far as to provoke a forceful reaction.

Were the EU to divide itself, then of course Putin would not hesitate for a moment to widen the cracks and push the Member States further apart. His policy has been one of extreme opportunism. Russia can only be a threat to Europe, in other words, if we allow it to be, if European politicians betray the values and interests of Europe – if EU governments break solidarity and let the Kremlin buy them, for example. Or if candidates in a presidential election while running for the highest national office show contempt for the national interest and wage their campaign with the support of Russian money and hackers, like the extreme-right Marine Le Pen in France in 2017. Which economic and political perspective can Putin offer to EU citizens that would beat staying in the EU? The Russian pension system? Conscription? Censorship? Putin's store is empty.

This is why it is a mistake to see the Russian intervention in eastern Ukraine as something that can easily be repeated in an EU Member State. Ukraine was a divided country: a large part of the population felt neglected by the government in Kiev, and in cultural terms had always looked to the East rather than to the West. And the country is not a member of NATO or the EU, nor will it receive an invitation to join. In those circumstances, what is now called "hybrid warfare" (which is but classic warfare, for since classical times propaganda and fifth columns have been as much part of war as the deployment of regular armies) could work. When a state does not offer them equality, then of course people will not consider it worthwhile to fight to defend that state's sovereignty. But that is not the case in any EU Member State. Not even in the Baltic states, which can offer their Russian minorities much better perspectives than what a return to Russia would imply (but these citizens have to be actively convinced of that).

Russia remains a nuclear power, and its conventional armed forces number 750,000 troops. That's why NATO remains important, because of the nuclear umbrella of the US (the British nuclear deterrent is closely integrated with the Americans; in addition the French "force de frappe" is an independent deterrent). In response to Russian muscle-flexing on the eastern borders of the Alliance, NATO has stationed troops from several Allies, including the US, in Poland, and the Baltic states. With a reinforced battalion in each of the Baltic states one cannot defend them, of course, but that's not the point. Militarily, the Baltic states cannot be defended against invasion, because they are where they are. The only reason why at the end of World War Two German forces in the region resisted until the end, is because the Red army bypassed them and marched straight on to Berlin – not a scenario that one wants to see repeated.

The point of prepositioning troops from all NATO Allies is that it renders a war with the Baltic states alone impossible. Whoever invades the Baltic states, thereby triggers Article 5, NATO's collective defence guarantee, and finds himself at war with all 29 Allies. That is the classic "tripwire" role of prepositioned forces, just the same as during the Cold War.[6] This deployment was and remains necessary, not just as a message to Russia, but even more so as a means of reassuring the political and military leaders and public opinion in the Baltics. Since the aim of these forces is to act as a tripwire, there's no point in increasing the numbers: the troops on the ground now are sufficient for this role.

Besides, the conventional armed forces of even the 28 EU Member States alone already count 1.5 million men and women. Those are not 1.5 million combat-ready soldiers – but neither are those 750,000 Russians. The Russian units that we have seen in action in Ukraine, and for the large-scale manoeuvres along the borders of Poland and the Baltics, are the tip of the spear. The shaft of the spear is rather mouldy, however. That is no ground for complacency. That Russia could not threaten the EU military even if it wanted to (quod non), is not because of any merit on our part, but simply because Russian forces are in even worse shape than our own. And because we have an alliance with the US. Russia is reinvesting in its armed forces, however (though its economic situation severely limits how far it can go). This is one of the reasons that Europe must indeed urgently step up its own military effort – we return to this in Chapters 5 and 6. Nevertheless, it does not serve our interest to present ourselves as weaker than we are. Military power means nothing without a sound economic foundation. According to the World Bank, Russia's GDP in 2016 amounted to $1,283 billion. Compare that to the figure for the EU: $16,000 billion. Even the GDP of just my own country, Belgium, at $466 billion, stands at well over a third of that of Russia.

Patient toward Russia

As long as the EU maintains unity among and within its Member States, there is no need for it to fear Russia. But how can it escape the deadlock over Ukraine?

Not reacting to the invasion and annexation of the Crimea and the stirring and arming of a separatist rebellion in eastern Ukraine, was not an option for the EU. Brussels was too involved itself already, and had offered too much encouragement to Ukraine to ignore it. And of course Russian actions constituted a very serious violation of international law, on the continent of Europe moreover. Therefore the EU adopted sanctions against Russia, be it hesitantly at first. Then on 17 July 2014 separatist rebels, most likely by mistake, shot down Malaysian Airlines Flight

MH17 above Ukraine, killing all 283 passengers and 15 crew members. That silenced all voices arguing that one should not react too strongly, and led to a sharpening of the sanctions. The low energy prices have probably hurt the Russian economy far more than the actual sanctions, since it is so preponderantly dependent on the export of energy. Nonetheless, the sanctions do have effect. For the EU is it difficult if not impossible to lift them without Russia offering a compromise.

The EU itself has already made an important gesture. The February 2015 Minsk Agreement that Angela Merkel and François Hollande brokered between Russia and Ukraine keeps silent about the Crimea. That serves as an indication that Europe will not legally recognise the annexation of the peninsula, but neither will it take action to undo it. We will learn to live with it, just like we have learned to live with the de facto autonomy of Abkhazia and South Ossetia, the two regions that with Russian assistance have separated from Georgia. The EU and NATO could go even further and formally state that they will not offer membership to Ukraine. They don't intend to anyway, for the country isn't ready for it and won't be for a long time. But before we can propose such "Finlandisation" of Ukraine (just like Finland after the end of World War Two could stay outside the Soviet sphere of influence on the condition that it remained neutral), Russia too must show some goodwill. For that, we are still waiting. The Russian argument that Ukraine is stalling the implementation of its obligations under the Minsk Agreement is not without ground. But the fact remains that Russia has provided weapons and covertly deployed troops in eastern Ukraine. Had it not, there would still have been a movement in favour of more autonomy, but never an armed rebellion – that was created by Putin.

For a moment it looked as if Europe (and the US) could have reached an agreement with Russia about ending the war in Syria. That might have created a positive atmosphere in which Putin would have been able to offer concessions on Ukraine. At some point in the war, European and Russian interests in Syria began to coincide, at least up to a certain extent. Europe more than anything else wanted to see a quick end to the war and gradually began to accept that this meant a ceasefire with Assad, no matter how morally problematical that might be. The alternative was for the war to grind on, killing even more people. Russia was fighting a defensive war in Syria, in order to prevent a repetition of the Ukraine scenario: that the regime would tumble and it would lose all of its influence at a stroke.

That war aim Russia has already achieved. It has nothing more or nothing less than before the war started, but thanks to its military intervention it is certain that Assad can stay in power. Thus Russian interests, notably the military bases, are guaranteed. Thanks to Russian (and Iranian) military support, Assad cannot be defeated, but he cannot win either: he is too weak to reconquer all of Syria's territory. Russia also therefore acquired an interest in consolidating its gains and ending the war. But instead of seeking cooperation, Putin began to see Syria as an additional theatre of confrontation with the West. Positive spillover to the Ukraine crisis thus became impossible. The American missile strikes against Assad's forces served only to further harden the Russian position.

All of this has made it even more difficult to break the deadlock, in Syria as in Ukraine. But the reason is also that Putin has manoeuvred himself into a dead-end street. Even an authoritarian regime must establish some basis of support with the population – repression alone is insufficient to stay in power. There's not much that Putin can promise the Russians in economic terms. That's why he has consciously played the nationalist card, positioning himself as the strong leader, who will return Russia to its rightful place in the sun, and for whom the weak Europeans tremble in fear. If that is one's only source of popularity, it is of course difficult ever to conclude a compromise with the other, even when that would be in your own interest.

As far as Ukraine is concerned, Putin could just conclude, however, that it is even more in his interest to simply not resolve the issue, turning it into yet another "frozen conflict". Eastern Ukraine would then end up in the same situation as Abkhazia and South Ossetia, and Transdniestria, an area that separated from Moldova, again with Russian help. In "frozen conflicts" fighting is no longer ongoing (which is not yet the case in Ukraine, which sees multiple casualties every single day). The situation remains permanently tense though, and violence can easily erupt again. In the eyes of Putin, this is an instrument which in the end is not that costly, and which makes it very easy for him to put pressure on Kiev whenever he feels like it – and, through Kiev, on Brussels.

The EU has no means of preventing this scenario, although the sanctions possibly contributed to the fact that the war in Ukraine has not escalated further (Fischer, 2017). It has no choice but to maintain its sanctions therefore, but it could link them more explicitly to the situation in eastern Ukraine (read: and silently accept the annexation of the Crimea). If the Russians would be willing to compromise after all, the EU could phase out its sanctions in successive steps. The 28 EU Member States have remained remarkably unanimous on the sanctions, given all the Russian efforts to play them apart. But the longer the crisis drags on, the more difficult it will become to stay united, certainly if at one point the US would reduce its sanctions as part of a deal with Putin – though Trump remains as unpredictable on this as on any other issue. More and more voices will call for an end to the sanctions and a quiet return to normal relations with Russia. But would it be in Europe's interest to abandon the sanctions if it gets nothing in return from Russia? Good-neighbourly relations with Russia remain the objective. That is the best way of safeguarding Europe's interests – but not every way of achieving good relations is in our interest.

A better option is to compartmentalise relations with Russia. That means that the two parties can discuss and even cooperate on every issue of mutual interest, without this entailing a change of position on the issue that is disputed between them. In time, the added value of cooperation may entice Russia to change its position, though this may require a change of government in Moscow. Many had hoped that a reassessment and a fresh start would already have been possible after the March 2018 presidential elections in Russia. However, the attempted murder in the UK of former Russian spy Sergei Skripal and his daughter Yulia two weeks before the elections, apparently ordered from Moscow, put an end to such hopes. Instead, the EU and the US expelled a number of Russian diplomats, to which Russia reacted in kind.

"Strategic patience" is called for toward Russia: "il est urgent d'attendre". This is what the *Global Strategy* says: "Substantial changes in relations between the EU and Russia are premised upon full respect for international law and the principles underpinning the European security order". But at the same time the EU can "engage Russia to discuss disagreements and cooperate if and when our interests overlap", including on "climate, the Arctic, maritime security, education, research and cross-border cooperation. Engagement should also include deeper societal ties through facilitated travel for students, civil society, and business".

The EU–Russia–China triangle

Meanwhile the EU, through a creative diplomatic approach, can try and involve other actors and convince them that it would be in their interest too to moderate Putin's "adventurous" foreign policy.

It must be pointed out that if other countries would join in the EU's effort, it would probably not be because they are outraged by the Russian invasion of Ukraine. True, it is the first time since the end of World War Two that a European state used force to modify the borders and annex part of the territory of another European state. Is that the beginning of a new era in Europe? It definitely means the end of the era after the end of the Cold War in which we thought that Russia would become "one of us", a country that slowly but surely would evolve toward the West. But didn't we know that already after the 2008 Russian–Georgian war? There's no point in assigning the blame to Russia or the West or both, but this certainly was a missed opportunity. It means though that the Ukraine crisis is not really the game-changer that redefines the entire European security landscape that some make it out to be.

Perhaps relations between Europe and Russia have simply returned to what in the light of history and geopolitics is "normal", ever since Peter the Great. Russia is too big to really be a part of Europe – it will always be a great power in its own right. Thus, Europe will always eye Russia with some degree of suspicion, while Russia will forever oscillate between seeking rapprochement with and distancing itself from Europe. Mutual distrust is peaking now, because of the Ukraine crisis, leading to military posturing on both sides. Over the years, this distrust will probably slowly dissipate again, until it reaches "normal" levels. As the then chief of defence, Yuri Baluyevski, said at an event at the Egmont Institute in Brussels in 2006: "Russia is Russia. Russia is not Europe, and Russia is not Asia. Russia is Russia".

Most countries outside Europe don't see the Ukraine crisis as a game-changer at all. In a multipolar world, this dispute between the West and Russia does not dominate international politics as it would have during the bipolar system of the Cold War. Most countries don't see the invasion as a particularly shocking or unusual event, which they should condemn more strongly than past crises. At an annual conference in Brasilia that the Egmont Institute co-organises since 2015, the prevalent mood among the South American participants was rather: in 2003 the Americans invaded Iraq, in 2014 the Russians invaded Ukraine, and for us one is not worse than the other, and we don't feel inclined to take a stand on either. The same holds true for China. Beijing certainly doesn't like surprises, and the Russian invasion is completely at odds with China's principle of non-intervention in other countries (which officially is a principle of Russian foreign policy too). But why should China publicly become involved? For China it is much easier and more profitable to stay out of this, observing how the EU, the US, and Russia are being absorbed by the crisis, and grasping every opportunity to benefit from their consequent lack of attention for other issues.

The EU has instruments though to make China realise that it if goes too far in supporting Russia (for that is what its silence amounts to), that is to the detriment of its own economic interests. One of China's most important projects is the Belt and Road Initiative (BRI), a massive investment in transport and communications infrastructure to reinforce connectivity between China and no less than 66 countries. On the one hand there's the "belt", the overland routes, including the "new silk road" that goes through Russia and central Asia to Europe and the Middle East. But there also are corridors to Pakistan and the Indian Ocean, and to southeast Asia. On the other hand, there's the "road", the maritime route through the Indian Ocean to the Middle East and Africa.[7] On 15 May 2017, China highlighted the importance it attaches to this project by organising an actual BRI summit in Beijing, in which no fewer than 40 heads of state and government participated. The BRI is a geoeconomic project par excellence: by investing, China is not just creating new markets, it's also gaining a lot of political influence, which it doesn't hesitate to use. But by investing, China also acquires a security interest in the regions that the BRI traverses. This is what the EU can make use of to influence the Chinese position.

The railway along "the new silk road" is becoming operational. Trains are arriving in Hamburg, among others, full of Chinese goods – and for now are mostly returning empty. From an economic point of view, the BRI is mostly in China's interest. Although there is a lot of talk about how the BRI could be linked to the European Commission's Investment Plan for Europe, in practice it still remains unclear how concrete cooperation will materialise. For Europe it is incalculably more important that the territorial disputes in the South China Sea are resolved in a way that does not affect the freedom of navigation. The land route will never replace the maritime route: almost 90 per cent of European foreign trade is seaborne. Nevertheless, the EU can show its goodwill and cooperate with China on the BRI.

Except that actually the EU cannot afford to, because the land route passes through Russia. Why would the EU volunteer to invest in it and make itself even more dependent on Russia than it already is (in the field of energy)? Given the current state of affairs between the EU and Russia, we simply cannot trust it – its foreign policy is just too unpredictable. That's not just Europe's problem, but

China's problem too, if it wants the BRI to succeed. For the regions that China sees as the western terminus of the BRI are exactly the regions, in Europe and in the Middle East, in which Russia is intervening in order to create a sphere of influence. That leads to instability, which is detrimental to China's economic interests. Beijing has been paying a lot of attention to Ukraine, for example, and already is the country's third trade partner, but the Russian invasion has blocked further development of their relationship, certainly when it comes to investment. This is the message that European diplomacy should get across to Beijing. The BRI is a Chinese, and not a European, priority. If China wants the BRI to be successful and seeks cooperation with the EU to that end, it will have to come out of the closet and engage with Russia itself in order to limit Putin's assertive policies.

There are many other factors that objectively should create tensions between China and Russia. To start with there's the fact that there are very few Russians living in the Asian parts of Russia, which is very rich in resources, but increasing numbers of Chinese (some legally, many also illegally). That could be seen as a long-term geopolitical threat to Russia, in a way in which the EU will never be. Putin's fear of the EU concerns the survival of his regime, not of Russian sovereignty and territorial integrity. He doesn't fear that the EU will invade Russia, but that one day his own citizens, impressed by the success of European society, will follow the example of the Georgians and the Ukrainians, and before them the Poles, the Czechs, and the Hungarians, and topple his regime. China's demographic dominance and the tempting presence of so many natural resources on the other side of the border is a geopolitical fact that Russia cannot ignore, even though China does not harbour any hostile intentions. Similarly, the ever-increasing Chinese presence in central Asia, which Putin also considers to be his preserve, cannot but cause irritation in Moscow.

Adding to the tensions in Russian–Chinese relations is the underlying realisation that for a while now the balance of power between them has been turned around. The Soviet Union already had a difficult relationship with China, which eventually became weary of toeing the line that the comrades in Moscow set, but the USSR clearly was the most powerful. Today China's GDP is nearly double the size of Russia's. The Chinese are often irritated to note that in spite of this the Russians still treat them as the junior partner. An intriguing example of these subterranean tensions between the two great powers is how in May 2017 Russia suddenly blocked access to WeChat, the Chinese version of WhatsApp. Usually Russia and China block the Western social media, but in this case they were blocking each other.

These tensions pulling at the China–Russia relationship should not be overestimated, however, for there also are very strong push factors that favour cooperation between the two (Lo, 2017). Living in what from their perspective still is a Western-dominated world order, Moscow and Beijing will not easily allow a wedge to be driven between them. Moscow has actually moved closer to China, because of the Ukraine crisis. Just weeks after the annexation of the Crimea, in 2014, both countries concluded an agreement on the export of Russian gas to

China after the negotiations had been dragging on for years. Russia wants to signal to the West that it can compensate for the effects of the sanctions and that it has alternative markets for its energy exports. Yet that should not be exaggerated: four years later, the gas agreement has still not been implemented, because low energy prices have rendered it economically unviable. In the face of Russian rapprochement, China has shown itself to be rather reluctant. It does what it takes to maintain good relations, but not much more.

Here lies an opportunity for European diplomacy therefore. The EU shouldn't hope to play China and Russia apart, like Nixon and Kissinger did in the 1970s. As yet their strategic interests are too convergent for that. But the EU could perhaps make China understand that tilting too far toward the other side, and tolerating Russian adventurism without further ado is not in China's interest either. Furthermore, there are opportunities for cooperation between the EU and China in the countries along the "new silk road", from central Asia to Ukraine, where Brussels and Beijing could certainly mount joint projects. The EU need not wait for the BRI to reach Europe while China is beginning to economically and politically dominate all the countries between Xinjiang (its westernmost province) and Brussels. We can proactively increase our own economic and political presence in these parts.

The multilateral context

As the EU strengthens its bilateral relations with the great powers, by flexibly cooperating whenever it can, it should continue to reinforce the multilateral dimension of international politics – in which the US is disinvesting. This is the fifth priority in the *Global Strategy*. Bilateral cooperation is the starting point. The EU can then try and build thematic coalitions, with different great powers and other countries jointly, and consolidate cooperation on a given topic by agreeing on rules to govern the issue, or even by creating an organisation to deal with it. A useful as well as promising area for multilateral cooperation is the freedom of access to the global commons, as indicated in the *Global Strategy*: the seas, the skies, space, and cyberspace. Mitigating the consequences of climate change, an area in which the EU already is a leading actor will remain another priority issue for multilateral initiatives. But then the EU must really take to the initiative. Opportunities for cooperation will not materialise by themselves – they must be created.

The other great powers are taking new multilateral initiatives as well. In 2015 China launched the Asian Infrastructure Investment Bank (AIIB), a multilateral bank that, as the name indicates, aims to finance infrastructure projects in Asia. The US (still under President Obama) openly called on its allies and partners not to join the bank. But why not? The EU can only be pleased if the great powers take multilateral initiatives instead of acting unilaterally. By joining the bank themselves, the European countries can co-direct its activities. And, of course, there simply is business to be done. Japan obeyed the American directive, but the Europeans (and Australians) rushed to join the AIIB. Naturally, the bank serves China's interests –

but it can benefit us, too. The alternative is that non-Western countries establish their own institutions, with their own set of rules, which inevitably will enter into a logic of competition with the existing international organisations. It is much cleverer to support and to shape the other players' multilateral projects. The more multilateral cooperation, the more interaction, and the more stability and predictability in the international system.

This is why the EU must continue to invest in the UN Security Council. The functioning of the Security Council is far from perfect. It is powerless when one of the five permanent members (the US, China, Russia, the UK, and France), which have veto powers, is itself involved in a conflict. And in a multipolar world the chance that the great powers will be involved in disputes, including with each other, is precisely becoming bigger and bigger. But the Security Council remains the core of the only organisation with nearly universal membership, which when it works, and that does happen, can impose measures to preserve peace and security, as provided for in the UN Charter. When Brexit becomes effective, the EU will be represented by France as a permanent member, and still by two or three out of ten temporary members (which are elected for a two-year period). In view of its important presence in the Security Council, the EU has an exemplary role to play, because for us multilateralism is both a matter of principle and a pragmatic choice. We, if anybody, must play by the book in order to demonstrate to the other powers that this way, too, one can safeguard one's interests.

The United Nations has many more members than the Western nations. The main added value of the UN is that nearly all states are members. That includes states with non-democratic political systems, some of which are indeed very repressive and violate human rights on a daily basis. The UN is a forum where everyone can speak to everyone. It is nonsense therefore to systematically oppose membership of authoritarian states in certain UN bodies, for that is directly at odds with the purpose of the organisation. For example, the fuss in the West in 2017 about Saudi Arabia's membership of the UN commission for women's rights was unjustified. Riyadh applied for this position itself. Rather than boycotting its application, it is a lot more effective to let the Saudis take up the seat and to use the workings of the commission to constantly ask them all the difficult questions about their own policies on women's rights. As the director of the Flemish section of Amnesty International put it: now that they got the seat, let them sweat in it (Degraeve, 2017). In a similar vein, there are many states in the Security Council that don't respect the Charter, but because they are there they can be called out. Avoiding dialogue is in contradiction with the idea of principled pragmatism. Nobody has ever had influence on another country by not speaking to it.

The EU has the political and economic weight to act as a great power among the great powers, both in the bilateral and in the multilateral arena. We must put to use our political and economic instruments to play a stabilising role in a world with a lot of potential for conflict. That is not to say we can neglect our military power. The moment is now for action: if the EU wants to realise its power potential, it must behave a lot more proactively than it has done hitherto.

Notes

1 The Russian population declined from 1991 to 2009; since then it has seen minimal growth. In 2017 there still were 4 million fewer Russians than in 1991.
2 One can find examples of close alliances between democratic and non-democratic states, such as between the French republic and the Russian empire before World War One, or between the US, the UK, and the USSR during World War Two.
3 Except for Eandis, the Flemish gas and electricity grid company, but that is the exception that confirms the rule. At the end of 2016 Eandis ultimately was not sold to China, although the deal was as good as done, one of the reasons being that Belgian State Security issued a warning against it (which was leaked to the press).
4 The scariest development in this regard undoubtedly is the "social credit system", under which every Chinese citizen would get a score based among others things on one's behaviour on the internet and social media, which would determine the level of access to public goods. Unfortunately, new technologies perfectly enable such totalitarian schemes.
5 Once a treaty has been signed by the representatives of the governments that negotiated it, it has to be ratified (i.e. approved by the parliaments of the states concerned).
6 The notion actually already existed in the mind of French general (and later marshal) Ferdinand Foch. When asked before World War One by British field marshal Sir Henry Wilson how many British soldiers France would need in case of a German invasion, Foch replied: "Just one, and we'll make very sure that he gets killed".
7 Initially known as One Belt, One Road (OBOR) or *i dai, i lu* in Chinese, which can also be translated as "one zone and one route".

References

Graham Allison, *Destined for War: Can America and China Escape Thucydides's Trap?* Boston, Houghton Mifflin Harcourt, 2017.
Robert D. Blackwill and Jennifer M. Harris, *War by Other Means: Geoeconomics and Statecraft.* Cambridge (MA), The Belknap Press of Harvard University Press, 2016.
Christopher R. Browning, "Lessons from Hitler's Rise". In: *The New York Review of Books*, Vol. 64, 2017, No. 7, pp. 10–14.
Wies Degraeve, "Dit is hét moment om verontwaardiging over Saoedi-Arabië om te zetten in actie". In: *Knack*, 2 May 2017.
Sabine Fischer, *A Permanent State of Sanctions? Proposal for a More Flexible EU Sanctions Policy Towards Russia.* SWP Comments No. 11. Berlin, Stiftung Wissenschaft und Politik, April 2017.
David Frum, "How to Build an Autocracy?" In: *The Atlantic*, March 2017.
Andrew Gray, "Macron on Trump Suggestion to Leave EU: 'You Can Imagine My Response'". In: *Politico*, 29 June 2018.
François Heisbourg, "The Emperor vs the Adults: Donald Trump and Wilhelm II". In: *Survival*, Vol. 59, 2017, No. 2, pp. 7–12.
Jonathan Holslag, *China's Coming War with Asia.* Cambridge, Polity, 2015.
Barry Posen, *Restraint: A New Foundation for US Grand Strategy.* Ithaca (NY), Cornell University Press, 2014.
James P. Rubin, "The Leader of the Free World Meets Donald Trump". In: *Politico*, 16 March 2017.
David Shambaugh, *China's Future.* Cambridge, Polity, 2016.
Peter W. Singer and August Cole, *Ghost Fleet: A Novel of the Next World War.* Boston, Houghton Mifflin Harcourt, 2015.
Peter Teffer and Eric Maurice, "Trump Calls Germans 'Bad' but Agrees EU Trade Plan". In: *EU Observer*, 26 May 2017.

Donald Trump, *Statement by President Trump on Jerusalem*. Washington, DC, the White House, 6 December 2017a.

Donald Trump, *The National Security Strategy of the United States of America*. Washington, DC, the White House, December 2017b.

Eszter Zalan, "EU Ready to Help China Fight Protectionism". In: *EU Observer*, 7 February 2017.

4

EUROPE AND ITS NEIGHBOURS

The EU has European neighbours to the east and non-European neighbours to the south. It's often seen as somehow politically incorrect to make this distinction, and so the *Global Strategy* doesn't. If political correctness blinds you to reality, however, it becomes counterproductive. For it's precisely because the one region is a part of Europe (historically, culturally, and geographically) and the other isn't that our eastern and southern peripheries are governed by completely different dynamics.

"Zwischeneuropa"

In most of our immediate neighbours on the European continent an important part of public opinion shares the EU's aspiration for these countries: that they would construct a society that guarantees everyone's equality, just like ours. As we have already seen in Chapter 2, this means that here the existing European Neighbourhood Policy can work, according to the principle of conditionality. This applies to Ukraine, Moldova, and, to a certain extent, Belarus; to Georgia; but less so to the two other countries of the South Caucasus, Armenia and Azerbaijan. Together with the EU these six states constitute the Eastern Partnership (EaP). The more these countries move toward democracy, the more assistance they can get from the EU. If these states opt themselves for the building of a democratic system, the EU has to support them. It has to, for democratisation is always in our interest, because it creates durable peace and stability – but only it if is their own choice, at the pace that they set. It's certainly legitimate to promote our model of society in these countries, but the EU should not attempt to artificially accelerate the process of change: *festina lente*.

The reason is that the chance of success is very low if the internal consensus in favour of democratic reform is not sufficiently strong. Change implies instability, which in the first instance can negatively affect people's livelihoods, so that they might turn against democratisation. Another reason is that our eastern periphery at the same time is the western periphery of Russia – it constitutes a "Zwischeneuropa" in between two great powers. As already seen, Russia considers this region to be its exclusive sphere of influence and therefore actively attempts to undermine EU policy. The EU doesn't have to accept that, but it should try to avoid that its relations with the states concerned provoke another clash with Russia like the one over Ukraine. That, in the end, is neither in our interest nor in the interest of our eastern neighbours themselves.

The EU's objective is not necessarily that the states of "Zwischeneuropa" would tilt towards Brussels instead of Moscow. Our aim is to safeguard these states' sovereignty: they should be allowed to make their own strategic choices, in all freedom, without illicit interference from any side. If it is their choice to primarily align with Russia: fine, so be it. Put frankly: the EU doesn't need these countries. But if they choose to (also) cooperate with us, we cannot allow others to interfere to prevent them from making that choice, certainly not if it also implies a turn toward democracy.

The EU does not require exclusivity. As far as Brussels is concerned, a country can build close relations with the EU and with Russia at the same time. In view of Russia's current irreconcilable attitude, we better build relations one small step at a time. A major trade agreement is anyway not possible with the countries that have joined Russia's own multilateral scheme for the region, the Eurasian Economic Union (EAEU): Armenia, Belarus, Kazakhstan, and Kyrgyzstan. An agreement can only be concluded with the EAEU as such. This is an example of how EU and Russian policies have become mutually exclusive. Consequently, countries are being put in a position to make a a choice that in most cases they don't want to make. Unless a neighbour steers in this direction itself, the EU should avoid having governments put in this awkward situation, for it can only produce internal divisions and instability.

Belarus can serve to illustrate this. President Aleksandr Lukashenko governs the country in a very authoritarian manner, which has led to the adoption of EU sanctions. Gradually though, Lukashenko has begun to distance himself somewhat from Russia. The country mostly still closely aligns itself with Russia, but from time to time it adopts a striking midway position. One of the reasons is that the Russian invasion of Ukraine has even unsettled the countries that traditionally favour Russia. They are not so pro-Russian as to volunteer to cede territory. The EU very cleverly played into this by lowering the sanctions (in 2016). Is Belarus going to become a democracy any time soon? Probably not. The EU remains critical of the human rights situation in the country, but at the same time it can gently encourage it to steer its own course. That in turn creates a margin of manoeuvre for the other EaP countries.

It should be pointed out that some countries gladly play off the EU and Russia against each other, in order to maximise their own advantage. If we respect their sovereignty, we have to accept this. But the EU can be strict once a country has opted for cooperation with us in a certain area, has accepted the aims and conditions of such cooperation, and has been granted EU means to that end. Then it must either stick by the rules or accept that assistance will be halted: you cannot have your cake and eat it, too. If a neighbour is ready to go very far in cooperating with us, the EU should on the other hand not show itself to be too stingy. The ENP budget for the period 2014–2020 enables the EU to spend €200 to €300 million per country per year. That's a nice sum, but it's not so huge as to allow one to dictate terms. It's quite easy for other players to outbid the EU, to the detriment of our influence.

If the EU would do well to offer more support to the countries that are willing to cooperate with us, EU membership is no longer in the offing. All countries of the Balkans will eventually join the EU – that's not very controversial. Geographically, they are already surrounded by the EU anyway. There is no need to rush things though: no accession before they are ready, in the political, economic, and in the security area, which will take quite a few years yet. Meanwhile, candidates for accession have to stand by what they have decided and implement the rules. It's their choice to apply for membership, but once that choice is made, they cannot at the same time make a big show of welcoming Russia. The EU would do well to keep a much closer look and prevent Russian infringement in future Member States. Beyond the Balkans, if ever Norway or Switzerland were to apply for membership, they wouldn't have to wait long before they would be accepted. But the story ends there.

Never say never, but offering EU membership to the countries of "Zwischeneuropa" would mostly just create problems, not in the least with Russia. In terms of economic and political development, these countries are lagging too far behind the EU to catch up quickly (read: in the coming decades). The EU already made the mistake once of allowing certain eastern European states in too soon, by allowing political considerations to take priority over the formal criteria for accession, with negative results for the internal cohesion of the Union.[1] The only southern neighbour to be a candidate country, Turkey, would do best to forget about accession as well – we return to this shortly.

According to the *Global Strategy*, our eastern neighbourhood reaches beyond our immediate neighbours and the Caucasus, into central Asia. The dynamics here are completely different from those in the EaP countries, however. First of all, central Asia, as the name says, is not in Europe. The European presence in the five countries of the region is limited: Kazakhstan, Kyrgyzstan, Uzbekistan, Tajikistan, and Turkmenistan. Most of these countries have very authoritarian regimes and lots of energy resources, which renders it difficult to exercise a lot of influence there. Perhaps there is a role to play for Europe in cooperating with China on the "new silk road" that passes through the region. Both European and joint European–Chinese investment would help make this a less exclusively Chinese project, and could ensure that it benefits both European interests and those of the local population. Central Asia has thus become the theatre (yet again) of a "great game", between three great powers this time: China, Russia, and the EU.[2] In terms of domestic politics, the challenge in the region for those who want to gain influence from the outside is more similar to that in Europe's southern periphery. There the EU is introducing a new concept: resilience.

Whose resilience?

In our southern non-European periphery, the neighbourhood policy must start all over again. Conditionality (become like me and I will reward you) has failed in the past and cannot work in the future. Not now that people in our southern neighbour states have become even more self-conscious political actors, as a result of the Arab Spring and the subsequent wars. People are not waiting for some outside actor to come and explain to them how they should organise their country. Often they blame these very outside actors for the malaise or even for the war in their country – usually not without justification. In the *Global Strategy*, the EU is carefully distancing itself from democratisation as a policy objective therefore. But are we sure that *resilience*, the most mentioned word in the *Strategy*, is a good alternative?

Resilience is a rather defensive notion. To increase someone's resilience is not the same as solving his problem. Hence the problem will hit him, but you will provide him with the means to quickly get back on his feet again when that happens, so that he can carry on. Read: and so that the problem ends there and doesn't affect you. In more classical geopolitical terms, a resilient neighbour would simply be called a buffer state. That sounds even less motivating. Congratulations: you have been selected as Europe's latest buffer state! Will this tempt our neighbours into cooperating with us, even if it comes with a nice little subsidy?

Whose resilience are we talking about anyway? In a democratic state, or a state that is in transition to democracy, resilience may mean something. One can attempt to reinforce democratic structures in order to make them resistant against internal and external shocks (our own democracies would benefit from that too). The problem remains though that even in a democracy this alone is not a very enticing programme. No politician in the EU would run for election on a platform of resilience. People rightly don't just want the government to make them resilient against problems – they expect the government to prevent and to solve problems. Most of our southern neighbours are not democracies in the first place. Whose resilience is the EU to strengthen then? That of the regime? The EU indeed cannot change the regime in Egypt, for example, but it should not be propping it up either. Or is the EU going to make the Egyptians resilient against their own government? It's not very clear what that means or how the EU would go about it.

Resilience, moreover, means different things to different people (Joseph, 2014; Soler i Lecha and Tocci, 2016; Wagner, 2016). The concept has long been used in the development sector, where it primarily refers to measures to help local communities become resistant against floods or droughts and other natural phenomena. The European Commission has been using the term in this sense for a long time already (European Commission, 2012). But people in the security sector mostly associate resilience with measures to protect oneself against foreign intrusion:

border control, surveillance, intelligence, and similar others – not really what we want to promote in states that are authoritarian already. In countries like Egypt, people are under enough surveillance. The *Global Strategy* doesn't really help in this regard, for, as we have seen, it contains many different definitions of resilience.

The vagueness of the concept causes confusion, to such an extent that in 2017 the European External Action Service (EEAS or the EU's "foreign ministry") in its internal proposals returned to the idea that the only truly resilient society is a democratic society. That may well be true, but the point of switching to resilience as the operating principle of the Neighbourhood Policy was precisely that outside Europe democratisation turned out to be well-nigh impossible. So we're back to square one – evidence that resilience is not a good basis for policy. Since the publication of the *Global Strategy* and the start of the debate on resilience, European subsidies have continued to flow, by the way, including to authoritarian states such as Egypt, simply on the basis of the previous policy. Isn't it about time for a more thorough reassessment?

As explained in Chapter 2, the notion of equality has a lot more potential as a foundation for our Neighbourhood Policy and for foreign policy in general. First of all, it is a positive notion, with a lot more power to motivate than the rather defensive notion of resilience. Second, it is a multidimensional notion, allowing the EU to explore with all of its neighbours areas in which interests (security, political, economic) coincide and cooperation is possible, without obliging a country to commit, or pretend to commit, to take steps in an area in which it actually doesn't want to (such as democratisation). In this manner, the EU can build a constructive relationship with every regime, without antagonising it from the start by putting a change of the political system on the table. At the same time, the EU must continue to critically assess the human rights situation in every country, and ensure that by cooperating it never becomes a party to human rights violations itself. That remains the absolute red line.

Many of our neighbours are not democracies, but many are not the most repressive states either. In many cases there is positive change toward more openness – think about Jordan or Morocco. In such a context, insisting on democratisation and trying to set deadlines for specific reforms, as the EU did under the Neighbourhood Policy, does not make much sense. It is much more advisable to let these countries follow the path that they have chosen at their own pace, in order to make sure that they can do so peacefully and without threatening their domestic stability. There are more than enough crises in the region as it is – the EU should be content that at least some countries remain stable. Addressing equality within these countries would precisely contribute to this stability.

We will sometimes feel uncomfortable cooperating with certain countries in our broad southern neighbourhood (which, according to the *Global Strategy*, reaches unto Central Africa, and in reality, also includes the Gulf). Saudi Arabia is a case in point. Principled pragmatism means that the EU must accept that it cannot change the domestic political system of Saudi Arabia. It can and must interrogate the Saudis about human rights violations, including publicly, in the UN Human

Rights Council in Geneva, for example. That may help to mitigate excesses, because even authoritarian regimes are sensitive about their image. But there's no point in making all cooperation conditional on Saudi human rights policy, for that will have no effect at all. Political, economic and even security cooperation with a country like Saudi Arabia must be allowed to continue, as long as the EU does not become involved in the human rights violations that the regime commits, be it at home or abroad. Only in the most flagrant cases (think of the circumstances under which R2P can be activated: crimes against humanity, war crimes, genocide, and ethnic cleansing) must cooperation be suspended.

Even in Turkey, an official candidate country for EU membership, our influence on domestic politics remains in the end very limited. Because of the prospect of EU accession, among other reasons, the country has made enormous progress. The role of the armed forces in politics has been notably reduced. It is unfortunate therefore that President Recep Erdogan is using his popular support to limit openness and democracy again. For a while now he has clearly been following the path to authoritarianism. But Erdogan has won successive elections and referendums (although in an atmosphere that has become less and less free) and is truly popular. Were the EU to try and interfere in domestic politics, by threatening economic sanctions for example, that would most probably be counterproductive. It would only serve to excite Erdogan's supporters and thus to strengthen his position.

Moreover, the EU has manoeuvred itself into a position of dependence by concluding an agreement with Turkey, in 2016, to limit the flow of refugees toward Europe. That may have been unavoidable, given the lack of support with the European public to host more refugees in Europe itself, and with most politicians opting for the easy way out: following rather than leading public opinion. The agreement will certainly not win any prizes though, and it makes it very easy for Erdogan to exert pressure on the EU by threatening to open the doors again. The EU can and must speak out against the limitation of fundamental freedoms in Turkey, but it cannot reverse the course of domestic politics – only the Turks can do that.

The prospect of EU membership for Turkey is now well and truly finished, however. Whether one was in favour or against, in reality we have known for several years now that the EU would never achieve the required unanimity of all current Member States – nobody just wanted to clearly state the fact. Since the July 2016 coup and Erdogan's reaction to it, effectively nobody in Brussels still counts on Turkish membership. That too weakens Europe's leverage over Turkey. In fact, the EU has begun to see Turkey as a buffer state. To which Ankara has said: fine with us, but then we want to be rewarded accordingly, for which one can hardly blame Erdogan. Thus, in the framework of the refugee agreement, the EU had subsidised Turkey for a total of over €6 billion by 2018. The accelerated path to EU membership that is also part of the agreement is just nonsense, however. Turkey cannot be a buffer state and a member state at the same time – it will most likely be the former.

It may sound counterintuitive, but principled pragmatism is a more honest approach than the EU's previous policy. Isn't it less hypocritical to stop pretending that we will democratise our neighbours, since we're not capable of that anyway? Outside Europe it has simply turned out to be impossible to engineer democracy from the outside. This doesn't amount to giving up on our values – it means we start applying them more pragmatically. It remains our duty to emphasise the universality of human rights, if necessary by naming and shaming regimes, in order hopefully to limit excessive violations. By at the same time cooperating where we can, under the heading of equality, we can actually have more concrete impact on the daily lives of citizens in our neighbours. Much more than by sermonising about democratisation, our belief in which we had abjured a long time ago ourselves – as our actions had already made clear a long time before our words changed.

"Allies" in the south

The foreign policy of regimes such as those in Ankara and Riyadh is another matter, though. When neighbours undermine the stability of the region or threaten our vital interests through their reckless or aggressive foreign policy, the EU has to act. In such cases it can act, because we can aspire to change their external policies (contrary to their domestic political system), by applying political, economic, and, when necessary, military means.

At the same time, in this respect too Realpolitik is the order of the day. It is easy to shout, as many in Europe do, that we should stop exporting arms to Saudi Arabia, just like it was easy to work up indignation about the country's membership of the UN commission of women's rights. Logical it is not, however, for as members of the anti-IS coalition, Saudi Arabia and the Europeans are taking part in the same military operations. What would it achieve, furthermore, if we were to no longer sell weapons to Riyadh, or even if we were to suspend all economic relations? The human rights situation would likely stay exactly the same, for the kingdom would not alter its domestic policy under external pressure. We may soothe our conscience this way, but once relations with Saudi Arabia would have been ruptured, would anybody at the political level still care about human rights in the country? Or would it be but gesturing? Criticising Saudi Arabia is mostly an easy way of avoiding self-criticism. Whatever the debate in Europe is, in May 2017 Trump concluded his first visit to Saudi Arabia by announcing arms sales of no less than $110 billion.

It would be a lot more pragmatic and effective to link European (and ideally American) arms exports to the country's foreign policy. Since 2015, Saudi Arabia and its partners are fighting a war in Yemen, where it supports President Abdrabbuh Mansur Hadi in his fight against the Houthi militias and former president Ali Abdullah Saleh (who was killed in December 2017). The Houthi in turn are supported by Iran, Saudi Arabia's competitor for dominance of the region. Military operations take place with scant regard for the civilian population. Furthermore, Saudi Arabia, just like Turkey, initially supported IS, which they saw as the most effective adversary of the Assad regime, until with the help of a little American pressure they realised that, like Doctor Frankenstein, they had created a monster they could not control. But even after coalition operations against IS had started, Turkey kept on importing oil from IS-controlled territory. Turkey has in fact been pursuing a Middle Eastern policy without taking into account its allies in NATO for years. In the war in Syria and Iraq, some of the Kurdish groups that were armed by the US and Europe were bombed by Turkey. All the while, NATO allies had deployed Patriot missiles to Turkey to assist the country with its defence.

The foreign policy of "allies" such as Saudi Arabia and Turkey is much less a subject of public debate than their domestic policy. Turkey itself is always the first to invoke Article 4 of the NATO Treaty whenever it feels disadvantaged by Europeans or Americans. That article allows an ally to ask for consultations when it perceives a threat to its "territorial integrity, political independence or security". Two can play this game: why shouldn't the European allies invoke Article 4 for once, and ask Turkey to explain how it reckons its Middle East policy contributes to the security of the Alliance? It would serve as a hint to make Erdogan understand that there are red lines in European foreign policy which he would better not cross.

The foreign policies of countries like Saudi Arabia and Turkey directly threaten European interests. This is the area therefore in which the EU, preferably in consultation with the US, but alone if necessary, should put pressure on them, by threatening to suspend military cooperation and arms exports, among others. Not just arms exports but trade relations in general can be put to use in a much more focused and effective manner. For example, 44 per cent of Turkish exports go to the EU. Erdogan may flirt with Putin, but Russia is not going to replace Europe's role in the Turkish economy anytime soon. This economic dependence provides us with the means to force Turkey not to diverge too far from NATO and EU foreign and security policy. The alternative is that the European members of NATO will stop seeing Turkey as a true ally, until it is a NATO member in name only.

European interventions

Before attempting to steer the foreign and security policies of Saudi Arabia, Turkey, and other more or less true partners in the region, the EU must define its own policy. In the security realm especially, clear policy is lacking, however. All too often the EU has defined grand projects for its southern periphery that ended where security problems began. That is nonsense, for one cannot create equality, or even resilience, in a country at war. This attitude is lethal for the credibility of the EU as a strategic actor. As so many of our southern neighbours are engaged in one or even several wars, they simply cannot take serious any actor that pretends to have a vision for the region but ignores those wars.

That said, the EU and its Member States are actively involved in various interventions to tackle the security problems of the southern periphery. The picture is certainly not entirely negative.

The most successful example of European security policy for the south probably is the commitment towards Mali. In January 2013, France, with the support of some allies, launched Operation Serval, deploying some 5,000 troops. In a sharp combat action these halted the progress of the Tuareg and jihadist militias that were poised to take the capital, Bamako. This initial combat-heavy phase was followed by a long-term counterterrorism deployment to the Sahel of some 3,000 troops, of which a third was in Mali: Operation Barkhane. Then came a military and a civilian EU mission: EUTM Mali, in which some 600 European troops are training the armed forces of Mali, so that in due course they can guarantee their country's security alone, and EUCAP Sahel Mali, training the police and gendarmerie. The UN deployed to Mali as well: Operation MINUSMA has over 15,000 military and police, mostly in the north of the country. French troops continue to constitute the tip of the spear of the international presence.

These military deployments are but one aspect of an integrated or comprehensive approach (in EU and NATO speak, respectively) that sees the EU aiming to stabilise the country both politically and economically, notably by obliging the government in Bamako to have an eye for the needs of the oft-abused Tuareg population in the north. Moreover, the EU is rolling out a regional strategy for the Sahel, and has deployed a civilian mission to Niger as well, assisting its police force: EUCAP Sahel Niger. Mali's problems are far from solved, but thanks to the international intervention they can be contained; the risk of spillover to neighbouring countries has been limited. And yet it appears that the presence of foreign troops on the ground will be necessary for a long time to come, and the EU and the other international actors will have to permanently provide economic and financial support (and put pressure on the government) before truly lasting peace and stability can be established.

The escalation of the situation in Mali was actually the direct consequence of a previous international intervention, in Libya in 2011, without which intervention in Mali would probably not have been necessary. France and the UK had insisted on military action in order to protect the civilian population from the troops of Khadafy, when he attempted to prevent a repetition of the revolutions in Tunisia and Egypt in his country by force of arms. Initially the US opposed the idea, so for once the Europeans had to convince the Americans of the need for military action. Air operations were started under a Security Council mandate – the first time a resolution was based on R2P; but under NATO command – that was an American demand. Once it had destroyed the Libyan air defence system, NATO initially chose targets very reticently, but inevitably it became the air force of the opposition, which consequently won the civil war. Khadafy was intercepted while on the run and killed by opposition forces.

Many of the mercenaries serving in Khadafy's army fled the country with their arms and equipment, and ended up reinforcing the various militias operating in Mali, among other places, resulting in the crisis that we know. This had not been foreseen: one of the considerations when intervening in Libya was precisely the assessment that the risk of spillover to other countries was very limited, given the fact that the Arab League had requested intervention itself and that the bizarre character of Khadafy meant that he had no real allies. The main reason to intervene, however, was that the West wanted to prove in Libya that it was on the "good side" after all, after its extremely hesitant reaction to the Arab Spring in Tunisia and Egypt, where it had only declared for the opposition once it had become clear that Ben Ali and Mubarak had irretrievably lost their positions.

Libya itself remains a country in crisis, alas. Being too internally divided, the opposition did not manage to consolidate a new political system, and before long the country disintegrated into territories controlled by rivalling armed groups. Libya soon counted nearly as many governments as my own complicated country, Belgium, the difference being that in Brussels they don't deploy armed militias. One thing most Libyan actors did agree on: no Western boots on the ground. The West was very pleased to avoid exactly that, but didn't really insist on relaunching the country economically and politically either. Military intervention alone can never generate any lasting effect, however, if it is not part of a broad strategy that integrates the political, economic, and security dimension. In spite of its wealth in natural resources, Libya is back to square one.

Not just in Mali, but in the Mediterranean too this outcome in Libya led to the need for another intervention. Because of the chaos in Libya, its borders, which under Khadafy had been strictly controlled, were turned wide open. The result was a gigantic stream of people, both war refugees and migrants from across Africa, who took their chances and tried to reach Europe from Libya by crossing the Mediterranean. Taking their chances must be taken literally, for instead of finding the promised land, thousands perished at sea. The various "authorities" in Libya had little interest in trying to control the situation, for human trafficking became big business, to the extent even that regular slave markets appeared. First Italy and then the EU launched a naval operation. Since 2015 European navies are patrolling the central Mediterranean: Operation Sophia. Yet all they can do is to try and save as many people as possible from drowning. Preventing them from crossing in the first place and ending the operations of the human traffickers they cannot, for that would require them to operate at least in Libyan territorial waters and probably even on the Libyan coast. But because the Security Council cannot provide a mandate (because of Chinese and Russian unwillingness) and Libya itself doesn't want to give permission, European ships have to stay in international waters, and the dramatic situation continues.

Libya is but one part of the refugee and migration crisis that the EU has been confronting for several years now. The civil war in Syria, too, generated an immense flow of war refugees (as seen in Chapter 2). As European authorities couldn't cope and the door into the EU was pried open, more and more people from further abroad, from central Africa to Afghanistan, tried to reach the EU through Turkey. In the end the EU closed off this route by concluding a deal with Turkey, as stated previously. Since 2016 a naval operation has been deployed in the Aegean as well, under NATO command.

To an extent the war in Syria as well is a consequence of our intervention in Libya. The Syrian opposition reckoned that if necessary we would support them militarily as well, which certainly was an important factor. We didn't though, because in this case we assessed that Western intervention would automatically lead to international escalation, since President Assad was being supported by Russia and Iran. But escalation happened nonetheless, as IS made Syria and Iraq into one theatre of war. This should not have been our war: not a single European state, but various states in the Middle East would have risked collapse if the progress of IS would not have been halted. But, as we saw, our allies in the region at first supported IS, in the framework of their proxy war against Syria and Iran. Obama probably had no choice, therefore, but to create an international coalition against IS, in September 2014, in order to force the countries from the region to face up to reality. Furthermore, IS attracted thousands of Europeans as "foreign fighters", so that Europe in a way became part of the problem. Russia intervened too, however, in order to prop up its ally Assad, as did Iran, which now has a presence on the ground in both Syria and Iraq.

Together with the different local groups that are all fighting for their own agenda, including the various Kurdish groups, this makes for an incredibly complex war in Syria and Iraq. The only thing that more or less binds all of the internal and external actors is their aim to destroy IS, but there the consensus ends. Successive attempts to arrive at a negotiated solution, by the Arab League, by the UN, and by Russia, Turkey, and Iran, have barely made progress. The international coalition as well (totalling 68 states) has only defined its mission as the total defeat of IS. To that end, European coalition members Belgium, Denmark, France, the Netherlands, and the UK have all deployed aircraft to bomb IS, in addition to logistic and other military support from other EU Member States. Many Europeans have also deployed special forces on the ground in order to train the local armed forces. Destroying IS is of course a legitimate objective – one cannot negotiate with IS because its sole reason of existence is to wage war to do away with the state borders in the Middle East and install a single kalifate. But what is the coalition's overall political strategy?

Neither the coalition nor the EU nor any of its Member States has an explicit view on the political end goal. They have not clarified to whom authority over the territories that have been reconquered on IS has to be transferred. There is no European view on the political end-state that would be best for Syria and Iraq and for the region as a whole. European governments continue to oscillate between the feeling that Assad has killed too many people for him to remain in office, and the realisation that an agreement with Assad probably offers the only realistic prospect of ending the war. They certainly don't have any concrete idea on how to end the proxy war between Iran and Saudi Arabia and return peace and stability to the wider region. The result is that the EU has remained as good as invisible in the international negotiations on the conflict. The coalition became a necessity, and European participation in it imperative. But the fact that years after the start of combat operations the desired political end-state has still not been defined is an illustration of the strategic incapacity of both the EU and the US.

Security guarantees

The EU and its Member States have always actively participated in all interventions that aim to control the security situation in our southern periphery. But there still is no overarching strategic view, even though several years ago already the Arab Spring had proved that the existing Neighbourhood Policy was bankrupt, and that any new vision should comprise a much more explicit security dimension, complementing the political and economic aspects.

As a result, the EU as an institution does not systematically take charge of security in the south. Every time a crisis emerges in our unstable periphery, it is a Member State or a group of Member States that initiates the reaction, but rarely the EU as such. Eventually the EU always has to become involved anyway though, because only the EU has the means to elaborate a long-term political and economic approach that should always follow upon any military intervention, or the latter will not score any lasting effect. If that transition fails, as was the case in Libya, the country will inevitably sink back into chaos. At times it almost seems easier for a state to decide on military action, however, than to come up with a comprehensive strategy. Military intervention demonstrates that one is "doing something". Once operations have come to an end, one feels that enough has been done, and attention shifts to the next problem.

The EU is struggling to operationalise its new concept, resilience, but that is insufficient to answer the security challenges in our periphery. In many of our neighbours, people are fighting for survival: in Iraq, Libya, Mali, Syria, and Ukraine. Actors there don't need advice on how to become more resilient. They are asking for real, tangible support: money, equipment, weapons, trainers, and combat troops. That doesn't mean that the EU should meet all of their demands. But the question is on the table. Pretending not to see it, would be unwise, for then we risk that in the eyes of our neighbours we become irrelevant. We don't need our neighbours to look up to us, but neither can we afford that they would look away from us. Too many interests are at stake in Europe's periphery to risk losing influence there.

A solution can be found in thinking through what the double concept of equality and sovereignty means for European strategy. The EU can cooperate with any country on one or more dimensions of equality, as long as it doesn't create new inequalities and does not itself become party to human rights violations. It's up to the neighbouring states to decide, in full sovereignty, whether they are interested in such cooperation or not. But promoting sovereignty also means that if a country gets into trouble and finds its sovereignty under threat because of its cooperation with the EU, we have an obligation to help it defend its sovereignty. On the one hand, this is a moral issue: if one encourages a country to embark upon a certain course, one cannot stand aside when that course leads it into stormy weather. On the other hand, it clearly is in our interest to protect the credibility of our strategy. Who would want to cooperate with the EU if we were to drop every partner at the least sign of resistance?

To rephrase the point: should the EU offer the neighbouring countries with which it has the closest cooperation a security guarantee? This is a question we never ask, because we feel so insecure that we ask for a security guarantee ourselves, from the US. But in the changing strategic context, the question does end up on our agenda. In the future, the US will be ever less inclined to intervene in Europe's periphery, because of its new focus on China and Asia. Washington rightly expects Europe to assume responsibility for the stability of its own backyard. From a US perspective, Mali was the optimal scenario: Europeans took the initiative to tackle a crisis, deploying their own means, and managed to contain the problem, while the US only had to offer some specific assets in support.

It obviously cannot be the intention to guarantee the security of all neighbouring regimes. It's not up to the EU to depose authoritarian regimes, that is up to their own populations, but neither should we be propping them up. But should neighbouring countries that have a democratic system, or that are evolving in that direction, and with whom we cooperate closely on all dimensions of equality, not be able to count on our support if they cannot defend their sovereignty alone? This is certainly not an easy question. If toward certain countries the EU responds positively, then first it needs the military capabilities that allow it to intervene quickly when necessary, including the command structures. Most importantly, it needs the political will to act: one who offers a guarantee but, when push comes to shove, withdraws it, has lost confidence forever. Yet if the EU responds negatively and declines to support certain countries, they will look elsewhere, because they cannot carry on without support. We may not like it where they turn to next: Iran, Russia, Saudi Arabia, or Turkey, for example. If the EU does not want to position itself as a credible and serious security actor, it may lock itself out of its own backyard, to the advantage of actors whom we would rather not see gaining influence there.

The situation in Tunisia can serve to illustrate this issue of security guarantees. People in Brussels like to mention Tunisia as the only good story to emerge out of the Arab Spring. The country where the first revolution took place, in the end, is the only country that is on the way to a hopefully durable democracy. But this remains a very fragile story. No less than 6,000 to 7,000 Tunisians have joined the ranks of IS and other armed groups as "foreign fighters". If a significant portion of those were to return with the intention of overthrowing the government, Tunisia would be faced with a very serious threat. Suppose that a democratically elected Tunisian government were to ask Europe for military support in such a scenario, should the EU answer that request? Support doesn't just mean equipment nor even just trainers and weapons (and certainly not just the author going over to give a lecture on European defence, like in Ukraine), but combat forces, that join the Tunisian forces in the fighting to restore order.

I have put this question several times to audiences of European diplomats and military, and usually received very similar answers: it's unlikely that the EU as such would reach consensus, but chances are France would take action in a case like this. In my hypothetical scenario, that might be a solution, but it cannot be the system. The stability of a neighbour like Tunisia clearly is in the strong interest of the EU as a whole. When there is chaos in Libya, to take another example, the resulting refugee crisis and the tensions within the EU which that in turn provokes have consequences for all Member States. It should be the EU, therefore, that assesses the threat and initiates common action if required. Leaving France to do the hard work, as was already the case in Mali, hardly shows a lot of solidarity, and is not a viable option for the long term. France no longer has the means to realise its indeed great military ambitions all by itself. Furthermore, action under the EU flag is perceived differently than action by a single Member State, certainly if that happens to be the former colonial power. And it is less complicated to integrate military action in a comprehensive political, economic, and security strategy if the EU is in charge from the start. It really is in our interest, therefore, to elaborate a common European view on our role as a security actor in our periphery.

The war in Syria and Iraq is another example of a theatre where European military support may be required – and a much less hypothetical one. Once the territory that IS held has been completely recovered, the war will most likely gradually start to fizzle out. In defeating IS the international coalition will have achieved its explicit objective (though IS will still exist as an idea, and we will probably see more terrorist attacks in Europe, but eventually IS, just like al-Qaeda before it, will fade away). The other external actors, Russia and Iran, have already nearly achieved their war aims in 2016: lasting influence in Syria for Moscow, and in Syria and Iraq for Tehran. Thus, they too will have an interest in consolidating their gains more than in continuing the war. Without external military support, neither the governments in Baghdad and Damascus nor the various armed groups can continue the fight for very long. Neither party can be totally defeated, neither party can win the war, so we will end up with a deadlock and a very fragile armed peace. Next to the governments of Syria and Iraq, various groups will hold effective control over specific territories. All of them will be looking for alliances and military support in order to ensure their autonomy.

Europe too will have to think about this carefully: do some of these groups merit our support, if only politically, and possibly with financial and economic means? Might it be in our interest to support some groups with equipment and perhaps weapons, and maybe even to assist them from the air and with special forces on the ground if their survival is threatened again? Or should we, on the contrary, withdraw our military as soon as possible after operations against IS have come to a conclusion?

Syria and Iraq are an incredibly complex puzzle. Ignoring this debate will not make the puzzle disappear. Ultimately a diplomatic solution is necessary, through the UN-led negotiations, in which the EU must play an active part. But before it can engage, the EU will have to decide for itself what its view is on the future political order in both countries. First of all, it will have to accept that at least in a first phase Assad will stay on as president – the Russian military intervention has rendered that unavoidable. A very specific question is whether the EU must support the different Kurdish entities in Syria and Iraq in acquiring or maintaining far-reaching autonomy within the existing state structures. The potential for conflict with Turkey is obvious. And what about the parts of Syria that are controlled by the so-called moderate opposition? A form of autonomy will likely be necessary here, too, and certainly in a transition phase, for one cannot imagine that these areas would simply revert to control by the Assad government, which continues to violate human rights on a daily basis. If the EU pronounces its political support for a certain entity, security support will probably have to follow in order to signal to other parties that the EU position is not to be dismissed.

Libya is an example of what can happen if the EU allows a vacuum to exist. Since 2017, one of the rivals for power, General Khalifa Haftar, is supported by Russia. The Libyan war too is a very complex issue without any evident solution. In international politics one has to accept that sometimes there is no entirely satisfying answer, and one has to choose from options that all have upsides and downsides. A military intervention on the ground in Libya would undoubtedly lead to a repetition of the Afghan scenario, with Western troops being sucked into the morass. But by not engaging enough with the Libyan question, Russia has been given the opportunity to acquire a bridgehead there. That can only serve to complicate the eventual resolution of the civil war and is therefore definitely not in our interest. The EU could arm the national unity government in turn, but that could lead to an intensification of the war, which can easily drag on for years. Are there other options to exert pressure and stabilise the country, so that eventually it can make its own choices, without any unwanted outside interference?

We're no longer used to posing questions of this nature, certainly not as the EU. But these issues will end up on our plate, whether we like it or not. Better to think about them, therefore, starting from our own values and interests. The specific question of which role we must play in the security of our periphery is part of a broader debate on the military level of ambition of the EU, to which we now turn.

Notes

1 The accession of Cyprus before the separation of the island in a Greek and a Turkish part had been resolved, was a strategic error as well. Once Cyprus had become a member, the EU had a lot less leverage to force the Cypriots into accepting an honourable compromise.
2 "The great game" is what the geopolitical competition between the UK and Russia was called. In the 19th century both attempted to extend their influence into central Asia and Afghanistan, with Britain being motivated by the desire to create a buffer for British India.

References

European Commission, *EU Approach to Resilience: Learning from Food Crises*. Brussels, EU, 2012.
Jonathan Joseph, "The EU in the Horn of Africa: Building Resilience as a Distant Form of Governance". In: *Journal of Common Market Studies*, Vol. 52, 2014, No. 2, pp. 285–301.
Eduard Soler i Lecha and Nathalie Tocci, *Implications of the EU Global Strategy for the Middle East and North Africa*. Future Notes No. 1. Barcelona, MENARA Project, July 2016.
Wolfgang Wagner, "Resilience as the EU Global Strategy's New Leitmotiv". In: *Contemporary Security Policy*, Vol. 37, 2016, No. 3, pp. 414–430.

5

EUROPE, MILITARY POWER, AND NATO

No great power is without military power. The EU too cannot do without military power if it wants to be able to defend its own interests. Often still the EU is presented as a special type of actor, a "civilian power", that can do without armed forces. That is sheer nonsense. Neither the EU nor its predecessor, the European Economic Community (EEC), has ever been a "civilian power". How could they have been, given that nearly all of their members have always been members of NATO at the same time? Europeans have never abjured the use of force. The only thing was that during the Cold War they bundled their military power in NATO, together with the US, and their economic and political power in the EEC. After the end of the Cold War, the EU began to unite all three dimensions of power under one roof again. That is a logical reorganisation, for in a multipolar world Europe will not always be able to count on the US. But is has not changed the character of Europe.

Possessing armed forces is not in itself morally reprehensible. Perhaps the opposite is true, for one who doesn't have an army just counts on someone else's army to protect him when necessary – or simply abandons his sovereignty. Neither option seems morally defensible vis-à-vis one's own citizens or one's allies. An actor without armed forces, moreover, sacrifices his options and surrenders in advance the capacity for action in circumstances when only military action is feasible. That is the same as saying that in such circumstances one will abandon people to their fate, including our own European citizens who might be in danger. Such pacifism plainly contradicts our values.

One can of course make a value judgement about the reasons why and the way in which the armed forces are used. This remains a very sensitive issue, and rightly so, because the use of force is the most absolute instrument that a state or the EU can deploy, and it must be used reticently. But the debate must be waged objectively. Many times have I sat in debates listening to people criticising Europeans for intervening in Libya, only to hear the same people criticise Europe for not intervening in Syria. In a similar vein, the same people who favour R2P and UN-mandated military action to protect civilians, in the domestic political debate often oppose investment in the armed forces. Who should implement R2P then, in their view? Postmen and train conductors wear uniforms too, of course.

Doctrine: the ways

If the armed forces are deployed, that must be done with the utmost circumspection.

In most interventions in which European forces take part, violence is not used unless in self-defence. Forces can be deployed with the objective of deterrence, on our own territory, like the troops that NATO has prepositioned in the Baltic states and Poland, or far away, like the American, British, and French ships and aircraft that regularly cruise through the area of the South China Sea in order to signal that we do not recognise China's claim to an exclusive sphere of influence. Forces can also be deployed with the consent of all parties involved, either preventively, to avoid a dispute from escalating into violent conflict, or after a conflict has been resolved, to make sure that the peace is not broken. This is classic peacekeeping, by UN blue helmets or other forces, which today is more often referred to as stabilisation operations. Increasingly, Europe is deploying its military (as well as police and other officials) to train and advise the military (and other actors) of a partner country. In the EU jargon, this is known as Capacity-Building for Security and Development (CBSD). This may involve accompanying the partner country's troops on operations in the field, but without deploying combat units from Europe itself. Europe also engages in various forms of military diplomacy and cooperation, such as port visits by navy ships, exchange of expertise, common exercises, or even common patrols. Finally, the logistical means of the armed forces are often called upon, for example, to support humanitarian efforts and disaster relief.

In certain scenarios, however, the use of force is the only way of forcing another actor to end its use of force: this is peace enforcement or crisis management. The use of force is of course also warranted to defend our own territory – that is defence in the narrowest sense of the word. But combat operations may also be required in order to create the circumstances under which other types of military and civilian deployments become possible. In their enthusiasm for CBSD, EU officials in Brussels tend to forget, for example, that in Mali no armed forces would have been left for the EU to train if it hadn't been for the French combat operation that stabilised the situation. If CBSD works, fine, but the EU will not be able to address all of its problems by training someone else to solve them for us.

As mentioned in the previous chapter, in all of these cases military action only makes sense if it is part of a comprehensive or integrated political, economic, and security strategy. In all three of these dimensions conditions must be created that are acceptable to all parties and that can produce a durable peace. For if inequalities that are unacceptable to one or more of the parties to a conflict are allowed to persist, tensions will inevitably mount again, and the chance of a renewed outbreak of violence will be very great, no matter how "successful" the initial military intervention. On its own, a military intervention can only address the symptoms, like the Euro–American air campaign over Libya in 2011 or, earlier, the American invasion of Iraq in 2003. "Mission accomplished", President George W. Bush declared on the deck of the aircraft carrier Abraham Lincoln on 1 May 2003, but 15 years later people are still fighting in Iraq. The need for a comprehensive approach does not just apply to the use of force but also to activities such as CBSD. In the end there is not much sense, at the tactical and local levels, in training battalions and creating good governance in a village if at the strategic and national level the army command and the government do not buy into the strategy. Afghanistan can serve as an example: one can train and equip hundreds of thousands of soldiers and police officers, but if they do not consider the government in Kabul to be legitimate, they will not fight for it. Indeed, many joined the opposite camp, taking their weapons with them.

My colleague at the Egmont Institute, Brigadier-General (Ret.) Jo Coelmont, has rightly pointed out that the total effect of one's political, economic, and military instruments is the result not of an addition but of a multiplication. In other words: if one factor equals zero, the total result equals zero (Coelmont, 2009). That works both ways, of course: often political and economic instruments cannot be put to use until the military instrument has stabilised the security situation. The military is nothing more, and nothing less, than a catalyst of a broader strategy, to use another of Coelmont's favourite expressions.

When violence is being used, it must be directed at its target as precisely as possible, in order to maximally avoid civilian casualties and damage to infrastructure and to the institutions of government. For except if another power invades Europe (which, as seen in Chapter 3, is very unlikely), we do not wage operations in order to defeat another state, let alone to destroy it, but rather to create a stable state, in order for it no longer to cause problems for us or for its own citizens. Ideally, military action is short and sharp, and very precise, so as to quickly eliminate the military capacity of the actors that are threatening peace and stability and to enable the deployment of political and economic instruments. The aim should be for the local actors to resume control of their own institutions at an early stage and maintain stability themselves (if necessary, supported by CBSD). Announcing the end-date of an operation beforehand can be counterproductive, however, for then the opponent will know how long he has to exercise patience in order to see the foreign troops leave. In principle, operations aim at an end-state, not an end-date. That also implies though that if the desired end-state turns out to be no longer achievable, operations should not be needlessly continued.

The principle that the security of the civilian population has priority, is known as *human security*. R2P is one expression of this: the Security Council mandates intervention, not just in a way that doesn't endanger the security of the civilian population, but precisely in order to safeguard it, if necessary against the will of the government concerned. Human security and the comprehensive approach are closely linked: no military intervention can stabilise a country if it antagonises the civilian population. All Western armed forces have integrated the principle of human security into their doctrine, their way of doing operations.

That should not lead to micromanagement, however. The idea, in certain European states, that for every bomb dropped by one of its aircraft parliament should check whether it didn't cause any civilian casualties, can only lead to the total paralysis of military operations. The illusion that such micromanagement is possible can in any case only exist in states that engage in "micro-operations". In a European country that deploys two aircraft here and 30 soldiers there, one can aspire to verify how every bomb and every bullet was used. For large-scale operations as a whole, that see hundreds of aircraft and thousands of troops deployed, that is simply impossible. In any case, every country that takes part in a multinational operation has a "red card holder" in headquarters. When, for example, a state's aircraft in the coalition against IS are assigned a target that violates its national rules of engagement, that officer can pull his red card and refuse the mission.

Let us not fool ourselves, however. Even though the European armed forces seek to avoid "collateral damage" (the common euphemism for civilian casualties) as much as possible when undertaking operations, there is no such thing as a clean war. But can there be a good war, a just war? Under which circumstances can the EU legitimately consider the use of force?

Fighting for Europe: the reasons why

Whether the use of the military instrument must be considered is determined by the scale of the threat to the collective vital interests of the EU. The *Global Strategy* defines these vital interests as our security and sovereignty, our prosperity, our freedom and democracy, and, in order to be able to safeguard these, a stable international order. By assessing the threat to these vital interests, we can decide on the priority tasks for Europe's armed forces.

The *Global Strategy* identifies these tasks as well. It mentions the protection of Europe, keeping our periphery stable, ensuring the freedom of access to the global commons, and contributing to the collective security system of the UN. These four priority tasks cannot be found in one dedicated chapter on defence, but are spread throughout the text. It was feared that a separate chapter on defence would trigger too much resistance, hence the defence implications are addressed chapter by chapter. This demonstrates that the EU still feels uncomfortable discussing military power. The *Global Strategy* turned out to be a lot more ambitious than expected though. The fear that Mogherini aimed to drown the issue of defence in a much broader document, which existed in many capitals, proved to be unjustified. Nevertheless, we have never had a real EU debate about the use of military force: how, when, and why can the EU deploy military force? As a result, the text of the *Global Strategy* is more ambitious than the state of the debate between the Member States warrants. Certainly not all Member States have integrated all of the choices made in the *Global Strategy* into their own thinking. Indeed, while some Member States have a systematic and substantial national strategic debate and a clear view on the use of the military instrument, many don't even have a clear national position, let alone any idea on what a collective EU vision could be.

In the military domain especially, therefore, Europeans have to learn again how to think about power in order then also to use that power aptly and effectively. This involves several dilemmas, which concern both our values and our interests. What could be the core of an EU view on the use of force within the context of the four priority tasks listed in the *Global Strategy*?

The very first consideration must be that deploying troops always means putting them at risk. This applies to all operations, including those at the so-called low end of the spectrum. Standing guard at the entrance to the base of EUTM Mali is still a lot more dangerous than sitting at home in Brussels writing a book on strategy. We have gotten used to the idea that Western states deploy the military somewhere overseas, where they quickly restore order and then return as heroes, without any body bags. That always was a dangerous illusion, with a neocolonial taste to it, moreover. Today what the French call "le zero mort", the notion that we can do military operations without incurring casualties, is definitely obsolete. Because of the spread of often cheap technologies and weapons, even irregular forces (such as militias and terrorist groups) have become dangerous opponents for the most advanced Western armies. At the same time, many states are investing in Anti-Access/Area Denial (A2/AD): the capacity to deny access to even high-technological military forces. The military-technological dominance of the West is as good as over.

All the more reason to be fully aware of what it really means to deploy our troops to use force: that they kill people, and may get killed themselves. In other words: this is war. Since World War Two, in Europe such wars have hardly been felt at home, with the exception of terrorist attacks. In my own country, before troops were deployed in the streets of Brussels (from early 2016 on) as a protection against terrorism, most Belgians who are too young to have been conscripted had never even seen a uniform, unless they happened to have a career soldier in the family.[1] But for our soldiers on operations, for the soldiers of the opposing party, and for the local civilian population, any expeditionary combat operation means precisely that: war. From the point of view of IS, for example, the coalition operations against it amounted to total war, for which they mobilised everything and everybody. We didn't bomb IS to force them to the negotiating table, we bombed them in order to totally annihilate the organisation and reconquer all of the territory that it controlled. IS fought for its very survival and therefore went to extremes. None of this implies that Europeans should begin to use the rhetoric of war. That might even be counterproductive and play into the hand of groups like IS, who ask nothing better than a chance to present their cause as a war between the West and Islam. But we must understand the character of this and every other war in which we engage, or we will not be able to develop the correct military strategy (except by stumbling upon it).

One doesn't start a war light-heartedly. Deploying armed forces, certainly on combat operations, must be seen as an instrument of last resort that can only be considered when other instruments can no longer have any effect. That doesn't mean that in a given crisis one first has to try out each and every instrument – time may not permit that – but that one can reasonably assume that it's too late for other instruments than force to be effective. Only then can military action be considered. The starting point of that consideration is the question: how big is the chance that military action will resolve the problem as compared to the chance that we make it worse or create new problems? Even when that assessment turns out in favour of intervention, one must still balance its potential positive effect against the cost, notably the risk of casualties, both among our troops and among the civilian population. Only when the chance of success and the expected positive effects of success are sufficiently large to justify the risk of negative side-effects and casualties can military action be decided upon. In case of doubt, it is probably better to err on the side of caution and not to intervene.

The conclusion is that unless our own territory is directly attacked by an armed aggressor, Europe's attitude toward the use of force should be one of minimal intervention.

Minimal intervention

Minimal intervention is not the same as non-intervention. Stating upfront that in principle one does not intervene is as much as signalling to less benign actors that they can do as they please. That undermines the deterrent effect of military power and therefore also limits our political and economic power, which will be a lot more effective if other actors have to take into account the fact that, ultimately, they may also have to face our military might. The EU Member States need a credible military capacity for both territorial defence and power projection, in other words, the means as well as the will to use them. The more credible that military capacity, the less we will have to revert to it because of its deterrent effect and its underpinning of our diplomatic and economic action.

Outside our own territory, minimal intervention means that we should abandon the idea that whenever and wherever a security problem arises, it is up to us to come up with a military solution. Outside the borders of the EU and NATO, Europeans should only intervene militarily when our vital interests are directly at stake.

What certainly is not a ground for military intervention, therefore, is regime change: forcefully altering the political system of another state. No matter how reprehensible a regime, only a state's own people can successfully initiate political change. It cannot be engineered or imposed from the outside, certainly not by force of arms. Even the outbreak of civil war or war between states does not automatically constitute a ground for military action. That should only be an option if that war directly threatens our vital interests: because hostilities would interfere with the freedom of navigation, for example, and cut a commercial shipping route. That was the case with the civil war in Somalia, hence the EU launched a maritime operation, Atalanta. Closest to home, a blockade of the Suez canal is the classic scenario in which military action may have to be considered, but such vital maritime choke points exist in Asia as well, notably the Straits of Malacca. Thus, safeguarding the freedom of access to the global commons is a task that our armed forces must be able to implement, not only in Europe's periphery but anywhere in the world where vital economic interests are at stake.

When assessed in the light of the doctrine of limited intervention, the 2011 Libya campaign, which I supported at the time, was a mistake, even though it was mandated by the Security Council. In the exhilarating atmosphere of the early Arab Spring the temptation to give the Libyan opposition a little nudge was strong. But actually it would probably not have directly affected Europe's interests had Khadafy won the civil war. That sounds very harsh, and a Khadafy victory would undoubtedly have ended in very severe repression – that was one of the most convincing arguments in favour of intervention. But by intervening we triggered an acceleration for which the country clearly was not prepared. The actual concrete results of the European–American intervention are the destabilisation of Libya, the destabilisation of Mali, and uncontrolled borders and a refugee and migration crisis, while it undoubtedly also helped to trigger the civil war in Syria. The estimate that the war would not engender spillover effects into other countries proved completely wrong. Did that serve our interests? It's always easy to judge with hindsight, but even so: does the Libya case not prove that it is smarter to adhere to the principle that when our own vital interests are not directly at stake, it is better to be cautious and not to intervene? In fact, the estimate that the chance of spillover was small should have been a reason to stay out of the civil war, for it meant that the chance that our interests would be threatened was small as well.

Rather ironically, since then Europe has remained very reticent, even though the refugee and migration crisis does directly affect us. Though we know full well that it will not stop the human traffickers and that people will continue to try and cross the Mediterranean, the EU's maritime operation Sophia strictly adheres to international law and stays in international waters. The maritime intervention is necessary. Not just because the EU needs to control migration (which, by the way, we need for our labour market – but uncontrolled migration undermines our societies) but because otherwise people will continue to drown. However, by obediently staying in the central Mediterranean, we condemn our operation to ineffectiveness, to the great frustration of the military involved, who understand perfectly the game in which they are playing an undesirable part. Could it not be acceptable, under the heading of principled pragmatism, to disregard the UN Charter in this instance and move our ships into Libyan waters? It's as good as excluded that the EU28 ever reach consensus on this option, for legal it is not. But if it's the only way to close this route of human trafficking and to stop even more people from drowning, would it not be legitimate?

Another instance therefore in which military intervention outside our borders can be considered, in addition to protect the freedom of the global commons is when a conflict threatens the peace and stability of European territory. For example, if the conflict's resulting chaos provokes a refugee stream of such a scale that our border security and asylum systems cannot cope, and our own societal cohesion is undermined, intervention would be warranted, or because in that chaos terrorist groups flourish that (also) target Europe. The latter is why Europeans have joined the coalition against IS. Protecting the security of Europeans citizens abroad is another instance, though in many cases evacuation will be preferred over direct intervention in the conflict itself. Obviously, the chance that a conflict within or between countries somehow spills over into Europe is the biggest in our periphery.

The 2001 American invasion of Afghanistan, far outside our periphery, was launched because the then-Taliban government harboured al-Qaeda, which had perpetrated the 9/11 terrorist attacks on US territory: a case of problems elsewhere directly affecting our territorial security. Europe too subsequently deployed tens of thousands of troops. Afghanistan also serves to illustrate, however, that one should never forget the original objective of an intervention. Long after al-Qaeda as a centrally led organisation had been destroyed, Western forces remained on the spot, in order to install Western-style democracy – which as we have seen is not a feasible objective of military intervention. And so it didn't work, in spite of one of the longest lasting deployments ever (longer than World Wars One and Two combined); Afghanistan has barely registered any fundamental progress toward good governance and democracy (Farrell, 2017). Once our goal was achieved – eliminating the direct threat to the US – we should have withdrawn our forces right away. Instead, after most troops had finally been pulled out in mid-2017, the US asked its NATO allies to send troops back in as trainers for the Afghan armed forces. Since nobody dares to refuse the US, the never-ending story goes on.

In order to maintain the stability of the European periphery, military support (from CBSD to combat operations) may further be considered when the sovereignty of a democratic partner country (or a country in transition to democracy) is under threat. As seen in the previous chapter, real democratisation, from the inside, is always in our interest, because democracy creates stability. If a neighbour gets into trouble precisely because it made the choice for democracy and close relations with the EU, military action can be an option, because under such circumstances abandoning it would amount to abdication. The EU would quickly lose all influence in its own backyard. We should therefore ask ourselves which of our neighbours we are willing to offer what amounts to a security guarantee. The intervention in Mali can be understood in this framework. On the one hand, the EU had to prevent the country from sinking into anarchy, which could easily have spilled over into its neighbours in the Sahel and from there to Europe. On the other hand, in return the government in Bamako was willing to accept the political and economic conditions set by France and the EU, which made a truly integrated approach possible. And of course our own prior intervention in Libya had partly caused the escalation of the crisis in Mali in the first place, which meant that we shared responsibility for solving it as well.

Within the doctrine of minimal intervention outside our own territory, three priorities can thus be discerned: (1) ensuring worldwide free access to the global commons; (2) preventing spillover effects of conflicts to European territory, especially in our periphery; and (3) maintaining the sovereignty of democratic partner countries in our neighbourhood. The more credible Europe's political will and military capacity to act in these cases, the larger the deterrent effect, and the smaller the chance that an actual intervention is necessary. To be clear: in these cases military intervention can be legitimately considered, because vital interests are at stake, but only ever as part of a comprehensive strategy and with maximum respect for human security. Preventive action (by military and other means) remains preferable, and the use of force can only be an instrument of last resort.

These are Europe's priorities, which doesn't mean that Europe should always act alone. If and when we decide to take military action, we preferably do so together with partners. But because vital interests are at stake, if necessary we must be able to act alone as well, at least in our own periphery. In this region, it is up to the EU, as a great power, to take the lead when it has to and maintain peace and stability. The doctrine of minimal intervention assumes however that in the first place it is up to the states concerned, and subsequently to the states of the region and their regional organisations (such as the Arab League and the African Union), to take charge of their own security problems. Their interests will obviously be even more directly at stakes than ours. The example of the war against IS, discussed in the previous chapters, demonstrates however that the local actors are not always willing to take the initiative. To the contrary: in this case, our partners at first contributed to creating the problem. There's a lot of hypocrisy in this debate, too: it's all too easy to condemn so-called Western interventionism after one has first let the problem rot oneself. Libya is another example of this: while the Arab League first asked for an intervention, many of its members made a U-turn when that led to the fall of Khadafy.

But, be careful what you wish for. When local actors do intervene, they don't always care very much for human security, as the Iranian and Saudi interventions in Syria and Yemen amply demonstrate. Many Arab countries have armed forces that are geared primarily to territorial defence and the protection of the regime from internal trouble; their employability for expeditionary operations is limited. In recent years, the trend has been for them to transform their forces and increase deployability (Biscop and Sassel, 2017) – but is that really what we want?

Fighting for justice

Minimal intervention can appear to be a harsh and selfish doctrine. But again: not intervening also means that our troops don't get killed, that we don't kill anybody, and that we don't generate any unpredicted side effects. One often hears the concept of "wars of choice" mentioned: wars waged not because one's territory is under attack, but as the chosen way of achieving a certain objective. If war really is a choice, one also has the choice of not opting for war – and then that must be the option that the EU chooses. Europe should only intervene militarily when it's really necessary and there are no other options.

That is not the same as letting anything go unpunished in those cases in which we don't intervene. It means that we do not employ the military instrument, but the EU can still use political and economic means of power to put pressure on the warring parties. Look at the sanctions against Russia: neither the EU nor NATO is going to fight a war against the Russians, but the EU and the US can impose economic sanctions in order to incite Moscow to implement the Minsk Agreement.

Minimal intervention thus actually implies a commitment to maximal diplomacy. The EU is well placed, moreover, to pursue a proactive diplomacy and to mediate (and to oil the process by economic means, if necessary) in order to alleviate tensions preventively or to bring combating parties to the negotiating table. The competition for dominance between Saudi Arabia and Iran is a good example: the EU did not choose sides and can therefore talk with both parties. Unlike the US: already during his visit to Riyadh in May 2017 Trump demonised Tehran, proof that for the US establishing normal relations with Iran remains difficult, in spite of the nuclear agreement and the election victory of the more moderate presidential candidate just days before Trump's pronouncements. Trump then pulled the US out of the nuclear deal in 2018. But where is the EU? European diplomacy, its crisis diplomacy especially, must urgently shift into higher gear.

Some difficult-to-answer questions will always remain, even if the EU were to commit to maximal use of its diplomatic and economic tools. The *Global Strategy* points out that maintaining the multilateral order in itself is a vital interest of the EU. It notably states that the EU must contribute more to UN operations, and very explicitly addresses the need to protect civilians in conflict, for example by consolidating local cease-fires. This fits within the principles of R2P, the adoption of which in 2005 was a major priority for EU diplomacy, lest we forget. R2P may contradict the doctrine of minimal intervention, however. The intervention in Libya was the first operation mandated by the Security Council on the grounds of R2P, but as we have seen it led to a result that ran counter to European interests.

A case in which a UN mandate did serve EU interests was the reinforcement of UNIFIL, the UN peacekeeping operation on the border between Lebanon and Israel, in 2006. After a short but intense war between Israel and the Hezbollah militias controlling southern Lebanon, the UN decided to reinforce its peacekeepers and asked the EU for assistance. The Europeans met this request and even deployed as blue helmets, because only the UN flag was acceptable to all parties on the ground. The stability of the Lebanese–Israeli border clearly is in the interest of the EU as well, hence its willingness to deploy several thousand troops.

There was much less enthusiasm to contribute troops for peacekeeping operations in the Central African Republic, where unrest threatened to escalate into massive violence against the civilian population. In 2014, the Council of Ministers of the EU did decide to deploy an EU operation, after France had already sent a national force, but in most Member States that political decision did not translate into any willingness to actually contribute. The force generation for the operation proceeded at a snail's pace therefore. The reason is that beyond maintaining international law and the principle of R2P, no specific interests were at stake for any EU Member State in a country in which none of them even have an embassy, with the exception of France (the former colonial power). A country, moreover, which has as its only advantage that its name tells you where it is, as a former colleague of mine once put it; otherwise, most people wouldn't know even that.

On the one hand, it truly is a vital interest of the EU to maintain international order and the collective security system of the UN that is supposed to guard it. Collective security can only be effective and credible if it addresses everyone's security problems and if everyone contributes. But on the other hand, as we have seen, there also is a strong case to be made that R2P alone is insufficient to justify military intervention. In every case the humanitarian and legal aspects should be assessed together with the potential impact on the other vital interests of the EU, especially if the use of force is being considered. Any automatism is out of the question, therefore: even in a case that meets the criteria to activate R2P, one must still assess whether military action would not make things worse. In any event, only the Security Council can decide to mandate the use of force to implement R2P, which means that the EU will always have to take a position, because through its Member States it is always represented in the Security Council.

The war in Syria is a tragic example of how the duty to protect the civilian population must still be weighed against the feasibility of military action. When the war started, our initial assessment was the opposite of the Libyan case: we estimated that European and/or American military intervention would immediately produce escalation and spillover of the war to other countries because of the involvement of Russia and Iran and the linkage to the situation in Lebanon. That analysis was not wrong, for we did see Russia intervene when it began to look as if the Assad regime might fall. When the war then did spill over into another country, Iraq, we intervened as well: to destroy IS, not to depose Assad.

As the war dragged on, more and more voices pleaded for the creation of safe zones, where the civilian population would be protected and essential services such as water, electricity, and medical care restored. Others called for humanitarian corridors in order to ensure humanitarian organisations access to people in need. All of this sounds nice, but militarily it is most demanding. If one just declares a safe zone by means of a diplomatic statement, one has done nothing but create a trap. People will convene there, only to see that nobody can or wants to protect them and that, actually, they have just become a very attractive target. We've done this before, in Srebrenica in Bosnia, during the Yugoslav civil war, when blue helmets were powerless to prevent a massacre.

A real safe zone demands the deployment of significant troop numbers on the ground, with serious firepower, backed up by air power and by ready reserves. Such a force must not necessarily seek out and destroy the enemy, but it must be ready to fight when the civilians for whom it is responsible are threatened. The same applies to humanitarian corridors: if the combating parties, who often purposely target the civilian population, don't want them to receive humanitarian aid, access will have to be enforced by military means. Noble intentions can thus imply large-scale combat operations. We made our assessment, and we didn't do it. Was that the right choice? If only it were that simple: in times of war there often are only bad options.

Take the example of the use of chemical weapons in Syria. In 2012, President Obama had warned that if that red line were to be crossed, the US would take military action. It was crossed, by Assad's forces in August 2013, but in the US there turned out to be but small appetite for intervention. The same in the UK, where parliament explicitly rejected that option. Only France was ready and willing to intervene. Russia used this Western hesitation to take a diplomatic initiative, which led to an agreement about the destruction of the regime's stocks of chemical weapons. That was probably a better solution, even though it meant that Assad went unpunished. In 2017 and 2018, however, chemical weapons were used again, apparently again by the regime. This time the US, under President Trump, did retaliate militarily, on both occasions. On the one hand, that seems legitimate: the interdiction of chemical weapons is an undisputed rule of international law. On the other hand, it may have rendered a diplomatic solution of the war even more difficult, and it certainly doesn't stop people from being killed by other means than chemical weapons. Again it's not easy to say what would have been "the right choice".

When we do intervene, every operation in principle requires a legal basis, because maintaining a rule-based international order is in itself an interest of the EU, and because of course the rule of law is an inherent part of our own values and societies. Therefore we either act out of self-defence (according to Article 51 of the UN Charter), or at the invitation of a state (as in Iraq and Mali), or under a mandate of the UN Security Council (as in Libya in 2011). As the example of the maritime operation in the Mediterranean shows, which cannot operate in Libyan waters, this principle too can generate dilemmas. Russia and China hold veto power in the Security Council and can thus block any request for a UN mandate. A country like Libya, to take another case, doesn't really want to acknowledge that it needs outside help. Once again, the EU can only assess on a case-by-case basis which interests weigh more heavily under the circumstances.

In 1999, Europeans and Americans intervened against Serbia in order to protect the civilian population of Kosovo, through NATO, and without Security Council authorisation. That intervention was heavily contested by Russia and produced some fierce debates in Europe, but abroad it provoked much less reaction than expected. Europeans solving a problem in Europe was rather seen to be in the nature of things. Should violence once again erupt on the Balkans, Europeans would undoubtedly do what it takes to halt it, by force of arms if necessary, regardless of the Security Council, because these countries are now (nearly all) candidates for EU membership and vital interests are directly at stake. Unauthorised military action outside Europe is much more sensitive, however. The absence of a sufficient legal base is one of the factors that can tilt the assessment of the potential use of force toward the conclusion that it would do more harm than good.

Defending Europe

If our own territory were attacked, we would of course defend our security and sovereignty with all available means, military force included. The European states have committed to a double obligation to assist one another if one of them would be the victim of aggression: under Article 5 of the NATO Treaty, and Article 42.7 of the EU treaty.[2]

Only NATO undertakes the military planning that would guide our reaction in case of a classic conventional attack on our territory, by the armed forces of another state. The Alliance has defined a level of ambition for collective territorial defence that should enable European and non-European allies together to deter and, if that fails, to resist any such attack. Only the multinational NATO headquarters are capable of commanding such by definition large-scale operations. The NATO command and control structure is capped by SHAPE, in Mons in Belgium, which oversees a series of headquarters totalling 8,000 military personnel. It is not now the intention that the European states would organise themselves for their territorial defence autonomously, through the EU, though that might be a long-term objective – we'll come back to that.

There is a whole series of threats and challenges to our internal security however that fall below the threshold from which Article 5 is activated. The EU is probably better placed to face this kind of threats than NATO. The *Global Strategy* stipulates that we must address "challenges with both an internal and external dimension, such as terrorism, hybrid threats, cyber and energy security, organised crime and external border management". In a democracy, it's not the armed forces that take the lead in tackling such threats, which is also why NATO, as a military alliance, has neither the authority nor the instruments to take charge of them. At most the armed forces have a supporting role, assisting the other security services, and acting as a measure of last resort in case of severe crisis. It is up to the individual states to decide whether to deploy their armed forces on their national territory, like Belgium and France have done in the context of protection against terrorism. Much more European cooperation is necessary, however, between military and civilian intelligence services, between national and European crisis response centres, and between police and gendarmerie forces, justice departments, coast guards, and the armed forces (notably when the latter operate at the external borders of Europe, such as Operation Sophia in the Mediterranean).

NATO Allies have activated Article 5 only once, in 2001, following the 9/11 terrorist attacks against the US. That demonstrated that collective defence also applies against non-state actors such as al-Qaeda and not just against other states. Washington rather haughtily rejected actual military support, however, and preferred to launch a national operation to destroy al-Qaeda in Afghanistan, with the support of individual allies like the UK. Only later, after the US had also invaded Iraq (in 2003) and began to realise that it was becoming overstretched, did it request NATO allies to send troops to Afghanistan. In the Ukraine crisis Article 5 has not been activated, for Ukraine is of course not a member of the Alliance. In the context of collective defence, NATO has prepositioned forces along our own eastern borders though, by way of deterrence.

The EU's mutual assistance clause, Article 42.7, has only been activated once as well, also because of terrorism. That was done at the request of France following the terrorist attacks by IS in Paris on 13 November 2015, in the Bataclan concert hall among other places. This demonstrates the inextricable link between internal and external security. Terrorism has two dimensions. There is an international dimension: the fact that IS proclaimed itself to be a state, controlled a territory, and waged a very active propaganda campaign. That is the pull factor, which attracted Europeans and others to join IS as "foreign fighters" in Iraq and Syria or to commit terrorist attacks in their own countries. But that pull factor would have a lot less impact if there were no internal push factor in our own countries: a feeling of exclusion, a lack of perspective, and frustration that creates a fertile breeding ground for recruiters and for self-radicalisation, and that pushes some on to acts of terrorism.

France did not request assistance in addressing the domestic dimension and securing its own territory, which would have been more in the spirit of Article 42.7. Instead it requested other EU Member States to support its military operations outside Europe, either by contributing more troops to the coalition operations against IS, or by replacing French troops in other ongoing operations (such as in Mali) so that France could focus on the fight against IS. That was a very broad but justified interpretation of Article 42.7. France put the question in the framework of the EU rather than NATO because traditionally it has a policy of promoting the EU as a security actor, but also because NATO as such couldn't really meet the specific French request, since operations against IS had already started, by the US-led international coalition. Not doing that under the NATO flag had been a conscious choice, in order to avoid creating the impression of a Western intervention, hence the option of an ad hoc coalition including countries from the region.

This first activation of Article 42.7 was rather improvised and in the end had mostly symbolic effect (Anghel and Cirlig, 2015). Since the EU until then had not defined any procedure for its implementation, that was invented on the spot. Unfortunately, the Member States gave a very narrow interpretation to the role of the EU institutions in the operationalisation of Article 42.7. Because France had invoked it, so went their reasoning, the article had been activated automatically, and no explicit decision of the Council of Ministers of the EU was necessary. In this instance there was no doubt of course that Article 42.7 applied – but that might not always be the case. Imagine a Member State that has been hit by a cyberattack and that invokes Article 42.7 against the alleged perpetrators in Russia. Would the other Member States not want to be absolutely certain that the Russian authorities were indeed behind the attack? Just like in NATO, in the EU too only the ministers collectively should be able to decide whether in a specific case the obligation of mutual assistance applies or not. Decisions on war and peace had better be explicit.

The same applies to the actions that have to be undertaken upon activation of the article. In this case the EU decided that it was up to France alone to initiate such action and to ask other Member States for specific assistance, on a strictly bilateral basis. The EU institutions did not play any part at all, not even a coordinating role. France did not in this instance undertake any action that was not legitimate. But again, not every future case might be as clear-cut. To stay with the example of a cyberattack: wouldn't the other Member States want to be sure that the Member State that was hit doesn't react disproportionately? Clearly not every cyber incident demands a military response. The EU should not just leave the decision on which action is to be taken to the Member State that was aggressed; NATO doesn't either. Because once Article 42.7 has been activated and the EU has become involved, all Member States are involved, whether they directly take part in any action or not. After 9/11, the US went its own way without its NATO allies and, following Afghanistan, also invaded Iraq – a decision with disastrous consequences, with which the region and we in Europe are still struggling today. Collective interests demand collective decisions.

In the end, in this first case of Article 42.7 being activated, assistance remained limited to rather symbolic contributions. Some countries deployed troops, like Germany for the UN operation in Mali, but those deployments had mostly been decided a long time ago, even though they could now be presented as a reply to the French request for assistance. If Europeans were ever to decide that in the future they need to take charge of their own defence in a more autonomous manner, they must seriously reconsider the purpose and method of Article 42.7. This constitutes yet another example of how the EU and its Member States really need to learn again how to think about military power, even in the context of something as evident and essential as self-defence.

The EU has actually created a second obligation of mutual assistance, in Article 222 of the Treaty on the Functioning of the EU, the so-called "solidarity clause".[3] This applies specifically in the case of terrorist attacks or natural or man-made disasters, but only provides for action to be taken on the territory of the Member State concerned. As France was requesting contributions to its actions outside the EU, activating Article 42.7 was the logical choice, even though Article 222 explicitly mentions terrorism. Furthermore, for Article 222 the EU had already adopted a detailed implementation procedure, which put the authority to decide what to do with the EU rather than with the Member States. That too appears to have been a reason that France, which wanted to retain full control itself, opted for Article 42.7.

My own country, Belgium, after the 22 March 2016 terrorist attacks on Brussels airport and on downtown subway station Maalbeek, invoked neither clause. On the one hand, the government didn't seem to have any specific request to address to the EU or other Member States. On the other hand it was reluctant to invoke the solidarity clause especially, because the implementation procedure states explicitly that it can only be activated if a Member State judges its own capacity to deal with the situation to be "overwhelmed". That's something that no government likes to admit. But it's also a superfluous stipulation, for it is quite possible that a Member State is not overwhelmed but that action is required that cuts across borders and, for practical or legal reasons, can only be done through or by the EU.

Belgium could have invoked either article in order to underline the urgency of its plea for more cooperation between European intelligence services, which it had proposed at various occasions but was always turned down. Knowledge is power: intelligence services regard information as coin to be used when they need specific data from another Member State. Systematic exchange of intelligence is very limited, and even if that would be improved upon, one would still face 28 services all pursuing their own priorities. It is quite justified to ask whether on top of the national services the EU doesn't need a European domestic intelligence service of its own, the equivalent of the French and Belgian *Sûreté* or the British MI5 (or a "European FBI", though not a "European CIA" as is often said in the debate, for the latter is the foreign intelligence service). Such an EU intelligence service could focus on a number of EU-wide threats, such as terrorism, and develop a common policy to address them.

The terrorist attacks in Brussels are a sad demonstration of how interlinked the security of the EU Member States is. The attack of 22 March 2016 was an attack against "European Brussels" as much as against "Belgian Brussels": half of the victims were Belgians, half came from all over the world. All were fellow human beings.

The military level of ambition

Safeguarding the worldwide freedom of access to the seas, space, air space, and cyber space (i.e. the global commons); preventing conflicts around Europe from spilling over to Europe itself; and guaranteeing the sovereignty of democratic partners in our neighbourhood: if these are the priority military tasks outside Europe, then the next question is how many troops it takes to effectively implement those. Put differently: which capacity for power projection outside our borders must Europe have? In addition, of course, we must be able to defend our own territory. Europe must define a military level of ambition therefore that allows it to defend itself at all times and, simultaneously, to project power when necessary.

For expeditionary operations, the EU agreed in 1999 already that the EU Member States should be capable, in an autonomous manner, of deploying 50,000 to 60,000 troops (about 15 brigades or an army corps, plus the required command and control, support, air, and maritime capacity), within two months and for at least one year. Approved at a European Council meeting in Helsinki, this level of ambition is known as the Helsinki Headline Goal – Headline Goal for short. This number (50 to 60,000) is an arbitrary number, which was inspired by the wars in former Yugoslavia. Had Europe wanted to intervene on the ground early in those wars, these are the troop numbers that would have been required. As many troops were effectively deployed in Kosovo after it had separated from Serbia in 1999, be it in cooperation with the US, and under NATO command. The Headline Goal is a land-centric target, therefore. Is this military level of ambition still sufficient to meet the priority military tasks of today?

Here is an example of an up-to-date level of ambition in terms of power projection. These are the expeditionary operations that Europeans should have the capacity to launch concurrently when necessary:

- Long-term capacity-building (CBSD) in several neighbouring states.
- Long-term cooperation activities with states across the globe, including in the maritime domain, and notably in Asia.
- Two long-term stabilisation operations (before or after a conflict), of a brigade each, in Europe's periphery.
- Two long-term contributions to UN peacekeeping operations (before or after a conflict), of a battalion each, beyond Europe's periphery.
- Three long-term maritime operations (before, during, or after a conflict) in Europe's periphery.
- One evacuation operation of EU citizens, of a battalion, anywhere in the world.
- One combat operation, of several brigades and/or air force squadrons, in Europe's periphery.

This list certainly is not overambitious: it is but the reflection of the operational rhythm of European forces since the start of the 21st century. It doesn't contradict the doctrine of limited intervention, for it doesn't mean that Europeans have to wage this many operations at any one moment, but that they need the capacity to do so if and when necessary. If Europe can credibly show that it is able to, this will in itself have a deterrent effect, notably in our periphery.

Can Europe do this today? Not alone. Yet the *Global Strategy* has stated, more clearly than ever before, that in the military sphere the EU needs "strategic autonomy". Not in the area of collective territorial defence, which we ensure through NATO together with the US, Canada, and our other non-EU allies. But the other priority tasks we must be able to do alone if necessary. As the *Global Strategy* explicitly states: "This means having full-spectrum land, air, space and maritime capabilities, including strategic enablers".

It is the strategic enablers in particular that Europe is lacking. Enablers are capabilities that enable one to project military power outside one's borders and to employ it with as much precision and as little risk for one's own troops as possible. That means, for example, substantial fleets of large transport ships and aircraft that allow one to deploy large troop numbers at once instead of just a small and vulnerable advance party. Also necessary are air-to-air refuelling aircraft in order to deploy combat aircraft for long periods over long distances. And precision-guided munitions or "smart bombs", which limit the risk for the civilian population. Finally, anything to do with information and intelligence (ISTAR in the military jargon), based on satellites, drones, radar aircraft, and the like in order to identify and locate the target in the first place. The *Global Strategy* explicitly mentions "investing in Intelligence, Surveillance and Reconnaissance, including Remotely Piloted Aircraft Systems, satellite communications, and autonomous access to space and permanent earth observation".

Europeans have invested far too little in these kinds of capabilities, as a result of which we are heavily dependent on the US, which does have strategic enablers in large quantities. For the 2011 Libya air campaign, for example, the US provided at least three quarters of the enablers, even though the two militarily strongest European states, France and the UK, were taking part. Without that American support, the Europeans might just have pulled off the air operation, but it would have started later, would have implied a lot more risk for our own forces, and would have been a lot less precise. And that was, after all, a relatively small-scale operation in Europe's backyard. The lack of enablers is a serious handicap therefore. The 28 EU Member States together may well spend over €200 billion per year on defence and maintain an impressive one and a half million people in uniform – but without strategic enablers they can hardly deploy any of them.

The readiness of many of the manoeuvre units (the actual combat units) leaves much to be desired as well, moreover. Many European states maintain capabilities that in reality are not capabilities at all, because as a result of understaffing, a lack of training, and a lack of modern arms and equipment they cannot be deployed outside their own borders. Troop numbers have been radically reduced in all EU Member States. That was logical and not unjustified, for after the end of the Cold War it was no longer necessary to maintain such huge, conscription-based armies. In most countries conscription was abolished (though in 2017 Sweden decided to reintroduce it, with an eye to the Russian threat). Even the 1.5 million troops that the EU Member States are paying to wear uniform today may be more than necessary, in view of our level of ambition. As armed forces were downsized, the tail (staffs, logistics, and support) shrunk much slower than the head (the combat units). Since the end of the Cold War European armed forces have lost massively in terms of firepower, and they continue to lose capability to this day.

Belgium and the Netherlands have all but abandoned their tanks and heavy artillery, for example. Many east European Member States are still employing Russian-made tanks, aircraft, and other equipment, of Cold War vintage, which mostly can no longer be deployed at all. The number of tanks in the EU has sunk from near 16,000 in 2000 to less than 5,000, including 2,700 of obsolete types (Andersson, Biscop, Giegerich, Mölling, and Tardy, 2016). The number of large warships has decreased as well, from 170 in 2000 to less than 130. Taking into account that many of the remaining ships are aging, the result is that Europe has trouble maintaining the EU and NATO operations in the Mediterranean and off Somalia, even though every operation counts but a handful of ships.

European air forces can serve to illustrate our capability problems as well. To start with, only 20 out of 28 Member States have combat aircraft, officially over 1,800. Five of those mostly or exclusively fly old Russian Mig aircraft, which cannot be deployed on any serious operation. Of the remaining 15, many, including the German *Luftwaffe*, are equipped with older Western aircraft that cannot be deployed for anything but reconnaissance missions outside the national airspace either. Taking into account which Member States have demonstrated the will and the capacity to participate in combat operations outside Europe, one arrives at no more than six or seven, which together can deploy just over 100 aircraft at any one time. The idea that is prevalent with many in my own country, that there are more than sufficient combat aircraft in Europe, hence Belgium need not replace its F16s, is completely wrong, therefore. There are many aircraft in Europe, but very few deployable ones, and there will be even fewer in the future, because the countries that are investing in new fighter aircraft are acquiring fewer than they have now (just like the Belgian government has announced it will replace 54 F16s by 34 F35s).

Conclusion: of the one and a half million troops in the EU, just a small percentage can be deployed on expeditionary operations, probably not more than 10 to 12 per cent (Horvath, 2011). Barely 150 to 180,000 out of 1.5 million: that's neither very cost-effective nor a very good use of taxpayers' money. Moreover, one has to take into account the need for rotation. Most European states deploy troops abroad for periods of no longer than four months, hence in order to maintain one soldier abroad, one needs at least three: one who is preparing to deploy, one who is deployed in theatre, and one that has returned for recuperation and retraining. So under normal conditions the EU28 can deploy no more than 50,000 to 60,000 troops simultaneously – which is just about the 1999 Headline Goal. Furthermore, an even smaller percentage than 10 to 12 per cent can be deployed for combat operations; a large share is capable only of less intensive missions.

The next conclusion follows from this: for the time being, the EU does not have strategic autonomy in the military field. The EU Member States collectively can deploy 60,000 men and women. At times since 2000 even up to 80,000 troops from EU Member States were deployed, if one adds up all ongoing EU, NATO, UN, coalition and national operations. But Europeans cannot do this alone – they can only do so if the US provides the strategic enablers to make deployment possible. Moreover, Europeans actually also count on the US to provide the strategic reserve for their deployments. It is good military practice to keep as many troops again as one sends out ready in a quickly deployable reserve, in case the troops in theatre run into trouble and must be reinforced or extricated. But once Europeans have 60,000 deployed, that's more or less it. Deploying more would see a lot of difficulties, and a lot of improvisation – so there are no deployable reserves.

The EU thus has not yet achieved the level of ambition of the 1999 Headline Goal, but the point is, moreover, that the Headline Goal is anyway no longer sufficient to meet today's challenges. The example of an updated level of ambition for power projection that I gave previously cannot be implemented wit 60,000 deployable troops. In fact, the Headline Goal should be doubled, so that the EU Member States can at any time deploy up to 60,000 troops and have as many again in a ready reserve, in case an ongoing operation goes wrong or a new crisis emerges that demands a military response. Furthermore, the rather land-centric Headline Goal, which was formed on the basis of the experience of former Yugoslavia, must be complemented with a stronger air and especially maritime dimension, in view of today's priority military tasks. Finally, the aim should be for the EU Member States themselves to have all the strategic enablers required to deploy a force of this size alone when necessary, without any help from the US or other allies and partners.

Doubling the Headline Goal: for an academic, that's easy to say. This means having 100,000 to 120,000 troops deployed or ready to deploy at any one time, which in view of the need for rotation requires 360,000 troops in order to sustain this effort for one year. Yet this still leaves more than a million of the troops that are currently on the payroll, so even a double level of ambition for autonomous expeditionary operations does not employ the full military potential of the EU Member States. More than enough troops remain, in other words, to fulfil our NATO commitments and to deter or defeat any attack on our territory at the same time. A higher level of ambition for autonomous expeditionary operations thus does not need to conflict with the needs of collective defence and the transatlantic alliance.

What about NATO?

Many continue to see the relationship between the EU and NATO as a competition, as if whatever the one gets automatically is to the detriment of the other. Of course, if one were to start from a blank page today, one would not create two separate organisations, but assemble European cooperation on all dimensions of foreign, security and defence policy under one roof. But we cannot. So, today Europeans organise our collective territorial defence in NATO, according to the mutual assistance commitment of Article 5, together with our North American and other non-EU allies. In addition, NATO can deploy expeditionary operations of any type anywhere in the world; in NATO jargon, these are simply called non-Article 5 operations. The EU as well, through its Common Security and Defence Policy (CSDP), can deploy all types of expeditionary operations across the globe. In EU jargon, these are the Petersberg Tasks, named for the Petersberg Declaration (itself named after the conference centre of the German government near Bonn) in which they have first been listed back in 1992. When a crisis demands a military response, the question thus inevitably arises under which flag Europeans will act. Neither NATO nor the EU have armed forces of their own – only states have armed forces. Both organisations must appeal to the same pool of capabilities in their European members for any operation.

As a result, a beauty contest has arisen between both organisations, which have almost come to see deployments as a market. Both absolutely want to maintain their market share and their consequent claim to their members' military capabilities. For example, there was great frustration in NATO headquarters in Brussels when after the November 2015 terrorist attacks France invoked Article 42.7 of the EU Treaty rather than NATO's Article 5. This was read as a direct threat against what NATO considers to be its exclusive market: the security of our own territory. Many in NATO also felt overshadowed by the EU's maritime operations. EU Operation Atalanta especially, against the Somali pirates, was the more effective one and it really didn't make sense for NATO to conduct a separate operation in the same theatre at the same time. In fact, it would have been a lot more logical to concentrate all European ships in a single operation from the start.

When the EU launched Operation Sophia in the Mediterranean, NATO perceived a new market and quickly followed up with its own operation in the Aegean Sea, between Greece and Turkey. That said, this is an operation that could not have been done under the EU flag, for that would have been unacceptable to Turkey, a member of NATO but not of the EU and highly critical of the EU's defence dimension. This already shows that the beauty contest is totally meaningless. Europeans cannot but assess on a case-by-case basis under which flag they can operate most effectively.

The EU for its part often feels marginalised, because when its Member States decide to launch combat operations they seldom if ever consider the CSDP as a framework. It goes further than that though: in fact states prefer to pass NATO by as well. The states that decide on combat operations prefer to conduct them themselves (such as the French in Mali) or through an ad hoc coalition outside the EU and NATO (such as the coalition against IS), so they can retain maximal control. Under the EU and NATO flag we patrol the seas, we train partner countries' forces, and we preposition forces in eastern Europe. But if there is any chance of combat, it appears their members prefer not to use either organisation – which makes the competition between them even more absurd.

Yet still the beauty contest goes on, even though 22 out of 28 EU Member States are members of NATO too. Of the remaining six, furthermore, five are partners of NATO, which amounts to a very close relationship: Austria, Finland, Ireland, Malta, and Sweden. Only Cyprus does not have any formal relationship with NATO: it is blocked by the enduring dispute about the partition of the island. Unfortunately Greece and Turkey abuse Cyprus' status in NATO (which Turkey limits) and Turkey's status in the EU (which Greece, though today many others too, seeks to limit) to fight out their bilateral disputes. Conversely, Albania, Canada, Iceland, Montenegro (whose accession was announced in May 2017), Norway, Turkey, and the US are members of NATO but not of the EU. After Brexit they will of course be joined by the UK.

In order to put a stop to the meaningless competition between the EU and NATO, everybody must first come to see what the nature of either organisation is, and how their tasks relate to each other. That seems obvious, but it is not. During the long years of the Cold War, NATO acquired such centrality in European foreign and defence policy, and in our relations with the US, that many cannot, or do not want, to see that this centrality has long since come to an end. Topping the agenda of Europe's foreign policy no longer is the threat of invasion, but climate change, energy dependence, international trade, terrorism, and the rise of China: all of them issues on which NATO has little or nothing to contribute. We do want to continue to have a dialogue with the US on these issues, of course, but we mostly do that directly between the EU and the US, outside the NATO framework.

The EU and NATO cannot be compared, in fact. The EU is a supranational organisation in which states share sovereignty. No EU Member State has abandoned any sovereignty, but on many issues Member States can only decide collectively, and by majority. Picture living in an apartment building (as your author does): inside one's own apartment, one does as one likes, within certain agreed rules and as long as one doesn't disturb the neighbours. But decisions about the staircase or the elevators and the building as a whole one can only take together with all the other owners. The owners' meetings can be tedious, but one better attend, for decisions are taken by majority and even if one isn't there, or if one is in a minority, one still has to implement them. NATO in this analogy is the neighbourhood watch, which not every neighbour in one's building has joined, and which includes neighbours from other buildings as well. The neighbourhood watch is very important, but it doesn't make any decisions on the future of one's building.

This means that the EU is a unique type of actor (*sui generis*, as the EU-studies crowd likes to say), something in between a state and an organisation. NATO on the contrary is an entirely intergovernmental organisation, where all decisions are taken by consensus, and there is no question of pooling sovereignty. In the EU this intergovernmental system applies only to foreign, security, and defence policy: in these domains European integration has advanced the least and the EU too for the time being operates in an intergovernmental way (though trade and the better part of development are governed by supranational rules). In general, however, the political centre of gravity of the EU is between Brussels and the national capitals, whereas in NATO it clearly is in the capitals (and in one capital in particular: Washington).

Consequently, the EU is an actor, whereas NATO is an instrument. The states remain the most important actors, of course. Each state wages a foreign policy and defines a strategy to that end. Through the EU, the EU Member States in addition pursue a collective foreign policy, the Common Foreign and Security Policy (CFSP, into which the CSDP is integrated), for which they have defined a collective strategy, the *Global Strategy*. If in a given case EU strategy requires military intervention, the Europeans always have several options to mount that. A military operation can be conducted by the EU itself (through the CSDP), but also by NATO (which can thus be an instrument of EU strategy), by European forces under UN command, or by an ad hoc coalition of Member States (and nonmembers). It can even be a national operation, conducted by one Member State with the logistic and other support of fellow members.

NATO does not wage its own foreign policy and therefore does not determine European strategy: EU strategy sets the context within which NATO operates, not the other way around. The only exception is collective territorial defence under Article 5, because for now the EU does not really play a role in this field. Hence for collective defence, and for that only, NATO is the forum in which Europeans and Americans together decide on strategy. For all other issues, Europeans set strategy through the EU, and Americans have their own US strategy. Many still think the opposite holds true, however, as if NATO in all areas determines the strategy within which Europeans, including the EU, must then act.

The Ukraine crisis can easily demonstrate that this latter interpretation is faulty. NATO conducts the military response to the crisis: prepositioning forces on our eastern borders, as a message to Russia and to our own public opinion. That response takes place within the framework of an overall vision on the future of Europe's relations with Russia, in all areas, including energy for example. This vision is not crafted in NATO. Europeans decide on this collectively in the EU, starting from their interests and priorities as Russia's neighbour, while the Americans develop their own views in Washington. The combination of those European and American visions then determines the margin within which the military instrument is put to use, via NATO.

Apparently though it remains difficult to accept this new reality, both for international officials working for the EU or NATO and for their Member States. Many in the NATO apparatus have still not come to terms with the Alliance's loss of centrality. Just like the NATO Allies who are not members of the EU, and a number of EU Member States, they refuse to see that in today's multipolar world European and American interests and priorities are too divergent to pretend there can be a single NATO view of the world. Moreover, in US strategy China and Asia is now priority number one, no longer Europe, hence the US (rightly) expects Europeans themselves to ensure the stability of Europe's periphery. So whether they act under the NATO flag or the EU flag: it will in any case have to be European states that take the initiative to resolve crises around Europe – the US will no longer automatically do that for us. At a stroke, this new American position renders EU–NATO competition entirely obsolete.

In such a context, the EU must be an autonomous strategic actor. This implies that NATO operates within a strategic framework that is determined by the US on the one hand, and by the EU on the other hand. And that NATO can be the instrument of an exclusively European or even EU strategy, if in a specific contingency only Europeans want to act and use the NATO command structure to that end. However, this implies as well that people in the EU administration and in the Member States must stop debating EU strategy as if the implementation of its military aspects is undertaken entirely through the CSDP, while the reality is that the majority of military operations take place in other frameworks.

Division of labour

In order to optimise EU–NATO relations and achieve the strategic autonomy that the EU absolutely needs at the same time, one must address the three main functions of security and defence policy. Leaving all dogmas and emotions behind, rational analysis can determine how to operate most effectively in each of these functions.

First comes the strategic function. In this area things are clear-cut: the European state wage a foreign policy through the EU and to that end define a grand strategy that integrates all dimensions (diplomacy, defence, trade, and aid). Only in the specific area of collective defence do the individual European states enter directly into a dialogue with the US and are the strategy and the military plans crafted in NATO. When a security problem arises in the periphery of Europe that may require a military response; in other words, in all non-Article 5 scenarios, it is through the EU as well that the Europeans states should assess the situation, in view of their values, interests, and priorities as codified in the *Global Strategy*, in order to decide what action to take. In doing so, they have to take into account their overall foreign policy toward all states concerned, a foreign policy which in any case they wage through the EU.

Second, there is the operational function. There is no doubt who will have to launch potential operations: increasingly, that will have to be the Europeans. Possibly with specific US support in well-defined areas (such as intelligence, special forces, and transport) as long as Europe itself does not possess all the required strategic enablers. But the condition for US support will be that the Europeans themselves take the initiative – if we don't act to resolve crises in our own backyard, the US is not going to either. Under which command Europeans will then deploy cannot be defined beforehand. It can only be decided on a case-by-case basis, depending on (a) the scale of operations and which command-and-control structure they require, (b) which countries want to participate, and (c) which flag is politically acceptable in the country where we have to deploy and which is not. There's absolutely no harm therefore in maintaining various options: the EU's CSDP, NATO, the UN, a temporary coalition, or a national operation by a single state, possibly with logistical support from others (like France in Mali).

A contentious issue in this context is whether the EU needs its own military headquarters. True strategic autonomy implies that one possesses all means that one needs to act, without being dependent on the means of other actors, so that one can always act when one wants to act. That does not just apply to the strategic enablers but also to the operational headquarters required to plan and conduct military operations up to the scale of the Headline Goal. Today only NATO is capable of that, with its extensive capacity for command and control. In addition, some individual countries have national operational headquarters that can conduct operations of some scale, and which can be made available to the EU on a case-by-case basis: France, Germany, Greece, Italy, and the UK.

The EU as such has within its structures but a small cell of just over 30 officers; it's not even allowed to call this cell a headquarters (though it doesn't really amount to one either) – the Military Planning and Conduct Capacity (MPCC). This is meant to conduct only non-executive missions, such as capacity-building and training. The EU announced its creation with great fanfare in the spring of 2017. The UK even temporarily blocked this move – a last gasp before Brexit, but London might have saved itself the trouble for it is a largely symbolic exercise. Many EU officials have declared that in time the MPCC can grow into a real headquarters, but for now we're very far from that indeed. Hence, when in a crisis, and Europeans decide to deploy troops under the EU flag, they must subcontract command and control, either to one of the five national headquarters, or to NATO, even though the EU retains strategic control and political direction over the operation.

And this is what the discussion is about: how certain can one be that one of those headquarters will always be available if and when Europeans want to launch an operation? Those five national headquarters are not automatically geared to conducting multinational operations. For them to be capable of running an EU operation in a specific crisis, staff officers from all Member States must be trained in all five, year after year, which is a costly affair. When a national headquarters is appointed to take charge of an operation, it will then temporarily be reinforced with officers from the participating Member States.

As regards the various NATO headquarters, the EU in principle has a guaranteed access, thanks to an arrangement between both organisations: the 2002 Berlin Plus Agreement. In practice, however, NATO decides on a case-by-case basis, hence many fear that a non-EU NATO ally could veto the EU's access. The non-EU NATO ally that most have in mind is of course Turkey. This is not just some hypothetical scenario. When in 2011 the British and the French had convinced the Americans to support the intervention in Libya, the US demanded that this would be a NATO operation. France had actually wanted to make this an EU operation, but Washington made it crystal clear: it would either be a NATO operation, or an operation without the US. France had to cede, only for Turkey then to state that it could not accept a NATO operation in that area. Washington then had to lean heavily on Ankara before NATO could finally assume command of the operation, which by then had already been going on for several days – far from an ideal situation. The US itself is very unlikely to refuse access to NATO command and control, because it wants Europe to assume more responsibility. But Washington will then of course have a lot of influence on those operations, because American officers occupy most key posts in NATO headquarters.

There are but two possible solutions. One option is that the EU creates a fully fledged operational headquarters within its own structures. In a way that is a duplication of NATO structures, which is why the UK has always blocked this option, but it's not necessarily an unnecessary duplication. As discussed previously, it is useful to be able to operate under more than one flag, since one can never know the exact circumstances of any contingency beforehand. But then each option has to be effectively available, which implies the necessary command-and-control structures. Moreover, the EU could use this opportunity to construct a civil-military operational headquarters, integrating all dimensions of crisis management – that would be a unique capacity.

The other option is to give the EU direct access to the NATO command structure. On top of NATO's operational chain of command is SHAPE, below which, as already mentioned, there are several headquarters. It's the latter that conduct the actual operations, whereas SHAPE operates more at the strategic level. The Libyan air campaign, for example, was run by the NATO headquarters in Naples. If the EU has recourse to the NATO command structure according to the Berlin Plus Agreement, it does not enter into communication with a headquarters like Naples, but with SHAPE, which passes on EU directives to the headquarters conducting the operation. As a result, the EU has but little control of its own operation. One could however grant the EU direct access to a headquarters like Naples, so that the headquarters is much closer to the political decision-making.

Even then the EU would need a military (or civilian-military) structure that links up the political bodies of the EU and the relevant NATO headquarters, but that can then be smaller than a complete EU operational headquarters.

This seems to be a very technical debate, but it actually is highly political: this is about the strategic autonomy of Europe – which, under the current arrangement, does not exist. In this debate, a lot of confusion is purposely created. One often hears, for example, that there are not enough European staff officers to man a potential EU headquarters. What one never hears is that NATO maintains an entire headquarters in the US (in Norfolk, Virginia), Allied Command Transformation (ACT), which employs over a thousand people, whom nobody knows very well what they are doing. The original idea was for the US to introduce innovations in military doctrine into NATO through ACT. In practice, ACT is too far removed from Europe to have any influence on the European debate. Even in NATO headquarters in Europe I have been told that if ACT were to stop working today, it would take quite a while for anybody in Brussels to realise it. But whereas one is confronted all the time with criticism of duplication of NATO by the EU, little or nothing is ever said about waste of means within NATO. In other words, there is more than enough capacity to create the headquarters that Europe needs. One just has to find the courage to make choices.

The third and final function is capabilities: it has to be decided which different capabilities in army, navy, and air force, and in which quantities, are required in order to realise the level of ambition. To this end, NATO has construed an elaborate mechanism, the NATO Defence Planning Process (NDPP), which defines precise capability objectives for each Ally and closely monitors performance. The Alliance defines a level of ambition for NATO as a whole, for all Allies including the US, for Article 5 (collective territorial defence) and non-Article 5 (expeditionary operations). That level of ambition is naturally higher than that of the EU-countries alone, which moreover includes only expeditionary operations, not territorial defence. What the NDPP cannot guarantee, however, is that the group of just the European NATO Allies (and partners) can act alone if necessary. NATO only looks at two levels: NATO as a whole and each Ally separately. One objective, for example, is for NATO as a whole to have sufficient strategic enablers, but the system is not built to ensure that those enablers are spread around the Alliance, and so they are not. Most strategic enablers are American capabilities. As a result, the sum total of the capabilities of all EU Member States that are members or partners of NATO does not suffice to allow that group of countries to mount operations by themselves, without US support. An additional cause is that no single European country can afford to acquire strategic enablers in numbers that matter. If the European Allies want strategic enablers, they will have to pool their means and acquire them collectively.

In order to achieve strategic autonomy, the EU Member States should therefore first define their own military level of ambition, an example of which I have already given: which operations do the EU countries always want to be able to launch, if necessary by themselves, without any support from the non-EU NATO

Allies? Which capabilities, including strategic enablers, does that then require? That collective capability target of the EU countries could then be incorporated into the NDPP, so that NATO can elaborate a mix of capability targets at three levels instead of just two: for NATO as a whole, for the EU Member States that are members or partners of NATO as a group, and for each individual NATO Ally. The result should be that the EU Member States collectively hold a range of capabilities that allows them to contribute to collective territorial defence together with all NATO Allies, to contribute to expeditionary operations with all NATO Allies, but also to launch and conduct certain expeditionary operations alone if necessary, in accordance with an EU-defined level of ambition.

Look upon EU–NATO relations like a set of Russian dolls, a matrushka (if that image is still permitted, given the state of our relations with Russia). The biggest doll is NATO as a whole. Inside it today is but one very small doll: the EU countries. So there is a lot of hollow space in between the little "EU-doll" and the large "NATO-doll". Filling that space by making the EU-doll bigger doesn't weaken NATO: on the contrary, it makes the Alliance less hollow. Moreover, a larger EU-doll can be taken out of the NATO-doll and perform on its own. In other words, defining an EU military level of ambition and enhancing the military capabilities of the EU Member States absolutely does not contradict NATO, not even if the EU Member States decide to acquire some capabilities collectively instead of each individually. Whatever strengthens EU Member States' armed forces ipso facto strengthens the military power of NATO.

Once the level of ambition has been defined, in NATO and in the EU, and translated into a detailed list of capability requirements, those capabilities (i.e. personnel, their equipment, and their doctrine and training) have to be developed and acquired. The question is: will the European states mainly continue to do that separately? Will they start by at least acquiring strategic enablers collectively? Or will they go further and start to integrate their forces, ultimately leading perhaps to a single European army? The next chapter addresses cooperation and integration of European armed forces.

The EU-doll can also be understood, more seriously, as the European pillar of NATO. Especially if the EU Member States were to integrate their armed forces ever more, a real European pillar will emerge, which can contribute to NATO operations together with the US and other non-EU Allies, but which could also mount operations alone – under the EU flag or the NATO flag, but relying on European capabilities only. In political terms, there really already are two pillars in NATO today, even though Allies like Canada and Turkey don't like to hear it: the US and the EU – the two strategic actors within the Alliance. But the EU as such is not represented in NATO. There is a lot of consultation between the two organisations, at different levels, from NATO Secretary-General Jens Stoltenberg and EU High Representative Federica Mogherini to the military staff and the civilian administration. The atmosphere between both is better than ever, though that does not necessarily mean that a lot happens in terms of concrete cooperation – then the beauty contest kicks in again. Mogherini and Donald Tusk, the

President of the European Council, are also invited to NATO summits of heads of state and government. Yet, fundamentally, the EU voice is not present in the Alliance.

As the European pillar solidifies, it would only be logical for the EU Member States to speak with one voice in NATO. Even though the EU is not a member of NATO, nothing prevents the EU Member States from sitting together prior to NATO meetings and agreeing on a common position. This has always been a red line for the UK, but after Brexit they will no longer be able to block this – if the remaining Member States would want to go that way. Constituting an EU block within NATO would definitely put the Europeans in a much better position to respond to the brazen behaviour of a president like Donald Trump. But above all, it would be but a logical consequence of the progressive development of the EU as a strategic actor. A great power acts as a great power everywhere.

Toward an EU–US alliance?

One question has been left unanswered: should the autonomous EU level of ambition be limited to expeditionary operations? Or should Europeans ultimately also be capable of defending their own territory – should the EU fully operationalise Article 42.7 akin to Article 5? Whatever the answer, Europeans do have to reinforce all of their capabilities, for collective territorial defence as well as for expeditionary operations. Because, as seen in Chapter 3, the reason that today we don't need to fear a direct invasion of our territory is not our own military strength but rather the military weakness of our potential opponents, especially Russia. And that we can count on the US, of course, thanks to NATO.

But will the latter always be the case? During his election campaign Donald Trump made it appear as if those who have not contributed enough should not count on the US anymore. Everybody noted that at the NATO meeting in Brussels in May 2017 Trump did not explicitly voice his support for Article 5, contrary to what most observers had expected. He subsequently did so at other occasions, and the US continued to increase the budget for its military presence in Europe. And yet it may not be unwise to start planning for the defence of Europe by Europeans alone, just in case. NATO could undertake such planning, or the EU, its European pillar. Not with the aim of abandoning the Alliance, but to ensure that there is a plan B, so that Europe is not entirely dependent on who happens to reside in the White House. For in that regard there are no more certainties – that much Trump's election has proved.

Perhaps Barry Posen's idea, which was discussed in Chapter 3, is in the end the best solution, because it is the most flexible: to replace NATO with a new alliance between the US and the EU as such (and other non-EU NATO allies could of course join this new format, too). In such a constellation, the EU Member States would define an autonomous level of ambition for all military tasks, including territorial defence, and build an integrated set of forces to that end, but they would maintain an alliance with the US at the same time. Our capacity to deter or defeat any attack would still be underpinned by an obligation of mutual assistance between the EU and the US, but if it comes to the worst, plans would be ready in order to defend ourselves alone. In this scenario, the various NATO headquarters could be transferred to the EU, while the US could maintain liaison officers (just like today there are European liaison officers in the different American headquarters). All of these headquarters would be under the strategic control and political direction of the EU. Only the strategic headquarters, SHAPE, could remain a joint EU–US headquarters, alternating between a European and American commander (whereas today the Supreme Allied Commander Europe, SACEUR, always is an American). NATO would thus be Europeanised, as it were (Howorth, 2017).

In an unpredictable world this does seem like a commendable option for the future. Furthermore, this probably is what it takes to really generate an autonomous mind-set in Europe. Because after the end of the Cold War, NATO just carried on, and Europeans never really stopped looking to the US to know what to do. That's our mistake, not theirs. In a balanced alliance, between the EU and the US, we could finally emancipate ourselves.

If full autonomy is what Europe wants, including as a military power, it cannot escape one further issue however: nuclear deterrence. It's not exactly a popular topic in Europe, where mostly we simply like to pretend that nuclear weapons don't exist. But they do exist, and since one cannot "un-invent" them, it's probably for the best if we retain some in our arsenal too. There is no need for more nuclear weapons, but the question is whether nuclear deterrence can be integrated into EU strategy. Once Brexit becomes effective, only one EU Member State will have nuclear weapons: France. From time to time the idea is raised that one could Europeanise the French nuclear forces, the "force de frappe". In the past, reactions have always been extremely reticent, notably in Germany. Since the British referendum and the election of Trump, a debate has gently started again. It would certainly make sense to extend the French nuclear umbrella to cover the EU, in return for co-funding, or to those EU Member States that are willing to co-fund it. This would greatly strengthen deterrence, as a part of Europe's collective defence, while ensuring that for France it remains financially feasible to maintain this enormously expensive capacity. That in turn will enhance its capacity to act as the driver of European defence, together with Germany. Next to a financial contribution, other EU Member States could also participate militarily though, for example by integrating units into the air force component of the French deterrent (which also has a submarine-based navy component). Does Europe dare to launch this debate?

Notes

1 I try to compensate by inviting military officers to speak in my courses at Ghent University (as well as diplomats). In Belgium conscription was suspended for men born from 1 January 1975 onward, so in fact from 1993. Born in 1976, I did not object: I am pretty

certain that I am more qualified to lecture for the military than to be in the military myself.
2 The EU Treaty states, "If a Member State is the victim of armed aggression on its territory, the other Member States shall have towards it an obligation of aid and assistance by all the means in their power, in accordance with Article 51 of the United Nations Charter. This shall not prejudice the specific character of the security and defence policy of certain Member States. Commitments and cooperation in this area shall be consistent with commitments under the North Atlantic Treaty Organisation, which, for those States which are members of it, remains the foundation of their collective defence and the forum for its implementation".
3 The latest amendment of the EU Treaty, by the Lisbon Treaty in 2009, divided it into a Treaty on European Union and a Treaty on the Functioning of the Union. The former comprises the rights and freedoms of European citizens, the competences of the European institutions, and the specific area of foreign and security policy; the latter all other policy areas in which the EU has competence.

References

Jan Joel Andersson, Sven Biscop, Bastian Giegerich, Christian Mölling, and Thierry Tardy, *Envisioning European Defence: Five Futures*. Chaillot Paper No. 137. Paris, EU Institute for Security Studies, 2016.

Suzana Elena Anghel and Carmen-Cristina Cirlig. "Activation of Article 42(7) TEU: France's Request for Assistance and Member States' Responses". In: *European Parliamentary Research Service Briefing*, 10 December 2015.

Sven Biscop and Julien Sassel, *Military Factors in the MENA Region: Challenging Trends*. MENARA Working Paper No. 6. Rome, Istituto Affari Internazionali, November 2017.

Jo Coelmont, *End-state Afghanistan*. Egmont Paper No. 29. Brussels, Egmont, 2009.

Theo Farrell, *Unwinnable: Britain's War in Afghanistan 2001–2014*. London, The Bodley Head, 2017.

Gabor Horvath, "CSDP Military Ambitions and Potentials: Do We Know What We Have?". In: *Studia Diplomatica*, Vol. 64, 2011, No. 1, pp. 55–60.

Jolyon Howorth, *Strategic Autonomy and EU-NATO Cooperation: Squaring the Circle*. Security Policy Brief No. 85. Brussels, Egmont, May 2017.

6

EUROPEAN DEFENCE AND MAYBE EVEN A EUROPEAN ARMY

If the 28 EU Member States were to spend the €250 billion that they dedicate annually to defence to create one European army, that amount could suffice to acquire all the capabilities that an autonomous European strategy requires. One European army means that the national armed forces cease to exist and are replaced with a single army, navy, and air force, with soldiers, sailors, and airmen on the payroll of the EU. On the use of such truly European forces, the Council of Ministers of the EU could decide, by majority even. It sounds far-fetched, but it isn't, for it is exactly what France, Germany, Italy, and the countries of the Benelux planned in 1950–1954: to create a European Defence Community (EDC). A treaty was signed to that end, so we know precisely what their European army would have looked like. Would have, for in the end the treaty was never ratified and so the project was forgotten, except by some European idealists, as an example of what might have been.

And should have been, for as a result of not going through with the EDC, we are stuck to this day with 28 mostly small national armed forces, which require 28 ministries of defence, 28 general staffs, 28 military colleges, 28 supply systems, 28 maintenance systems, and so on and so forth. There are a great many useless duplications between Europe's armed forces. A further consequence of this fragmentation is that all national forces spend an ever-larger share of their budgets on the tail – maintenance and support – rather than on the head, the actual manoeuvre units. The reason is that as our forces have become smaller, not all costs have decreased at the same pace as the forces have shrunk. Whether an air force operates 10 fighter aircraft or 100, it still requires an airfield and a school to train its pilots. Whether at a military academy I lecture for 10 students or 100, my fee remains the same, and I still need a classroom. As a result, less money is obviously available to invest in research and technology and in the acquisition of new arms and equipment. And even when they do invest, states don't always buy the best equipment or the equipment that they need. Often they buy what their own national defence industry produces, or what generates status and prestige, rather than investing in the strategic enablers that Europe so direly needs. In the defence domain, protectionism remains an enormous obstacle to further cooperation and integration. As discussed in the previous chapters, many Member States hang on to useless units and obsolete equipment, which can no longer be deployed but continue to cost money.

Duplication and fragmentation: those are the reasons that EU Member States can spend €250 billion per year on defence and still are not capable of mounting autonomous operations. Unfortunately, a large share of that €250 billion is just money wasted.

Budgets and percentages

The solution to Europe's defence conundrum is not to spend more money therefore, or at least that can only ever be part of the solution. If we don't change the wasteful way in which we spend our defence budgets, a large share of any additional spending will simply be wasted as well. And yet an increase in defence spending is high on the political agenda. A major increase even, to 2 per cent of GDP, while the European average is barely 1.5 per cent. As regards my own country: Belgium's defence expenditure has sunk below 1 per cent of GDP. But Germany too, to name another example, in 2017 spent just 1.2 per cent on defence – but of a very large GDP, of course.

In his first speech to the NATO Allies President Trump insisted that all Europeans should effectively spend 2 per cent. (When he came back to Brussels for the July 2018 NATO Summit he suddenly even stated that it should be 4 per cent, but that was just another example of an improvised "Trumpism" that the other Allies quietly ignored.) The 2 per cent was indeed agreed at NATO's Wales Summit in September 2014 – or not quite, for what the summit declaration actually states is that Allies should "aim to move toward the 2 per cent guideline" by 2024. That's not the same as spending 2 per cent in 2024. What the Allies did agree on very explicitly is that the decline in defence spending should be halted. In that regard, Belgium clearly went against what was agreed, for the new government that came into office just after the Wales Summit cut the defence budget. Most other countries have been gradually increasing their budgets, mostly as a reaction to Russia's assertive behaviour. And not really because of Trump's visit to Brussels: that's how Trump chose to spin it, but in reality the turning point had been reached before.

But even if every country were to spend more on defence, as long as they all do it separately, on a purely national basis, the added value will remain very limited. No single European country can afford on its own to acquire expensive strategic enablers in numbers that can make a difference. Without such enablers, Europe will still not be able to launch expeditionary operations alone, and will thus remain dependent on the US, even if we reach the 2 per cent target. It is not a very useful benchmark, therefore. Do the defence needs of a country decrease when its GDP decreases? Probably the opposite is true. What good does it do to spend 2 per cent if that money is not allocated to addressing the priority shortfalls that the EU and NATO have identified, but instead to prestige projects or acquisitions whose main purpose is to keep the national defence industry alive? What does the 2 per cent matter if a state is unwilling to contribute its forces to operations? Greece, for example, spends more than 2 per cent but rarely participates in operations. The Greek armed forces serve in the first place to deter another NATO Ally: Turkey. It reminds me of the World War Two Chinese general who told his American military advisor: why would I deploy my American-equipped army against the Japanese – I'm not going to risk losing all of that beautiful equipment (Peck, 2008)!

The problem is that the 2 per cent norm has become a fetish in the defence debate. NATO officials always emphasise that it's not just how much you spend, but what you spend it on and what you are willing to do with that. The Wales Summit notably confirmed that however much one spends, 20 per cent should always be allocated for investment. And still everybody is fixated on the 2 per cent idea, including Donald Trump, a man who (witness his perennial orange hairdo and red necktie) takes his fetishes seriously. Both Democrats and Republicans in the US Congress want to see the Europeans spend more, however, so every American president would stick to the 2 per cent standard. And as Europe remains dependent on the US, for lack of its own enablers, the American president can easily retaliate if we don't reach that target. The current incumbent is not favourable to Europe in the first place, so he will not mind "punishing" us, unless his advisors can dissuade him.

It would be very easy for the US, for example, to reduce its share in the common NATO budget, which today amounts to 22 per cent. This budget serves to fund NATO headquarters in Brussels; the NATO command structure, including SHAPE; and all support systems and infrastructure. It's not a very large sum (€2.2 billion in 2017, though that is not that much less than the entire Belgian defence budget), but reducing the American share would send a clear signal to Europe without endangering American leadership and prestige. The message could also be gotten across in much harsher ways, however. The next time Europeans want to launch an operation in their periphery, in a non-Article 5 scenario, the US could refuse to deploy its enablers. Or they could send us the bill for their deployment. You need so many air-to-air refuelling aircraft for so many flying hours? Fine, we'll send an invoice. This option was actually briefly considered, but in the end not acted upon, during the Libya campaign in 2011.

The Europeans did sign up for 2 per cent in Wales. Perhaps they shouldn't have, even though the 2 per cent norm is not defined as sharply as everybody now seems to think. At the Summit, only Belgium had a caveat enacted, because at the time the country had a caretaker government (that tends to happen). Outgoing Prime Minister Elio Di Rupo announced that he could not really commit his successor. Reaction from the other European Allies: silly Belgians! Nobody feels committed, but you don't have to tell the Americans that – just sign and smile, 2024 is a long time away. But now there's an American president who takes the 2 per cent norm very seriously, as any American president would do. Europeans cannot just say: dear American friends, we've thought this over, and in the end we're not going to go for the 2 per cent after all.

What Europeans could and should say, however, is: dear US, instead of increasing our defence spending to 2 per cent of GDP, we are going to integrate our armed forces and thus generate a lot of additional capability while spending less than 2 per cent.

Military sovereignty

Defence is often presented as the last bastion of national sovereignty. That doesn't make much sense, for, with the exception of France and the UK, military sovereignty in Europe is an illusion. Not a single European country can mount significant operations on its own, except for the British and the French. Even they quickly reach the limits of their capabilities, as the intervention in Libya proved: without US support they would have had great difficulties launching it, let alone bringing it to a good end.

What does military sovereignty mean today for the average European state? It still has negative sovereignty: it can in all freedom decide not to do something. But even that is relative. Consider the NATO intervention in Afghanistan. Which country could have said to the Americans: Afghanistan? That's rather far away, we don't think we've lost anything there – so we're not joining the operation. In theory it was possible not to participate, but any European Ally would have paid a heavy political and probably also economic price for such independence of thought. For most, if not all, European states, even the capacity just to decide which actions to join and which not is limited therefore by the fact that they are members of NATO and/or the EU. The average European state's positive sovereignty – in other words, the capacity to take action autonomously – is simply nonexistent. There's but one operation that my own country, Belgium, can undertake completely on its own, without any support from other countries. We mount it every year again, on 21 July: the national day parade. It's a large-scale operation, numbering thousands of troops, and a joint one, including army, navy, and air force. And we need just a single American to do it: the US ambassador, who has to come and watch it, along with his colleagues of the *corps diplomatique*. There ends Belgium's military sovereignty, and the same applies more or less to most European states. It goes further even: EU Member States that have adopted the Euro must have their national budget approved by the European Commission before it can be implemented, including the defence budget. So what does this famous sovereignty that we keep referring to really mean?

And yet, in practice the focus of defence policy in Europe remains strictly national. When it starts to matter, states forget that they are members of the EU or NATO or both. When national defence planning is being decided upon, doors and windows are closed and states determine on an almost exclusively national basis in which capabilities to invest and which capabilities to terminate. Once finished, the plan is shared with fellow EU and NATO Member States. Only then will some, but not even all, states explore whether there aren't any opportunities for cooperation with other countries. But by then many opportunities will have been foreclosed because of the national choices already made. This system worked – during the Cold War, when all European states had much larger armed forces, with large numbers of conscripts, and each separately had the scale to maintain a wide range of capabilities. But that's more than a quarter century ago now. Today we are facing fragmentation and duplication. Only integration can put a stop to that.

Military integration: enablers

Integration goes further than cooperation. All EU and NATO Member States cooperate closely, on a permanent basis, in order to ensure the interoperability of their armed forces. That means that they can participate alongside each other in multinational military operations. This is necessary, but no longer sufficient. In the 21st century effective military integration is required: harmonising and merging national capabilities.

To start with, European states should turn their practice of defence planning upside down. Instead of first making national defence plans, everyone for himself, EU Member States should begin by drafting a common defence plan, as if they had a single set of armed forces. Only in a second stage should they outline in a national plan which contribution each of them will make to the common plan. With all of them together, the EU Member States should be capable of fielding the full range of capabilities in army, navy, and air force, but not every state must necessarily contribute to every capability. The larger Member States can contribute to nearly all capability areas, but the smaller ones can choose.

The objective of such an integrated EU defence or capability plan would be to deliver an integrated set of forces that can achieve the EU-military level of ambition as outlined in the previous chapter. An integrated European force should thus be able to act through NATO, together with the non-EU Allies, for self-defence under Article 5 as well as for expeditionary operations in non-Article 5 scenarios. But it should also be able to act alone, for autonomous European expeditionary operations (and in due course perhaps also for our own territorial defence). Once the defence planning of the EU Member States has been integrated, the actual capabilities can be integrated as well, at two levels.

The first level is that of the large strategic capabilities, the strategic enablers that countries need in order to be able to deploy their forces beyond their borders and project power. In view of the military level of ambition, the EU Member States should collectively decide, as early as possible, which and how many strategic enablers they need in order to be able to mount autonomous operations, without relying on non-European assets. Then they can have the required platforms (drones, aircraft, satellites, etc.) designed and built by a European defence industry, and acquire them, again collectively.

Strategic enablers are the most urgent, for in this area our dependence (on the US) is the greatest. In a way, it is also politically the most feasible area, because in the first instance this is not about combat capabilities but about crucial support. The EU is already progressing with a project on a satellite for military communications, for example, which is less politically sensitive, as is another project on air-to-air refuelling. But then again, this is very political, because in each of these expensive areas, Europeans can only afford one project, which can only be entrusted to one consortium of defence companies. If every Member State just continues to protect its own defence industry, this is not going to work. The old model is that of the "national champion": a defence firm that survives by supplying only its own government. Both the states and the governments have to accept that this model is no longer viable. National markets, even those of the biggest Member States, have simply become too small. Only big European consortia can mount big European projects, for a large number of Member States together, so that sufficient numbers will be procured in order to make it economically viable to design and to produce a new platform.

Ideally, Member States would not stop at the collective procurement of new equipment. Once acquired, it would be better not to divide the new platforms up among the Member States that took part in the project. That would lead once again to fragmentation. It would be much more efficient to keep the acquired platforms together in one collective capability, such as a European fleet of drones or transport aircraft or ships, or a European satellite programme. Then only one command-and-control structure, and one structure for supply and maintenance, is required, and training can then be organised collectively as well. Imagine a dozen EU Member States co-funding the development and procurement of a number of drones. Each Member State would of course retain ownership of the drones that it funded, but it would be a lot cheaper to group them together in a single fleet, to which every participating state has access when engaged in operations that require drones. Technically it is perfectly feasible to calculate at the end of the year which state has used more capability and which less, and to allocate costs accordingly. By permanently pooling all drone capability, its availability will moreover be larger than when it is fragmented across several Member States.

The existing European Air Transport Command (EATC) in Eindhoven in the Netherlands is going in this direction. EATC coordinates the use of the transport aircraft of the participating countries: France, Germany, Italy, Spain, and the Benelux. The principle is very simple. Imagine a Belgian aircraft has to pick up a load in Kinshasa while a French aircraft has to deliver a load in neighbouring Brazzaville. Instead of employing two aircraft that each fly empty on either the outgoing or the return flight, EATC ensures that a single aircraft will deliver its cargo to Brazzaville and then pick up the other cargo in Kinshasa: money saved. In the future, EATC could be deepened: in addition to coordinating flight movements, maintenance, supply, and the training of pilots could be merged.

Cooperation of this kind will lead to a setting in which Europeans in the future systematically develop a single platform for all their capability needs. One fighter aircraft, for example, instead of several that then compete against each other. That is still the case today: the development of the Rafale by the French company Dassault, the Gripen by Swedish Saab, and the Typhoon by the British–German–Italian–Spanish Eurofighter consortium has each cost an enormous amount of money. Logically, the price per aircraft increases, but the European market has become very small, making it very difficult for the companies to earn back their investment. Meanwhile Lockheed Martin's F35 Joint Strike Fighter, which has already earned back the investment on its American home market, is a strong competitor for the European aircraft. The same applies to land platforms: several European countries are developing more than 20 different types of military vehicles, as if they were planning to sell commercial cars. In reality, of course, the European market has become far too small to accommodate so many different types, and indeed not every country needs its own type of vehicle.

Developing new high-tech platforms takes a very long time. If a group of European countries were to decide today to develop and build a new fighter for example (an intention that France and Germany have expressed in July 2017: the Future Combat Air System or FCAS), it would probably only enter into service in 20 or 30 years. There is no time to waste, therefore. If we want to avoid ending up in the same situation as today the next time we need to replace our fighter aircraft, decisions have to be made today.

Military integration: combat units

As the example of combat aircraft shows, European military integration should go beyond the supporting strategic enablers. Europeans should increasingly anchor their combat units, in army, navy, and air force, in permanent multinational formations, under permanent multinational headquarters. The actual combat units can remain fully national, with soldiers from one Member State only: an infantry or tank battalion, a fighter squadron, a frigate. But all support functions (supply, maintenance, intelligence, education and training, as well as command and control) can either be merged, or a division of labour can be organised. This implies that national structures in these areas be abolished: new multinational structures must replace national structures, not become another layer on top of them. In this manner, the European defence effort would become a lot more cost-effective.

Belgian–Dutch naval cooperation is an existing example of how such a combination of merging or pooling on the one hand, and a division of labour or specialisation on the other hand, can work in practice. Both countries contribute frigates and minehunters, which either sail under the Belgian flag with a Belgian crew, or under the Dutch flag with a Dutch crew. There is only one common headquarters though, and one navy operational school, both located in the Dutch naval base in Den Helder. The Netherlands take charge of all training, maintenance and supply for both navies' frigates, and Belgium does the same for the minehunters. Moreover, Belgium and the Netherlands operate the same ships. This case of military integration has now gone so far that it can actually no longer be undone. In theory it could, but not in practice, because neither Belgium nor the Netherlands has the means to recreate national structures and to resume tasks that in the current set-up they are no longer doing alone or even not at all. In order to maintain the same degree of integration, Brussels and The Hague should acquire the same type of ships in the future as well, which is indeed what they are currently planning. This model of integration is very far-reaching, and has saved a lot of money for both countries. And yet each country retains a large margin of manoeuvre when it comes to deploying its naval capabilities. If Belgium decides to participate with a frigate in EU Operation Atalanta, the Netherlands is in no way obliged to also send a ship. But all of the staff in all the support structures have to do their jobs, regardless of which of both countries is deploying a ship.

The same model can easily be applied to air forces. The Belgian case can again serve to illustrate this. In 2018 the Belgian government made the decision to acquire 34 F35s to replace its F16s. An important factor when choosing which new type to buy is which partners operate the same aircraft that Belgium could integrate into its own future capacity, along the lines of Belgian–Dutch naval integration. Each country can contribute a number of aircraft, which will have the national flag on the tail and will be piloted by a national. But those aircraft can be concentrated on a reduced number of bases, where maintenance and supply can be merged. In this way smaller countries such as Belgium can maintain a combat capacity in their air forces in a cost-effective manner.

The model offers a solution for small-scale armies, too. To continue with the Belgian example: the Belgian government's Strategic Vision 2030 seeks to maintain the current seven battalions – five battalions of motorised infantry in a motorized brigade, and two battalions of paracommando and the special forces group in a special operations regiment. But as the troop numbers of the armed forces are set to continue to be reduced, down to 25,000, this will not be self-evident. It will be very difficult indeed to at the same time maintain all support capabilities in the Land Component. One option could be therefore to anchor the Belgian Land Component into a larger multinational structure, to which Belgium contributes its seven manoeuvre battalions, but in which certain support functions are assured by a combination of pooling and specialisation. In this way Belgium alone would no longer have to field the full range of support units and could maintain a significant combat capacity. The result would further be that all participating countries would spend a smaller share of their defence budget on support and would thus have more funds available for investment and, of course, actual operations.

The Eurocorps, in which Belgium, France, Germany, Luxembourg, and Spain participate, could be a perfect framework. It is probably one of the best-known examples of multinational military cooperation, but currently integration actually does not go very deep. In fact, the Eurocorps today mostly is a multinational land headquarters that can conduct land operations. But it has no units permanently assigned to it, hence there can be no integration between the land forces of the participating countries. The Eurocorps is not alone in this: there is a multitude of frameworks for cooperation between small groups of European states, but only a few exceptional cases have already reached effective integration.

Europeans should then also use these multinational formations as the framework to generate a force for deployment each time they envisage a military operation. That seems logical, but it rarely happens this way today: countries mostly do defence planning on their own, then they cooperate with other countries to develop capabilities; and mostly they launch operations with yet other countries, in ad hoc constellations. In the future, countries should do defence planning, capability development, and operations in the same framework. That would create an upward spiral: not just countries' arsenals and practices, but their thinking will align more and more, enabling ever-deeper integration.

Military integration benefits all European states, big and small. The smaller countries (which is nearly everybody) win in terms of relevance. By anchoring their forces in larger multinational formations, they no longer need to field all types of supporting capabilities themselves. That enables them to continue to contribute, and deploy, significant combat units, which directly translates into influence at the decision-making table. Moreover, most smaller countries can thus maintain a combat capacity in all three forces – army, navy, and air force – in an affordable and cost-effective manner. While smaller EU Member States do not need to contribute to each and every capability area, maintaining at least one deployable combat capacity in each force is a necessity in order for these governments to retain the possibility to contribute to every operation to which they want to contribute. If a country would abolish the combat capacity in one of its forces, it will quickly end up in a situation in which it wants to be part of an operation, but has nothing of relevance to contribute. Think of the air campaign against IS: how can a country without fighter aircraft make a noticeable contribution? Willing to help but not being able to is a very uncomfortable situation, and will result in immediate loss of political influence. Burden-sharing between Europeans does not just mean that each state should contribute financially according to its means but also that each should assume its share of risk – and must therefore deploy combat forces.

Larger countries must constitute the core of the multinational formations into which the smaller countries can plug in. But they win too. A country like France, for example, still has a very high national military level of ambition, but it can no longer afford all of the strategic enablers that it needs to maintain its very high operational rhythm. But if other EU Member States participate, Europeans can acquire collective enablers, which can support the operations of individual or groups of countries. Moreover, this will in turn lead to a much more competitive and consolidated European defence industry.

Just as in many other domains of European integration, military integration is about regaining rather than abandoning sovereignty. By pooling their sovereignty, the European states will collectively win back the capacity to act that most individual countries have long ago lost. What are they waiting for?

A role for the European Commission

This is indeed not a new story. Since 1999 already the EU has been pursuing its own defence policy. Back then, already all shortfalls in the European inventory were identified, and proposals launched to collectively address them. Two decades later the Member States have still made little progress. Meanwhile Europe's military power has further declined, as budgets (until about 2016) and the size of the forces continued to decline while arms and equipment became more expensive. Initially countries confronting this challenge attempted to maintain the full range of capabilities by slicing off a little bit of each: they cut a little from the budget for each area. Many years later a lot of capabilities have become so tiny that this is no longer an option. Governments in many cases no longer have to choose on which capabilities to save money, but which capabilities to abandon altogether. Everybody has known for a long time that only far-reaching military integration can reverse this trend, but nobody dares to make the first move. Now that defence expenditure in most European countries is rising again, the opportunity should be used to take collective initiatives in order to make the best possible use of the extra funds.

What is new, and might make a big difference, is that the European Commission has begun to play a strong role in the area of defence. Traditionally the role of the Commission was limited to regulating the defence market, just like it has the authority to watch over the functioning of the market and competition in other sectors. Since the 2014 European elections, the Commission, led by President Jean-Claude Juncker, has begun to actively plead for a European defence union. In June 2017, the Commission unveiled a detailed plan for a European Defence Fund (EDF). On the one hand, the Commission will provide funds for defence research, up to €500 million per year for the next budgetary period (2021–2027), starting already with €90 million per year for the remainder of the current period. Defence research does not directly lead to new military capabilities, but is meant to develop new technologies that in due course will be integrated in the equipment of the future.

In the other dimension of the EDF the Commission also plans to provide €1 billion per year from 2021 for actual capability projects – in other words, for the development and procurement of new equipment (starting with €500 million for the current budgetary period). The Commission seeks to create a multiplier effect: it will not fund entire projects, but can co-finance up to 20 per cent of multinational projects that involve at least two EU Member States and three companies and that address one of the priority shortfalls that the EU has identified. Obviously, these Commission funds in the end also come from the Member States, which pay into the EU budget. But by thus creating a collective defence budget that the Commission will manage on behalf of the Member States (which is a form of common funding), the Commission acquires an instrument to steer Member States' defence efforts. It will be the very first time that states can get money from the EU for investing in military capabilities, but only if they invest in the capabilities that the EU needs, of course, and if they do so collectively, together with other Member States. Or such ought to be how the EDF is used for it to be effective.

Of course, ultimately the ones deciding whether and wherein to invest will remain the Member States. The success of the EDF is still entirely dependent on the political will of the capitals, therefore. But it is a potentially very important new factor in the area of European defence. Only a short while ago such common funding could not even be discussed – now, thanks to the push by the Commission, it is ready to be implemented.

One thing must be made very clear, though. If the Member States go along this road, and effectively start collective capability projects, to acquire strategic enablers first of all, and then also begin to integrate their combat units, this will not allow them to spend less on defence. In time, however, the integration of their defence efforts will allow them to generate more capabilities and launch more operations with the same budget. Many participants in the debate on European defence don't seem to be able or willing to understand this. In many national debates it is made to appear as if one can safely disinvest in national defence because European defence will appear instead. But European defence will not just fall from the sky. It will be the result of the addition and integration of the national defence efforts. If that integration is organised effectively, one plus one can equal three, thanks to synergies and effects of scale. But zero plus one will always equal one. Those that have nothing to contribute cannot participate in European projects, therefore. What would be the added value for the other Member States if a state joins in that refuses to commit to any effort?

All EU Member States must allocate a reasonable amount of money to defence. Achieving 2 per cent of GDP is perhaps not really necessary if, but only if, Europeans truly integrate their defence efforts. But there is a necessary minimum defence budget as well. Spending 0.9 per cent of GDP, the level to which Belgian defence spending has sunk, is not reasonable, because it is insufficient to maintain a ready force and to be an attractive partner for other Member States. The Belgian case can serve as a warning, for its defence budget has decreased so much that its partners in existing frameworks of cooperation have begun to doubt even those. The odd thing is that conceptually Belgium has always been at the forefront of the European defence debate. It owes it to itself to play a part, and to play a leading part even, now that European defence is actually beginning to materialise.

A puzzle

If the European countries would embark on a process of military integration as previously proposed, that would still not lead directly to one European army (technically one should say, of course, European armed forces: an army, a navy, and an air force). Rather, a complex puzzle would emerge, of differently organised capabilities.

Strategic enablers are the most promising area for real integration because industry can only develop and build them if there is a critical mass of Member States willing to acquire them in sufficient numbers. In time, Europe could arrive at a single collective fleet of transport aircraft, a single drone fleet, a single satellite programme and so on, each with a single structure for maintenance, supply, training, and command and control. At least 10 to 15 Member States should participate in such fleets to make them feasible. Those who do can then have recourse to this common pool of enablers when they launch operations. In addition to the large clusters that acquire strategic enablers, Member States can constitute smaller, partially overlapping clusters in which they anchor their combat units in larger multinational formations while pooling the supporting capabilities and/or organising a division of labour. To illustrate this with the Belgian case: Belgium will undoubtedly continue its naval integration with the Netherlands, but could anchor its Land Component in a more integrated Eurocorps, with France, Germany, Luxembourg, and Spain. Depending on which countries buy which fighter aircraft, it can integrate that capacity with one or more partners as well. One way or another, most Member States will in the end probably anchor all of their capabilities in a multinational framework. Only the largest Member States, notably France, will be able to maintain certain purely national capabilities, but even they will become increasingly dependent on collective strategic enablers that they can no longer afford alone.

Military integration can happen under various flags. First of all, two or more countries can simply make an agreement among themselves, like Belgium and the Netherlands have done in the maritime domain, and more recently also for air defence (with both countries now defending their airspace together). Such cooperation takes place outside the formal framework of the EU or NATO, but the capabilities created can of course be deployed for either, as well as for the UN or ad hoc coalitions. Countries can also cooperate in the framework of NATO, where they now collectively exploit a fleet of airmobile radars: the AWACS fleet. The Alliance does not actually have that much experience with multinational capability development, however. NATO's focus remains the individual Ally; the sum total of the national capability targets of each member must achieve the level of ambition for NATO as a whole.

The EU is much better placed to undertake collective capability development. Fragmentation of defence efforts is, after all, a European problem, which must be solved among Europeans by integration. The Belgian Land Component can be integrated with its neighbours; it won't be integrated with the US Army. Moreover the Treaty on European Union provides for a specific mechanism for defence: Permanent Structured Cooperation (PESCO). This was introduced by the Lisbon Treaty, which entered into force in 2009, but initially wasn't used. The idea was for a core group of Member States to agree to binding criteria between themselves and to generate more capabilities more quickly by integrating their defence efforts more closely under the aegis of the EU, making use of the EU institutions.

The Brexit referendum and the election of Trump revived interest in this mechanism. France and Germany, joined by Italy and Spain, accelerated the pace and tabled a detailed proposal for the implementation of PESCO in the summer of 2017. In December 2017 this was subscribed to by no less that 25 out of 28 Member States: all but the UK, which is leaving; Denmark, which does not participate in the CSDP; and Malta. It is rather more than a core group, which makes PESCO far more unwieldy then foreseen, since within PESCO all decisions still have to be taken by unanimity. The first list of 15 capability projects that was announced together with the decision to activate PESCO immediately demonstrated the pitfalls, for most of these would be implemented anyhow, PESCO or no PESCO, and do not address any of the strategic shortfalls. The unprecedented speed of decision-making leading to activation was thus followed by a rather slow start. On the good side, the participating states are now legally bound to increase their defence budgets in real terms, in order to reach "agreed objectives". What those are is not spelled out, because everybody knows that many Member States will never reach the one agreed-on objective, the NATO norm of spending 2 per cent of GDP on defence. But having formally signed up to the 2 per cent standard in NATO, one can hardly sign another document in the EU that would say that 1.5 per cent is enough.

Much more important, because it's more realistic and mentioned explicitly, is the commitment for 20 per cent of total defence spending to be invested. First of all, investment is key to kick-starting PESCO. Second, this forces states that now spend two thirds or more on salaries to increase defence spending anyway. And in the EDF, states now have an important incentive to fulfil this obligation (and the Commission can co-finance up to 30 per cent of a project instead of 20 per cent if it takes place under PESCO). Some pundits belittle this, stating that €1 billion per year is not much compared to the more than €250 billion that the EU-28 spend on defence. But compared to the €45 billion or so of this total that is spent on investment (€35 billion without the UK), it is a sizeable amount of money. If it is put to use to launch a limited number of key projects, it can really orient the decisions of the participating states. Furthermore, under PESCO, states would commit to multinational projects as the default option and launch national projects only when no other option is available.

Given the need for European strategic autonomy, the EU option undoubtedly is the most logical. It would also produce the most rational construction. If the EU Member States integrate their capabilities in the framework of the EU, a European military pillar will emerge, the strategic direction for which will be provided by a European grand strategy, which will also guide a European foreign policy, trade policy, development policy etc. This European pillar could operate under NATO-command, together with non-EU Allies, but also alone if necessary. This would also fit into the long-term perspective of the EU assuming responsibility for its own territorial defence and, ultimately, concluding a new alliance between the EU as such and the US.

What counts, however, is not which flag or logo is put on things, but that Europeans implement effective military integration. The states of Europe must drop all taboos and do really common defence planning, abolish useless structures, and merge supporting structures and/or divide labour. The aim is clear: to liberate means to create additional capabilities. If PESCO turns out to be just a new label but Member States don't change their way of doing things, we might as well not have activated it. But if PESCO leads to real integration, which goes beyond the current degree of cooperation, it can be the start of an effective European defence pillar. We definitely need to give PESCO a chance, therefore (Biscop, 2018).

References

Sven Biscop, "European Defence: Give PESCO a Chance". In: *Survival*, Vol. 60, 2018, No. 3, pp. 161–180.

Graham Peck, *Two Kinds of Time*. Seattle, University of Washington Press, 2008.

7

BREXIT, STRATEGY, AND THE EU

Britain takes leave

When as a young boy I was asked what I wanted to be later, unlike many others of my age I never chose to be a fireman or a truck driver. For years, my answer was: I want to be an Englishman. I guess I read too many books about the history of the British Empire at too young an age. Since then I have read a lot more, but I do still see myself as an Anglophile (even though successive British governments do their best to dissuade me). I feel absolutely no Schadenfreude over Brexit, therefore. Brexit is bad news for the EU and a disaster for the UK. In the area of foreign policy and defence on which I focus here, the consequences will be far-reaching and the cost very high, for both Brussels and London.

In the beginning

In the beginning, however, in the immediate aftermath of World War Two, the UK was a strong proponent of European cooperation. None other than Winston Churchill, in his 1946 speech at the University of Zürich, stated, "We must build a kind of United States of Europe." That was the task the UK saw – for the others. For itself, the UK saw a different role.

Financially and economically exhausted by World War Two, knowing that the Empire was entering its final stage (India, the jewel in the crown, gained independence in 1947), Britain fundamentally changed its grand strategy. Instead of an independent global role, the UK opted for the part of permanent (and, certainly in its own eyes, essential) ally of the US. The war had seen the start of the Anglo-American "special relationship". The UK had started out as the dominant partner, but as the US mobilised its enormous war potential, the relationship had turned around. After the war, the US was left as the only Western superpower, with Britain a distant second (even though it acquired the atomic bomb). But while many in the US were initially inclined to demobilise and let Europe take care of its own defence,

Britain played a key role in convincing the Americans of the need of a permanent transatlantic alliance, NATO, as a continuation of the war-time alliance.

The UK did engage in European cooperation. In 1947, it signed an alliance with France, called the Treaty of Dunkirk, followed the next year by the Treaty of Brussels with France and the Benelux Countries. Britain's view of the latter was largely shaped, however, by the fact that the US had put a European initiative as a precondition to start the secret talks with Canada and the UK that would lead to the creation of NATO (in 1949). In the end, the UK remained outside the main track of European integration: the European Coal and Steel Community (ECSC, 1951), the failed European Defence Community mentioned in the previous chapter (EDC, 1954), and the European Economic Community (EEC, 1957) that grew out of that failure. It did join the Western European Union (WEU, 1954) that succeeded to the Brussels Treaty and added West Germany and Italy as members, but that organisation quickly became an empty shell as NATO and the EEC took off.

At first sight, it may seem as if having decided to leave the EU, the UK has come full circle. But a closer look reveals that the choice for Brexit actually is a fundamental break with past British strategy. In the 1940s, the UK sought a permanent transatlantic alliance in order to guarantee permanent American involvement in the security of Europe, because it knew very well that a strong and secure Europe was a prerequisite for a strong and secure Britain. Hence London was in favour of cooperation between the other states of Western Europe, even though at that time it did not join their main project itself. In the area of defence, the UK did opt for an Atlantic rather than a European-only strategy. But from 1945 through 1955, the UK did not distance itself from Europe. It had just fought a major war to liberate Europe from the Nazis.

That is a completely different attitude to Europe than the anti-European stance of the core Brexiteers, who in June 2016 forced Brexit upon the UK.

Illusions

At times it almost appears as if the Brexiteers would want the EU to collapse, just to prove that they were right. They need proof, because so far all they have managed to create is uncertainty. Not even those who shouted the loudest in favour of Brexit actually expected to win the referendum, so there was no plan.

One reaction to this predicament is fatalism. At a seminar, I heard a Conservative MP confess, when asked what the desired end-state of the Brexit negotiations was, that he had no idea where the UK wanted to land, but that in any case there was no alternative now but to see it through, since "the people have spoken". Others try to mask their fear or ignorance with bravado and, like former Foreign Secretary Boris Johnson, talk about a "glorious future". But I am very much afraid, for the UK, that all the talk about "global Britain" as an independent actor in world politics is nothing but hubris. The mistake that the Brexiteers are making is to assume that they can return to the status quo ante, and that there are many options available for British grand strategy.

The reality is that Britain's strategic options have been severely limited ever since the end of World War Two. Already during the Greek civil war (1946–1949) London was forced to ask Washington to take over its military commitments in the country (in support of the non-communist camp), because it simply no longer had the means to carry on. This is exactly why after the end of the war the UK did not opt for an independent grand strategy, but for the role of permanent "deputy sheriff" of the US. The 1956 Suez crisis was the last gasp for Britain and France as independent powers. When these countries militarily occupied the canal zone, they were immediately called back by the US, and duly retreated.

Many Brexiteers see the Commonwealth as Britain's natural constituency that can support its global role, but that is a very loose grouping of countries. Or they refer to the "Anglosphere", but even countries like Australia, Canada, and New Zealand have a much more diverse population than 70 years ago and a much looser emotional link with the UK. The Queen may still be the Head of State, but when push comes to shove, they will choose the national interest over the British legacy. Canada is economically dependent on the US, Australia on China, and for their security, both look to America. Pretending that even these key members of the "Anglosphere", let alone the Commonwealth as such, can replace the EU in British trade and foreign policy is not very realistic.

Of course, the UK still is an important country. But it is not a great power – not anymore. Britain enjoys a strong diplomatic position. It has a permanent seat on the UN Security Council and is a member of the G7, the club of the world's seven biggest economies, but the same applies to France, and Canada and Italy are members of the G7, too. Nobody pretends that any of these countries can play a major part in world politics by itself. The players that matter are countries the size of a continent, or countries that have grouped together to achieve that size: the US, China, Russia, and the EU. This holds true in the military domain too. The UK entered World War Two with a Royal navy of over 1,400 ships. Today it counts less than a hundred. Both in absolute and in relative terms (compared to other major actors), the UK doesn't even come close to the power that it had even in 1945.

Furthermore, the centre of gravity of the world system is shifting to Asia, where even the EU as a whole has difficulties being heard. Nobody in Asia is waiting for new initiatives from a single European country. Yes indeed, China has already stated its willingness to negotiate a new bilateral trade agreement with the UK once Brexit becomes effective, but on different terms than those that apply to China and the EU. Read: on terms that are more advantageous to Beijing.

The conclusion should be obvious: the option for the UK to return to an independent great power strategy no longer exists. The UK could of course try and return to the period before its accession to the Union, in 1973, and once again opt for the role of "deputy sheriff" to the US as its key strategic part. The Brexiteers certainly like to play up the "special relationship". But is the US itself still interested in having a country as a deputy that has lost so much power?

Suppose the US fights a limited war. Then it doesn't need the UK, except maybe for political reasons. American military might is such that it can project its power anywhere in the world without the help of allies and partners. Whereas if the US were to fight a truly major war, with China for example, the UK has become too small to make much of a difference. The UK was much more important to the US as a Member State of the EU so as to ensure that the EU would not diverge too far from Washington's guidelines. That part the UK has always played excellently well, notably by continuously putting obstacles in the way of autonomous structures for European defence. That's one of the main reasons the EU still has but very limited command-and-control capacity within its structures, and why the European Defence Agency never received the budget it would have needed to really play the role it was intended to. The UK also has always been the greatest proponent of Turkish accession to the EU, and of EU enlargement in general. In the strategic debate on whether the EU should be deepened first (by integrating more) or widened first (by allowing in more members), the British view has won out – and now the Brits are leaving. Thus Washington loses its closest ally within the EU. And the UK loses a lot of its interest for the US.

Unless, that is, a British government would join forces with President Donald Trump, who has welcomed Brexit, to actively undermine the EU. The UK could attempt to sabotage collective EU decision-making through bilateral deals with individual Member States. Perhaps this is what some Brexiteers are dreaming of, just like some seem to covet the American model of society. That's a model in which the welfare state is being dismantled, a tax cut massively favours the rich and undermines the future functioning of government, and the state does less and less to assist those who are worst off. Probably not exactly what most of those who voted for Brexit had in mind.

But such an anti-EU policy would be very risky, for it would be directly at odds with British interests. It would also go against centuries of British grand strategy, which has always considered a divided but stable European continent to be a precondition for a stable UK. Britain could only focus on its global role and the Empire as long as it was not in any way directly threatened in Europe. Therefore it regularly intervened on the continent, and often played the decisive part in restoring the European balance of power, from the War of the Spanish Succession (1701–1714) to World War Two. The need for a strong EU may understandably appear counterintuitive to many British, because in the past restoring the balance of power always meant preventing a single great power from dominating the continent of Europe. But the EU is unique, because it is of course a voluntary coming together of states that choose to pool their sovereignty, rather than the subjugation of Europe by a single state, as Louis XIV, Napoleon, Wilhelm II, and Hitler have attempted. Today it is precisely the unravelling of the EU that could once again lead to war in Europe, in which sooner or later the UK would inevitably be involved. For the first time in history, a (voluntarily) united Europe serves the British interest better than a balance of power between individual European states.

By choosing to leave the EU, the UK may paradoxically have become more useful to the EU than to the US. To the extent that the "special relationship" endures and the UK has more influence in Washington than any other European country, the UK could perhaps play a part in moderating some of the more eccentric of Trump's views on Europe and the world. The attempt would certainly be worthwhile, for British interests often coincide much more with EU interests than with those of the Trump administration. But does Trump really listen to anybody who doesn't agree with him in the first place? As long as he remains president, a "special relationship" may be an illusion, sadly for both the UK and the EU.

Out of the EU, but in NATO

In addition to emphasising the importance of the "Anglosphere" and the "special relationship" with the US, the Brexiteers always stress the fact that the UK will of course remain an ally in NATO and will continue to play a key role in the security of Europe. But the UK will soon find out that in NATO as well it will no longer be able to play its traditional part.

Once Britain effectively leaves the EU, it will at a stroke lose its direct influence on EU decision-making on security and defence, and thus also most of its influence on relations between the EU and NATO. After Brexit, London will quickly realise that its views will no longer automatically be heard in the EU debate. Just like any other third country, if the UK will want to be heard, it will have to lobby. And those who undertake demarches only in order to block proposals have a lot more difficulty in gaining attention than those who table constructive proposals. Bilateral relations with individual EU Member States will obviously remain, not in the least with France and Germany. But EU decision-making has its own dynamic. In the end, one is a part of it – or not.

In this regard, too, the UK is set to lose a lot of its usefulness to the US. Brexit will affect Britain's standing in the Alliance. This may have an effect on the posts that Britain holds. Currently, NATO's military number two, Deputy SACEUR, is always a British general. It is already being debated whether this has to change, because Deputy SACEUR is automatically in command when an EU military operation has recourse to NATO command and control. Should not that officer, therefore, come from an EU Member State?

Most importantly, as long as it exists, the political centre of gravity of Europe is, and will remain, the EU, not NATO. And the EU will carry on, with or without the UK. As long as France and Germany seek "ever closer union" (the phrase in the European treaty that the UK objected to from the start), closer union is what we'll have. This is because the Franco–German axis is not just the engine of the EU, but its essence. The process of European integration was launched precisely to create a reconciliation, and then a partnership, between France and Germany, in order to prevent a third world war from ever starting in Europe. In this geopolitical sense, the UK is in the periphery rather than in the core of the European project, hence the project can continue without it, while it would tumble the moment France or Germany gave up on it.

Many in the UK do not seem to understand this and are under the illusion that other EU Member States will do anything to keep the UK on board. But certainly for the founding members of the EU, this is about vital interests, so they cannot but prioritise the continued existence of the Union. This should have been clear to the UK even as the referendum campaign was still ongoing. Initially, encouraged by Prime Minister David Cameron, the referendum was not given that much attention in Brussels. It was just generally assumed that the British people would vote the "right" way. When it became apparent that they might not, and that Brexit was becoming a real possibility, Brussels quickly came to a conclusion: we'd rather not have Brexit, of course, but if Brexit it is, we will carry on with the EU. This crucial realisation, even before the outcome of the referendum was known, meant that there was never any possibility of the Brexiteers' mirage becoming reality. Not just Brussels and the founding members, but all Member States have to take a similar stance, because of the interests at stake: you cannot expect to leave a club yet retain all benefits of membership, otherwise it would be the end of the EU. You can't have your cake and eat it, too: that the British of all people should know.

Yet many Brexiteers still seem to think that people in Brussels and the other capitals wake up every morning and go to bed every night thinking: how are we going to solve Brexit? The unsurprising reality is that the first item on the agenda of the EU is – the EU. Since the referendum, the EU debate has focused on the future of the European project. Brexit is first and foremost a British problem: the UK has chosen to leave and must now search for its own path. The EU is absolutely right not to allow Brexit to dominate its agenda. A team has been appointed to wage negotiations with the UK on behalf of the Union, so that the EU as such can focus on its own future. That is a big enough challenge.

Out of the EU, but in Europe

None of this means that there cannot be an enduring close partnership between the EU and the UK. In the area of defence, this would definitely be in their mutual interest. The UK accounts for no less than a quarter of the defence expenditure of the EU-28, and 10 per cent of the total troop numbers. Moreover, excellently trained and highly experienced British forces constitute a very high share of the relatively small number of European troops that are actually deployable on expeditionary operations. The quality of the British defence effort is also reflected in the fact that the UK spends some €155,000 per soldier as compared to the EU average of €130,000. Together with France, the UK is the leading military power in Europe. It is very much in the interest of the EU therefore to ensure that the UK continues to contribute to the security of Europe.

The British armed forces will not, of course, disappear. When the clock strikes midnight on the eve of Brexit, British tanks will not change into pumpkins nor frigates into watermelons. And, come Brexit, Britain will have left the EU, but it will still be in Europe. Any military threat against Europe will thus also constitute a threat against the UK. Continuing cooperation in the field of defence is as much in Britain's interest as in the EU's, therefore.

This implies that the Brexiteers cannot use the security argument in order to get a better deal from the EU. Some have made the case that the UK is entitled to better conditions from the EU because it makes a more-than-average contribution to NATO. But this is not how it works. NATO and the EU are separate organisations: one cannot ask for a discount in one club because one already pays fees into another. Besides, then the EU should somehow also reward other Member States that have a larger defence budget than the EU average (such as Greece). The threat of abandonment cannot work either. The UK can hardly refuse to contribute to European security since that is still its own security. If a certain threat against Europe requires a military response, it is still much more likely than not that the UK will be part of that response.

When in a given crisis Europeans engage in *combat* operations, they increasingly do so in ad hoc coalitions, outside the formal framework of NATO or the EU. Brexit will likely reinforce that trend. Of the two key military actors in Europe, one, the UK, will no longer be a member of the EU, while the other, France, is not going to turn its back on the EU and channel its entire operational commitment through NATO. At the same time, troops on other types of operations will of course continue to be deployed under EU, NATO, and UN command.

A practical question, therefore, is whether, after Brexit, the UK will still be willing to contribute to EU operations if in a specific contingency the other Europeans opt for the CSDP as framework for deployment. Even today though the British contribution to military CSDP operations represents just 3.6 per cent of the total (and 5.8 per cent for the civilian missions). There already is an arrangement for the participation of non-EU Member States in CSDP operations. Many countries, from Asia to South America, have contributed ships to the EU's anti-piracy operation, Atalanta, for example. London has already made it understood, however, that it considers this arrangement to be insufficient, as it allows third countries to contribute capabilities to an operation, but not to be involved in its strategic direction. (And many other third countries have also expressed their dissatisfaction, actually.) In view of Britain's military weight in Europe, some sort of special arrangement does seem advisable. But if London wants a special status, it will have to offer something special, more than other third countries. For example, the UK could continue to make its operational headquarters in Northwood available to the EU after Brexit. Only in return for permanent concrete contributions could structural involvement in decision-making on CSDP operations be envisaged, for example by offering the UK a seat – but without voting rights – in the relevant EU bodies.

After Brexit, Britain will continue to participate in European military operations, under various flags, possibly even that of the EU. It's a different question, however, whether the UK will be able to play the same leading role as before in *initiating* operations. Until now, it has usually been London and/or Paris that took the initiative to mount an operation and forge a coalition to that end. But as British decision-makers will be absorbed by the Brexit negotiations, and the many domestic issues that Brexit also entails, there will be less and less bandwidth left for strategic initiatives. The question for the EU is then whether France alone can play this role, and whether Germany may gradually grow into it. Because of the country's history, German public opinion remains very reticent to see the armed forces deployed abroad. Nevertheless, Germany has made singular progress. German troops are deployed in Afghanistan, Iraq, and Mali – 20 years ago, that would have been unimaginable. Berlin will have to play an even stronger leading role in the area of defence though, if it really wants to strategically underpin European defence together with Paris.

For the further development of military capabilities in Europe, Brexit will probably not matter much. If anything, Brexit has in fact had a positive effect, because the debate on military cooperation and integration in Europe has accelerated since the referendum. For the wrong reasons: it's not because of the UK's departure that the remaining Member States will miraculously agree on everything. True, the UK has traditionally vetoed certain initiatives, mostly those having to do with setting up new structures. A permanent military headquarters for the EU, for example, remains a red line for the UK, which sees this as a superfluous duplication of NATO. But the UK never opposed multinational schemes to enhance capabilities through cooperation and even integration. It most likely would not have participated in most of such schemes itself, but neither would it have stopped other Member States from doing so. On the other hand, many Member States who were not actually that enthusiastic themselves were always able to hide behind the UK. It was easy to pretend to support an initiative even if one opposed it in order not to complicate relations with those that tabled it, if one knew that the British would veto it anyway. After Brexit, those Member States will have to come clean.

European defence has momentum now, as the activation of PESCO shows. The non-participation of the UK will not have much of an impact on PESCO's eventual success, since nobody expected it to join in the first place. Britain and France were at the origins of the idea, back in the days of the European Convention and the 2003 Constitutional Treaty, but London had long lost interest. Now that PESCO has started, it may have an effect on the UK though. Britain has never been very keen on big multinational projects or on far-reaching integration, but it has constructed some very close bilateral military cooperation arrangements. In 2010, it notably concluded the Lancaster House Agreements with France, in the context of which a Franco–British Combined Joint Expeditionary Force (CJEF) has been created. The CJEF is about cooperation to increase interoperability, not integration to create multinational capabilities; it basically allows a British and a French brigade to be deployed together. On the British side, the very same forces constitute the British contribution to a similar scheme with Denmark, Estonia, Finland, Latvia, Lithuania, the Netherlands, Norway, and Sweden: the Joint Expeditionary Force (JEF). If in the future, however, France, or one of the countries participating in the JEF, were to effectively integrate some of the capabilities concerned with those of other countries in the framework of PESCO, then the British in the CJEF or JEF would no longer just cooperate with a purely national capability but with a multinational European one. Technically this is perfectly feasible.

At the same time, as the January 2018 Franco–British Summit showed, Brexit need not prevent bilateral defence cooperation from being deepened. French President Emmanuel Macron's European Intervention Initiative, announced in the autumn of 2017, even seems to aim at a new scheme for cooperation on expeditionary operations outside PESCO and the EU, and will involve the UK. It would be much more advisable for France to pursue this initiative inside PESCO, however (where a very similar Crisis Response Operational Core, or CROC, is also envisaged), in order to prevent a fragmentation of effort. The UK, like other third states, cannot take part in the overall decision-making process on PESCO, but it could participate in individual projects, such as the CROC, on a case-by-case basis.

As PESCO and the EDF gather pace, the British defence industry, unlike the British government, will likely want to join in. If, thanks to PESCO and the financial support from the EDF, the EU Member States effectively managed to harmonise their defence efforts and, in the future, start just a single collective project to build each of the next generation of major platforms, then these will dominate the European market. It remains a big if, but if it works out as intended, British firms will have a major interest in participating in the industrial consortia that will develop and build Europe's future arms and equipment. As usual, the British will probably wait and see, and jump on the wagon only if PESCO and the EDF clearly are successful.

All things considered, Brexit may not affect EU defence policy that much. Brexit does imply that the UK will no longer contribute to the EU budget, including the EDF, nor to the EDA. Either the other Member States compensate by increasing their own contribution, or budgets from other lines will have to be reallocated to defence. Brexit will also mean that many British staff will leave the EU institutions. British citizens who have permanent appointments as EU officials are likely able to stay. Even so, quite a few are applying for Belgian nationality. (Who would have thought that people would feel it's better to be Belgian than British?) However, one third of the posts in the EEAS, and all posts in the EU Military Staff, are held not by EU officials, but by seconded national diplomats and military officers. From this category, all British personnel will automatically disappear. It so happens that it's precisely the UK that sends many excellent people to the EU. A British general once told me that among the staff that Member States second to Brussels, there are swimmers, floaters, and sinkers. In my experience, Brits have always been overrepresented among the swimmers.

But what about foreign policy?

There seems to be more debate about the colour of future British passports then about the substance of its foreign policy after Brexit. But even though it is talked about much less than defence policy, it looks a lot more complicated to keep the UK involved in the EU's CFSP. That there is a mutual interest in this area, too, is evident. The UK is an important diplomatic actor. Any EU position to which the UK also subscribes and that its extensive diplomatic network and experienced diplomats can support will carry a lot more weight. If the EU were to adopt economic sanctions against a third country, any divergence between EU and UK sanctions regimes would only be to the profit of the targeted state.

Conversely, there is not that much space for an independent British foreign policy outside the EU framework. The UK may be able to exercise significant influence on some specific issues or individual countries with which it has special ties. But what impact do the Brexiteers think the UK on its own will have on the major issues of world politics: the Ukraine crisis, the wars in the Middle East, the rise of China? The UK alone, just like any other European country, no longer has sufficient power to aspire to significantly influence any of these.

Imagine that on a major issue, the EU adopts a clear-cut common position, enters into a dialogue with the US, and that Brussels and Washington coordinate their views and take joint action. What will the UK do – the opposite? On the big issues, London's margin for manoeuvre will be limited to the choice between joining EU and US action, or simply not doing anything at all. If the EU and the US adopt opposing points of view, which, with Trump in the White House, is not unlikely, London will be in an even more uncomfortable position, forced to choose between one or the other or, again, to remain inactive. This is happening already: in reaction to Trump putting in doubt the nuclear agreement with Iran, the UK sided with France, Germany, and the EU to stress its importance. The conclusion is obvious: the UK would do well to seek a close partnership with the EU in foreign policy as well as defence.

There is as yet no arrangement for involving third countries in EU foreign policy. Certain countries, notably candidates for accession, subscribe to EU positions on a nearly systematic basis, but they don't really participate in EU decision-making. Moreover, this mechanism mostly concerns diplomatic statements and rarely the operational decisions on election observation, sanctions, civilian missions, or military operations. One can certainly imagine pragmatic solutions. The EU could allow the UK to maintain its seat on the Foreign Affairs Council (FAC) and all preparatory bodies, but without voting rights. In this manner, London could contribute its views to the EU decision-making process from the start, instead of just being able to choose whether to subscribe to an EU decision at the end of the process. Such an arrangement would certainly benefit the quality of EU foreign policy.

A new "special relationship"?

Arrangements to continue to involve the UK in CFSP and CSDP post-Brexit, and, of course, continued consultation through NATO, could amount to an EU–UK strategic partnership – a new "special relationship", as it were.

Unfortunately, it is far from certain that all concerned will be sufficiently pragmatic to agree on workable solutions. On the EU side, no matter how unjustified, the fact is that there exists in many corners a certain revanchist attitude: the idea that the British deserve to be punished. They will have to beg for it, on their bare knees, was how a general from another Member State reacted when I first vented my idea to maintain a British seat in the FAC. Another general, not without reason, warned against repeating the experience of the now-defunct Western European Union (WEU), which in the end had so many associate members, associate partners, and observers that the actual full members lost their autonomy of decision-making.

An EU–UK partnership will have to be clearly defined, therefore. First of all, a Euro–British "special relationship" must be just that: special. It cannot be seen as a precedent for similar arrangements with any other state (which, for most Member States, means: with Turkey). That is easy to justify, if necessary: after Brexit, only one non-EU European state will have a permanent seat on the Security Council, so only that one state qualifies for this type of strategic partnership.

Second, as the UK has always strongly opposed free-riding, it cannot now do so itself. A seat in the FAC, even without voting rights, cannot come for free. The CFSP remains an intergovernmental area of EU policy: decisions require unanimity. In practice, Member States hardly ever vote in the FAC or its preparatory bodies, but either take decisions by consensus or don't decide at all. A seat without a vote thus actually comes very close to having a normal seat. Therefore, it would be but logical that in this scenario the UK would continue to abide by all treaty stipulations on the CFSP, and continue to pay into the CFSP budget. An "opt-in" into the CFSP cannot be partial: it would have a very negative effect on decision-making if the UK subscribed to one EU common position and not to another. Having a seat implies subscribing to *all* CFSP decisions, and defending them in all other forums, just like the Member States.

This would send a strong signal to the other powers, such as Russia and China, that in diplomacy even after Brexit there will be but one Europe, which would be in the interest of all European states. The UK would also benefit because it would retain an important asset in its relationship with the US. And the EU Member States would benefit because if the UK remains fully involved in the CFSP, they need not fear the emergence of new parallel circuits that would bypass the EU. Smaller Member States especially would not be keen on the UK trying to influence foreign policy from the outside through bilateral relations with the other big European players, France and Germany. At the same time, it would be clear that if one leaves the Union, one cannot come back in on the cheap, so this would strengthen Brussels' hand in the Brexit negotiations.

Third, with regard to the CSDP, British involvement would only concern the EU operations and missions in which it would take part, and not capability development. Decisions on capability development will henceforth shift to PESCO, of which the UK is not a member, but it could contribute to individual projects.

Pragmatism versus emotion

Both sides stand to gain from a pragmatic partnership. There's no point in debating who needs the other more. If we don't manage to create an EU–UK strategic partnership in foreign policy and defence, both sides will lose – that's what counts.

The biggest obstacle to such a partnership, however, is the British themselves. The British government, in *Foreign Policy, Defence and Development: A Future Partnership Paper* (September 2017), expressed a very positive view of CFSP and CSDP. One almost wonders why it would wish to leave. Unfortunately, and contrary to the British reputation for pragmatism, in the debate on the EU and Brexit, ideology and emotions prevail. That renders it very difficult for the British political leadership to adopt a nuanced stance. Prime Minister Theresa May's electoral defeat in June 2017, against all expectations, demonstrated how volatile British domestic politics has become. This certainly doesn't make the Brexit negotiations any easier.

Not just in foreign and defence policy, but in many other policy areas there are very good reasons to maintain practical cooperation between the UK and the EU even after Brexit. Cooperation between police and intelligence services and justice departments in the fight against terrorism is an obvious example. The problem is that when every British ministry draws up the list of what it still wants to do with the EU after Brexit, and London then assembles all those lists, the result will look very much like membership. That will be politically unfeasible, even though every individual item on every list will be perfectly logical. This demonstrates the sheer absurdity of Brexit: after years of negotiating on how to leave, the UK will then have to start another round of negotiations on how to link back up with the EU in a whole range of areas.

If the general atmosphere in the negotiations were to turn permanently sour, the risk is that foreign and security policy will suffer as a consequence, and that none of the pragmatic solutions on offer will be implemented, to the detriment of both sides of the Channel. A "hard" Brexit is a definite possibility. At the same time, there still is a slight chance that in the end Brexit will not happen. Once the negotiations have been concluded and an agreement is on the table, it will most probably become very clear very quickly that this will not quite bring the golden future that the Brexiteers promised. By that time the economic impact of Brexit will have become clearer as well. For now, the impact is limited, because governments and companies are waiting to learn what the future status of the UK will be. Gradually, however, the flow of investments to the UK will slacken – nobody is going to embark on a major investment without knowing whether the UK will remain in the single market.

Perhaps, if offered the chance to vote again, British citizens will prefer to stay in the EU after all. Meanwhile, however, the EU itself will (one hopes!) have advanced and made new steps towards more integration. Even if the UK were to remain, which personally I strongly hope for, something, sadly, has been broken between the UK and the rest of the EU.

8

CONCLUSION

Which Europe are we doing this for?

When I was just about halfway writing the original Dutch-language version of this book, the second round of the French presidential elections took place, on 7 May 2017, between centre candidate Emmanuel Macron and extreme-right candidate Marine Le Pen. Macron won convincingly with two thirds of the votes cast (though many didn't vote), and I had expected as much. About a year earlier, the vote for Brexit had come totally unexpected for me. I had not foreseen the election of Trump either, but after the outcome of the British referendum I was better prepared, so the shock was less great. When it rains in Paris, it trickles down in Brussels, or so a Belgian saying has it, but clearly there can be rainstorms in Washington and London and a clear sky over Paris.

Fretting

And yet, I've been fretting ever since the French presidential election. Had Le Pen won, I could have thrown away the half of the book that I had already written. An extreme right president in France would not immediately mean the end of the EU, but it would undoubtedly lead to a grave systemic crisis. A nationalist, anti-EU French president could block EU decision-making, and could even refuse to continue to implement existing European legislation. The EU could come to a complete standstill. European foreign policy, which this book is about, would be finished for a long time to come. All attention would have to focus on saving the Union. A Le Pen victory was never likely, but neither was it impossible. The fact alone that she made it to the second round should set alarms bell ringing. What will happen at the next elections, in 2022, if Macron will not be as successful, for the sake of Europe, as we hope?

No matter how I turn things, I always arrive at the same conclusion, and it worries me greatly: the EU still is much more fragile than I had assumed. Since the

2008 financial crisis and the resulting problems in the Eurozone, observers outside the EU like to predict the imminent end of the Union. My answer to these preachers of doom has always been, and still is, that integration has proceeded so far that it cannot easily be undone: not only because the economic cost of abolishing the Euro, the single market, and the Schengen zone (of no internal borders) would be enormous but also because the European idea has become part of our identity. I still am convinced of that. But in spite of it all, in the year of the 60th anniversary of the Rome Treaty that founded the EEC, it depended on the outcome of a single election in a single Member State whether European integration would continue or come to a halt.

Even worse: our democracies themselves remain very fragile. In the US, an unworthy man has been elected president, even though already during his campaign he had proved not to hesitate at inventing "fake news" to discredit his opponents, nor at slinging the rudest insults at individuals, as well as entire groups of citizens, who didn't please him. And still he won. He obviously has no shame at all, witness how even as president he continues to insult people on Twitter. In the UK, during the campaign for the EU referendum, the Brexiteers told obvious lies and made huge promises (notably that £350 million per week could be allocated to the National Health Service if only the UK would leave the EU), which they shamelessly withdrew the day after the vote. Does anybody still have the capacity to feel ashamed? Certainly not Hungarian Prime Minister Viktor Orbán, who, without any ado, has announced that he seeks to create an "illiberal democracy" in his country. Obviously, no such thing exists. Whatever populists claim: the choice is between democratic and non-democratic government. Yet Orbán has been elected twice already without any problem. And in France, in 2017, a third of the voters chose the extreme right.

The voter is not always right. Whoever in a democratic election votes for an undemocratic candidate, or for a candidate who through his shamelessness just ridicules democracy (which amounts to the same thing), is just very, very wrong. And such a voter clearly has no sense of history whatsoever. This, for me, is the gravest threat to democracy and therefore to peace in Europe.

The dangerous geopolitics of populism

European integration started off as a small club of just six democratic states: the EEC. NATO, originally, was actually less squeamish about values, in spite of the reference to "democracy, individual liberty and the rule of law" in the preamble to the Washington Treaty. The authoritarian Portugal of Prime Minister Salazar was a founding member in 1949. Greece and Turkey have been allies since 1952, even as they went through periods of authoritarianism. Strategic necessity trumped values. That assessment began to evolve with the accession of Spain to NATO in 1982, and of Spain and Portugal to the EEC in 1986, following the democratisation of both countries. The end of the Cold War definitely changed things: democracy now *is* a strategic necessity. The consolidation of democracy in central and eastern Europe has become a key objective of NATO and EU enlargement. So what do NATO and the EU do when some of their members revert back to authoritarianism?

The authoritarian trend creates a fundamental problem for NATO, because it is at odds with how its basic purpose has evolved since the end of the Cold War. The purpose of NATO today is to defend not just the territorial integrity of its members but also the model of society that they have constructed on their territories. If an ally no longer upholds this European way of life, then what exactly is NATO supposed to defend? A government that undermines its country's democracy thus ipso facto puts its security at risk too. The more authoritarian a government becomes, the more it puts the bond of solidarity in the Alliance into question. To put it very starkly: which democratic government could justify to its citizens putting its forces in harm's way in order to defend an eventual dictatorship in another NATO country?

This, of course, is obvious to NATO's potential adversaries, too. Russia definitely will not hesitate to use any opportunity that presents itself in order to weaken NATO, if only to stop the Alliance from interfering in its strategic design of reestablishing predominance in the former Soviet republics. Hence Russia actively supports various populist actors. In most cases, populist tactics include Euro-scepticism. It is both acceptable and necessary in a democratic polity to criticise EU policies, and even the EU project as such. But when countries decided, by democratic means, to join the EU, they subscribed to a set of objectives and limitations. If a government no longer is willing to abide by them, it cannot expect that its country's status in the EU will remain unaffected, even if such were the free and informed democratic choice of its citizens (which today is questionable). Therefore, if the EU adopts sanctions against a government that violates the basic principles that it subscribed to when joining the Union, this does not constitute a violation of the sovereignty of the state in question.

But certain governments not only violate the EU's values but also actively undermine EU policies, notably the CFSP. What is worse, they appear to be doing so under the influence of foreign powers such as Russia and China. In full contradiction with their nationalist rhetoric, some governments have willingly become instruments of outside actors. Worryingly, not only proto-authoritarian but even some fully democratic governments are undermining the EU in this way, having become hostage, it seems, to Russian energy or Chinese financial power. As a result, it has become increasingly difficult for the EU to take a resolute and united stance in issues involving China and Russia. Certain governments even undermine EU positions on general human rights policy, directly affecting the core of the Union's value-based foreign policy.

NATO and the EU can no longer be disentangled. If one weakens the bond between nations in the EU, ipso facto one weakens ties in NATO. Or do proto-authoritarian governments really think that they can constantly frustrate other EU member states, and yet those same states will come running to their assistance through NATO when they are in need? Today, there can no longer be a strong and united NATO without a strong and united EU. Thus, undermining the EU undermines collective defence just as much as undermining democracy does.

A geopolitical void

The governments concerned may think that they can always count on the US to protect them. But how certain can they be? In July 2017, President Trump happily let himself be fêted in Warsaw, and in his speech even seemed to support the Polish government against "bureaucracy" – a thinly veiled reference to the EU. But just a week later he made his appearance as the glowing guest star at the Bastille Day celebrations in Paris, where president Macron will have given him a totally opposite view of the EU.

Even without the suspicion surrounding Trump's links to Russia, it hardly seems wise to put one's faith in a president who chose a campaign slogan that originated with extreme right isolationists in the 1930s: "America First". Under the Trump administration, the US has increased its military presence on the eastern borders of NATO. But given Trump's less-than-enthusiastic views on institutions such as NATO and the EU, and his apparent links with Russia, can he really be counted on to counterbalance Russian attempts to unravel these organisations and to gain major influence in specific central European countries (by other than military means)? Especially if some of the European governments concerned seem to have de facto enabled Russia themselves?

What anti-EU, undemocratic governments are at risk of doing, therefore, is to slowly create a geopolitical void in central Europe. By antagonising fellow European states in NATO and the EU, at a time when the US is less than fully invested in Europe's institutions, they are actually isolating themselves. At the same time, by artificially stirring anti-EU feeling, they are rendering their citizens more vulnerable to Russian propaganda. In a worst-case scenario, these states might end up detached from the West, and entering into the same geopolitical limbo as Ukraine, an uncomfortable buffer zone between the West and Russia. This is probably not what citizens in Poland and Hungary have in mind.

The consequences may not be limited to the current proto-authoritarian states. If authoritarianism is not stopped, it may well affect ever more European states. Already, the existence of proto-authoritarian regimes within the EU has greatly undermined the legitimacy and effectiveness of EU foreign policy. It may well end up paralysing EU decision-making altogether and, consequently, cause the flight ahead, if not the breakaway, of the remaining democratic member states. At that point the cohesion of NATO too will crumble. What is more, authoritarian tendencies in Europe and in the US may become mutually reinforcing. Many

American observers fear similar developments in the US as are now happening in Poland and Hungary. In a reversal of history, a strong democratic EU can act as a beacon for democratic forces in the US. But a divided and progressively less democratic EU and US may end up pulling each other down.

This is a dark scenario, but not an impossible one, which is why NATO and the EU have to guard against it.

Back to basics

To offer an answer to all of these challenges far surpasses my expertise. But I am sure of one thing: even the best foreign and security policies will not remedy this situation. Unfortunately for me, perhaps, since I made my career in this area, but in the end this is not what keeps people awake at night. The answer will have to come from social and economic policies, at the EU level especially. As I have already said, our European society distinguishes itself from most others because of the centrality of equality as an objective, in the security, political, and economic fields. That is what people expect from government. But many have the impression that the EU no longer sincerely aspires to equality, or have even come to see the EU as a threat to the welfare state. An ambitious social agenda could convince European citizens again that the EU can exactly be the ultimate guarantor of their social security (Vandenbroucke, 2014).

In the classic promo-talk for the EU, the welfare state is usually forgotten. We sell the success of the EU by referring to the end of internal borders, the introduction of the Euro, and, since 15 June 2017, the abolishment of roaming tariffs for use of mobile phones. All of these are very concrete and easy-to-explain advantages. And it is great, of course, that one can travel across nearly all of Europe without meeting a customs officer or having to change money. It's equally great that, thanks to the Erasmus programme, more and more European students spend a semester or longer studying in another Member State. So many of my students have a foreign boyfriend or girlfriend. University students truly are European, or even global, citizens. But not everybody studies at university, and not everybody travels. Even in a wealthy country like Belgium, a quarter of the population simply never travels because people just don't have the means (JNS, 2017). What does the Schengen zone matter to them?

In our usual story on the EU, we have forgotten a very large group of people, because we have forgotten half of the European story itself. The founding myth of the EU as usually told talks of the wise forefathers who, having lived through the horrors of World War Two, desiring to prevent that from ever happening again, put the states of Europe on the path of integration, rendering war between them practically impossible: "simultaneously the dullest and most daring trick that statesmen had ever attempted" (Morris, 2014, p. 342). This story is true, but it's only half of history. The same wise forefathers had also seen the economic crisis of the 1930s. European democracies had no answer to the crisis, inequality increased dramatically, and the cohesion of society fragmented, to the advantage of the extreme right and the extreme left. In most European countries, democracy collapsed already before the war, and fascist dictatorships took power. In order to prevent the lure of "the strong man", who will bring all hail, from ever again tempting Europeans, the same wise forefathers, in those same years after the war, created not just European integration but also the comprehensive welfare state. The social buffer that the welfare state provides protects equality, particularly in times of crisis, so that political extremism cannot catch root and democracy will not be threatened. The welfare state, therefore, is as much a part of the European peace project as European integration itself.

Many have come to consider the welfare state to be but a luxury product, however: nice to have when you can afford it, but easily discarded when thing are going badly. While precisely the opposite is true: the worse things are with the economy, the more vital the welfare state becomes. That's why when the EU after the 2008 financial crisis initially pressured Member States into cutting back on social security it had such a dramatic negative effect on the legitimacy of the Union. Moreover, we now have a single market and a single currency, which implies that the welfare state can no longer just be a national project. The EU must not only guarantee the national welfare state but must develop a social policy of its own as well. I don't want to be naïve: creating an effective EU social policy will not be simple, and even if we do, it will not convince everyone of the merits of the EU at a stroke. My surname may mean bishop, but I don't believe in miracles. But I am convinced that without this social dimension, the EU will never work.

Equality is a positive project, but at the same time the EU should probably also be more severe – more severe for Member States that no longer respect the political equality of their citizens and that are undermining democracy and the rule of law. It's not easy for Brussels to call back Member States when they are acting within their national competences, be it against democratic principles. The Commission is fighting back. Yet the impression persists, inside and outside Europe, that governments like that of Orbán are getting away with it. However, it should be crystal clear that one cannot just stay in the EU when one no longer respects democratic rules, even if one stays within one's national competences. Perhaps the EU should resort to sanctions quicker and suspend the voting rights of Member States that deface European democracy. The alternative is that fake democrats not only harm their own countries, but begin to actively undermine EU decision-making. If the EU does not enforce its own values internally, it can hardly pretend to pursue a value-based foreign policy.

A core group?

Opponents often say that the EU's answer to criticism usually is that we need more EU. But that just happens to be true. Of course, the EU is not free from criticism. And it is obviously not the intention to transfer all competences to the EU. Each competence must be exercised at the level where governance can be the most effective. For many issues that today are still mainly dealt with by Member States, that level actually is the EU. In a world dominated by great powers the size of continents, we Europeans have no choice but to unite in a continental union if we want to retain a modicum of influence.

Ideally, the EU as whole, with all 27 Member States remaining after Brexit, will take the necessary great steps in further integration. Unfortunately, that is unlikely. Then creating a core group or an avant-garde, smaller group of Member States that in the first instance are willing to go further than others is the second-best option. The Eurozone and the Schengen group started out as smaller groups as well, but now the majority of Member States has joined both. A new core group would preferably comprise a number of Member States that want to take new steps in several domains at the same time: economic, financial, social, foreign, and defence policies. If we create a separate group for each area, the EU risks becoming a confusing tangle without an obvious centre of gravity. With PESCO, we have already created a distinct group for defence, but as it counts 25 Member States, it's not unlikely that a de facto core within PESCO will emerge, of the states that participate in all key capability projects and that are willing to go the furthest in defence integration. The foundation of any core group must be the Franco–German axis, which, as in the past, will continue to be the engine of European integration.

A multispeed Europe is probably inevitable, but it does carry a cost. Therefore, a multispeed EU should be a positive choice, a way of moving ahead with a view to all member states re-joining the core eventually. It should not be a negative choice, a way of casting aside those that have come to be seen as obstacles to progress. That would create long-lasting acrimony from which the EU might not recover. Relations between Brussels and Budapest and Warsaw are bad as they are because the Commission constantly has to tell off both governments for their undemocratic decisions. Now who will join a comprehensive core group (in terms of policy areas covered)? The six founding members, surely, plus Spain and Portugal, probably, as well as some of the northern members – but most likely not a single east European country, which would be a first. The challenge will be to maintain an EU-wide identity and political dynamics in spite of this.

Since it does come at a cost, a core group must take really big steps once formed to make it worthwhile. Launching a core group only to fiddle in the margins: then we'd better not do it at all. The core cannot be hollow.

Big politics

This certainly applies to the EU's grand strategy, and to its foreign and defence policy. The *Global Strategy* that Mogherini presented in June 2016 operates at the level of grand strategy. This is about Politics with a big "P" – great power politics. But that's not what the EU has been doing since then. If someone without too much prior knowledge would read the *Global Strategy*, he or she would probably be curious to learn how the EU deals strategically with the US, China, and Russia; how the EU addresses the wars in its periphery; and how it attempts to shape the future global order. That is indeed what the EU should be doing. It certainly has the capacity, as I have argued in this book. In reality, however, the EU in implementing the *Global Strategy* has focussed not so much on great power politics as on procedures – with a very small "p". The EU has started processes, created procedures, and written plans for implementation, which in turn have generated more processes and procedures. It's as if the EU hesitates to use the power that it does have. The aim is not to play power politics and copy the ways of the other great powers, of course, but to put the EU's power to use to pursue a distinctive European grand strategy and a positive agenda for world politics.

"It is easier to deal with an open objection than with a profession of agreement in principle which covers an underlying reluctance to translate it into practice. While clear opposition presents an obstacle that can be surmounted, hesitant acquiescence acts as a constant break on progress" (Liddell Hart, 1965, p. 73). These words from British strategist Sir Basil Liddell Hart refer to British army reform in the interbellum years, but they perfectly apply to European foreign and defence policy today. All too often EU Member States subscribe to a proposal in the full knowledge that actually they have no real intention of implementing it. The *Global Strategy* is a case in point. It doesn't really happen that often that an initiative is completely blocked. More often, it will be watered down and put into vague and general conclusions, with which all capitals can concur, and then everybody leaves it at that. Since 1998 already Member States keep repeating that more defence cooperation is the only way of achieving European strategic autonomy. Sometimes I feel the policy-makers concerned would rather have my job: they talk about it, they write about it, but they don't do it.

It doesn't help that in foreign and defence policy, EU decision-making still requires unanimity. The result is that EU policy often is reduced to the lowest common denominator. There is no good reason, in fact, why EU Member States could not decide on foreign policy by majority, as they do in so many other areas. Not on launching military operations: here majority voting would only be possible if we had a real European army (i.e. when our soldiers are on the payroll of the EU). But on all other dimensions of grand strategy, why not? Unfortunately, Belgium is more or less the only Member State that is formally in favour of majority decision-making in the CFSP.

It does feel at times, as a Belgian, as if we are the last of the Mohicans, the last ones to be optimistic on European integration. But in the end, I don't think that's true. Besides, it's not a very enviable position, for those who have read James Fennimore Cooper's book know how it ends: the last of the Mohicans die, and the British win. In spite of all obstacles and all the reasons one can imagine why it wouldn't happen, Europeans have made enormous progress in the EU, and will continue to make progress. But that's exactly the point: we have arrived at a moment when another major step is an absolute necessity. We don't need to make Europe great again. Europe *is* great. Let's keep it that way.

References

JNS, "Kwart van de Belgen kan niet op vakantie door geldgebrek". In: *De Standaard*, 16 January 2017.

Basil H. Liddell Hart, *The Memoirs of Captain Liddell Hart, Volume II*. London, Cassel, 1965.

Ian Morris, *War! What Is It Good For? The Role of Conflict in Civilisation, from Primates to Robots*. London, Profile Books, 2014.

Frank Vandenbroucke, "Een Europese sociale unie". In: *Samenleving en Politiek*, Vol. 21, 2014, No. 5, pp. 24–37.

INDEX

Abbas, Mahmoud 41
Abe, Shinzo 53–54
Abkhazia 58
Afghanistan: democracy, imposition challenges 11, 84, 89; NATO intervention influence 115; US invasion, post 9/11 89, 94
Alliot-Marie, Michèle 17
al-Qaeda 32, 45, 89, 94
al-Sisi, Abdul Fatah 17, 18
Arab League 75–76, 77, 90
Arab Spring 11, 17, 28, 76
Armenia 15, 67–68
Asian Infrastructure Investment Bank (AIIB) 63
Assad, Bashar: political alliances/opposition 18, 77; Russian support crucial 42, 58, 80, 93
Australia 53, 63–64
authoritarian states: EU members, political influence 140–141; flexible cooperation, mixed potential 27–28; political justification of governance 12–13, 16, 52, 65n4; undemocratic volatility 24, 26
Azerbaijan 15, 67–68

Baltic States: EU and Russian interests 56–57; Joint Expeditionary Force (JEF) 133; NATO deployment 39, 57
Baluyevski, Yuri 60
Bannon, Steve 43
Belarus 15, 67–68

Belgium: anti-IS coalition 77; Belgian-Dutch naval cooperation 118–119; Brussels terrorism attacks 86, 96–97; CETA dispute 54; EATC participation 117; European Defence Community (EDC) 112; Land Component and Eurocorps 119, 123; military capabilities 99, 119–120, 123; NATO budget contributions 114
Ben Ali, Zine El Abidine 11, 17
Berlin Plus Agreement 106
Bolton, John 43, 44
Bouazizi, Mohamed 17
Brexit: EU prestige loss 12; Euro–British "special relationship" 135–136; European defence, operational impacts 132–134; peripheral to EU agenda 130–131; strategic illusions and realities 127–130; strategic partnership, obstacles 137; UK and EU foreign policy 134–136; UKIP involvement 13
buffer states: resilient neighbour 70; Turkey for EU 72
Bush, George W. 44, 84

Cameron, David 130–131
Canada 38, 53, 54
Capacity-Building for Security and Development (CBSD) 83–84
Central Asia states and EU 69
China: America's Asia Strategy and Chinese relations 38–40, 49, 104; Asian Infrastructure Investment Bank (AIIB) 63;

Index

authoritarian nationalism 12–13, 28, 52, 65n4; Belt and Road Initiative (BRI) 61–62, 65n7; EU and the BRI, political bargaining 61–62, 69; EU, existing and potential relations 50–52; EU's investment negotiations 49; global rise 14, 39; human rights sensitivity 23, 36n1; influence in North Korea 41; Russia's geopolitical importance 61–63; South China Sea, claims and opposition allies 8, 50–51; student's European insight 25–26; UK, post-Brexit proposal 128; US economic sanctions 38

Churchill, Winston 126
Clinton, Hillary 38–39
Coelmont, Jo 84
Cold War Europe: NATO/US led strategies 9–10, 82, 102, 110
Common Foreign and Security Policy (CFSP): EU members, authoritarianism issues 140–141; pursuance of interests 1–2; UK's conditional involvement 135, 136; values and strategy determination 2, 103
Common Security and Defence Policy (CSDP): deployment conditions and activation 101, 102, 103; UK involvement, post-Brexit 132, 136
Comprehensive Economic and Trade Agreement (CETA): Canada and EU 53, 54; criticisms of 54–55
Cooper, Robert 8
Cyprus 69, 81n1, 102

Delor, Jacques 3, 4n3
democracy: democratisation objections 22; equality and flexible cooperation 26–27; geopolitical tensions, Ukraine 11, 15, 19; imposition challenges, former Soviet states 11, 30, 67–68, 140; resilience, interpretation issues 70
Denmark 77, 123–124
Di Repo, Elio 114

Eastern Partnership (EaP) 14, 19n1, 67
Egypt: Arab Spring events 17; opposition movements and EU support 15–16, 17, 70; post-Arab Spring alliances 18
equality: flexible cooperation 26–29, 71, 78–79; social and economic objectives 27–28, 142–143; soft power benefits 25–26; sovereignty defended 29–30, 78
Erdogan, Recep 72
Eurasian Economic Union (EAEU) 68
Eurocorps 119–120, 123

European Air Transport Command (EATC) 117
European Commission: China, investment negotiations 49, 50, 61; European Defence Fund (EDF) 121–122, 124, 134; resilience, interpretation 70; Ukraine trade agreement 5
European Defence Community (EDC) 112
European Defence Fund (EDF) 121–122, 124, 134
European defence, present and future: budgets and spending, reality and possibilities 113–115, 121–122; duplication and fragmentation issues 112–113; Eurocorps 119–120, 123; European Air Transport Command (EATC) 117; European Commission, funding strategy 121–122, 124, 134; military integration, combat units 118–120; military integration, planning and capabilities 116–118, 122–125; military sovereignty 115–116; Permanent Structured Cooperation (PESCO) 123–125, 133; strategic enablers 116–117, 122–123; UK military cooperation, post-Brexit 131–134
European Economic Community (EEC) 82, 127, 139
European External Action Service (EEAS) 71
European Intervention Initiative 134
European Neighbourhood Policy (ENP) 14, 67, 69
European Security Strategy (EU) 8, 10–11, 14–15
European Union (EU): bilateral partnerships and conditionality 14–15, 16–17, 19, 67–69, 81n1; core group proposal 143–144; effective multilateralism 51, 63–64, 91; equality, pragmatic values and actions 26–31, 142–143; financial crisis and austerity 11–12, 143; geopolitics, value underestimated 8–9; intelligence service gaps 96–97; interests, political and security dimensions 1–3, 23–25, 144–145; mutual assistance, security articles 94–96; NATO security and the "Maginot Complex". 47–48; political status, possible threats 138–139; populist movements, growth in 13, 141; positive governance model and weaknesses 10–13, 15–16; post-Brexit credibility 12; postmodern 'security community' 8; power potential 2–3; pragmatic review, strategy gaps exposed 14, 16–19; strategic

partnerships 14, 19n2; UK's impact on defence options 129; Union interests paramount 130–131; UN security commitments 91–92, 93; values and strategy determination 21–25

European Union (EU), Eastern and Southern neighbours: Arab Spring, post event interventions 17–18; Eastern Partnership (EaP) 14, 19n1, 67; Libyan security intervention 75–76, 98–99, 106; Mali, security intervention 75, 83; Middle Eastern and African cooperation issues 70–74; peripheral neighbours and security policies 78–81; refugee and migration crisis 12, 72, 76, 88; Saudi Arabia, compromised relations 17, 28–29, 64, 71–72; Saudi arms as bargaining chip 73–74; Southern non-European states, security issues 74–78; Ukraine relations and crisis 5–7, 56, 57–58, 60–61; Union for the Mediterranean 14, 19n1

European Union (EU), *Global Strategy* 2016: effective multilateralism 34–35, 51, 63–64; *Global* context 36n3; internal security, EU responsibility 94; military power, priority tasks 85–86, 98; principled pragmatism 31–32, 52, 72–73; priorities and shared interests 32–35; realistic implementation 35, 48, 144–145; resilience, interpretation issues 70–73

European Union (EU), world power relations: AIIB membership 63–64; Asian trading strategy and geoeconomics 53–55; CETA with Canada 53, 54; China, investment negotiations 49; China's BRI, cooperation opportunities 61–62, 69; China's problematic policies, decisive strategy 50–52; foreign investment and economic vulnerability 49–50, 65n3; Middle East, diplomatic role 42, 91; multipolar world, US alliance and beyond 46–48; relations with Japan 53–54; Russian relations, "strategic patience" 57–60; Russian tailored sanctions 18, 57–58, 91; Russian threat reassessed 55–57; Trump's anti-free-trade agreement stance 37–38; Trump's unrationalised dealings 43–46, 141

Farrage, Nigel 13
Flynn, Michael 42, 44
Foch, Ferdinand 65n6
France: anti-IS coalition 77; Article 42.7, terrorism related activation 94–96, 101; Chinese investment concerns 50; EATC participation 117; Eurocorps 119; European Defence Community (EDC) 112; European defence operations 133; European Intervention Initiative 134; FCAS project 118; joint expeditionary force agreements, UK 133–134; Libyan security intervention 75, 106; "Maginot Complex" 48; Mali, security intervention 75, 80, 83; NATO relations 10; nuclear force under EU 110; PESCO implementation 123–124; Syrian war responses 42, 93; Tunisia and its security 17, 79–80

free-trade agreements (FTAs): CETA criticisms 54–55; EU and Asian trading strategy 53; EU/Canada CETA dispute 54; Trump's appraisal and protectionism 37–39, 47, 53

"frozen conflict" 59

Gaulle, Charles de 10, 36n4
geoeconomics 54
geopolitics and strategic thinking: democracy, imposition challenges 11, 30, 67–68; EU's dependence on NATO/US 9–10; EU's underestimation 8–9; *Global Strategy* 2016 priorities 33–34; populist influence 139–141; power politics and proxy wars 7–8; Russia's exclusivity, ex-Soviet regions 6–7; Ukraine, EU's trade agreement mistakes 5–7

Georgia: EU adoption challenges 15; EU non-exclusive relations 67–68; Russian backed divisions 7, 58

Germany: Chinese investment concerns 50; EATC participation 117; European Defence Community (EDC) 112; European defence operations 133; FCAS project 118; mutual assistance, UN in Mali 96; national military HQ 105; PESCO implementation 123–124; Trump's anti-free-trade discussions 37–38

global governance: EU's multilateral strategy 34–35; maritime access, safeguarding 87–88

Greece 102, 105, 114
Gulf Cooperation Council (GCC) 34

Hadi, Abdrabbuh Mansur 73
Haftar, Khalifa 81
Harmel, Pierre 9–10
Hollande, François 58
human rights: state violators, compromised relations 29, 71–72, 73; undemocratic

regimes, pragmatic response 23, 28–29; universal value 21–22
Hungary, populist influence 13, 141
Hussein, Saddam 44, 45

Iran: EU diplomatic relations 34, 42; Houthi support, Yemen 73, 90; security related sanctions 18–19; Syrian war involvement 77, 80, 90; US strained relations 34, 42, 45
Iraq: American invasion and crisis 42, 44, 45, 84, 96; democracy, imposition challenges 11
Islamic State (IS): anti-IS coalition strategy 86, 88–89; fighter's European alienation 9, 77, 95; Paris terrorism attacks 94–95; religious narrative 12; Syrian and Iraqi conflicts 77, 80
Israel 41
Italy: Chinese investment concerns 50; EATC participation 117; European Defence Community (EDC) 112; national military HQ 105; PESCO implementation 123–124; refugee and migration crisis 76

Japan, EU and US relations 53–54
Johnson, Boris 127
Judt, Tony 25
Juncker, Jean-Claude 121

Kelly, John 44
Khadafy, Muammar 18, 75–76, 88
Kim, Jung-Un 41
Kissinger, Henry 17, 22
Kosovo, NATO intervention 93
Kushner, Jared 44

Lebanon 91
Le Pen, Marie 56, 138
Libya: Arab Spring 11; destabilisation and spillover impacts 76–77, 88, 93; EU/NATO security intervention 75–76, 78, 84, 98–99, 106; Khadafy opposition, Western support 18; Russian interests 81; UN mandated R2P 75, 88, 91
Liddell Hart, Basil 145
Lukashenko, Aleksandr 15, 68
Luxembourg 112, 117, 119

Macron, Emmanuel: European Intervention Initiative 134; presidential election 138; Trump's anti-free-trade discussions 38; US/Iran relations 42
"Maginot Complex" 48

Magnette, Paul 54
Mali, security intervention 75, 79, 80, 83, 89
Malmström, Cecilia 49, 50
Malta 124
Marshall Plan 43
Mattis, James 44
May, Theresa 137
McMaster, Herbert 44
Merkel, Angela: Minsk Agreement 2015 58; Trump's anti-free-trade discussions 38; US/Iran relations 42
Middle East and Gulf States: anti-IS coalition 18, 77, 80, 86, 88–89; Arab Spring events 11, 17–18; EU as diplomatic broker 42, 91; geopolitical tensions 8, 9; Southern non-European states, cooperation issues 70–74; US policy, friends and foes 41–42, 45, 91; see also individual nation entries
Military Planning and Conduct Capacity (MPCC) 105
military power, European forces: Anti-Access/Area Denial (A2/AD) 86; Article 42.7, terrorism related activation 94–96, 101; Capacity-Building for Security and Development (CBSD) 83–84; Common Foreign and Security Policy (CFSP) 103; Common Security and Defence Policy (CSDP) 101, 102, 103, 132; deployment conditions and strategies 83–85; essential security 82; EU states, capabilities issues 99–100; EU Treaty obligations and amendments 111n2–3; EU-US alliance, operational options 109–110; *Global Strategy* 2016, priority tasks 85–86; Helsinki Headline Goal 97, 100–101; *human security*, civilian protection 84–85, 93; intelligence service gaps 96–97; internal security, EU responsibility 94–96; Military Planning and Conduct Capacity (MPCC) 105; minimal intervention, strategic reasoning 87–90; NATO/EU, operational contests 101–102; NATO/EU, operations and strategy differences 102–104; NATO headquarters, EU access 106–107; NATO's defence of Europe 94; NATO/US led Cold War 9–10, 82, 102, 110; nuclear deterrence 110; Operation Atalanta 87, 101, 132; power projection, expeditionary operations 97–98; risk assessment and war last resort 86–87; strategic autonomy, functions and relational operations 104–109; strategic

enablers, lack of 98–99, 107, 113; UN security commitments 91–92, 93
Minsk Agreement 2015 58, 91
Mogherini, Federica 14, 31–35, 85, 108–109
Moldova 15, 67–68
Mubarak, Hosni 17

nationalism, global spread 12–13
NATO: Aegean Sea operation 102; Allied Command Transformation (ACT) 107; authoritarian members and risks 140–141; EU interests insecure 47, 109, 141; Europe, armed defence and Article 5 94; formation conditions 127, 139–140; Kosovo intervention 93; Libyan security intervention 75–76, 98–99, 106; NATO Defence Planning Process (NDPP) 107; NATO/EU, operational contests 101–102; NATO/EU, operational relations 107–109; NATO/EU, operations and strategy differences 102–104; Russian threat reassessed 56–57; SHAPE operations 94, 106, 110; Trump's assessment 47; Turkey's selective membership 74; UK, post-Brexit role 130; Ukraine crisis 6; US led policy, Cold War Europe 9–10, 82, 102, 110; Wales Summit and budget agreements 113, 114
Netanyahu, Benjamin 41
Netherlands: anti-IS coalition 77; Belgian-Dutch naval cooperation 118–119; European Air Transport Command (EATC) 117; European Defence Community (EDC) 112; military capabilities 99
North Africa: Arab Spring events 11, 17; Egypt, post-Arab Spring alliances 18; Egypt's opposition movements, EU support 15–16, 17, 70; Libya, EU/NATO security intervention 75–76, 78, 84, 98–99, 106; Libyan intervention impacts 76–77, 81, 88, 93; Mali, security intervention 75, 79, 80, 83, 89; refugee and migration crisis 76, 88; Tunisia, Arab Spring and after 11, 17, 18, 76, 79–80
North American Free Trade Agreement (NAFTA) 38
North Korea, nuclear issue 41

Obama, Barack: AIIB, against membership 63; anti-IS coalition 18, 77; Syrian war responses 93; Trans-Pacific Partnership (TPP) 38–39
Operation Atalanta 87, 101, 132

Operation Sophia 76, 88
Orbán, Viktor 139, 143

Palmerston, Henry, Viscount 47
Pence, Michael 43
Permanent Structured Cooperation (PESCO) 123–125, 133
Philippines 51
Poland: NATO deployment 39, 56; populist influence 13, 141; Trump's unpredictable policies 44, 141
Pompeo, Mike 44
Portugal 139–140
Posen, Barry 47, 109
Putin, Vladimir: nationalist policies 13, 59; non-Russian intolerance 12, 62; populist influence 13; relations with Trump 42; Russian threat reassessed 56; Ukraine/EU relations opposition 5–6, 30, 59; *see also* Russia

realpolitik: concept 31; EU's approach, *Global Strategy* 2016 31–35
refugee and migration crisis: EU states' mixed response 12; limitation agreement with Turkey 72, 76; maritime Operation Sophia 76, 88; North African and Syrian exodus 76
resilience, EU's interpretation issues 33, 70–73, 78
Responsibility to Protect (R2P): human security, civilian protection 84–85, 91; Libya intervention mandate 75, 88, 91; principles 30
Rochau, Ludwig von 31–35
Russia: authoritarian nationalism 12; Eurasian Economic Union (EAEU) 68; EU relations, "strategic patience" 57–60; EU's tailored sanctions 18, 57–58, 91; exclusivity policy, ex-Soviet regions 6–7, 29–30, 56, 59, 68; geopolitical tensions with China 61–63; global threat reassessed 39; Libyan interests 81; Putin-Trump relations 42; Syrian war involvement 18, 42, 58, 77, 80, 93; threat to EU reassessed 55–57, 140; Ukraine/EU relations, Putin's opposition 5–6, 30, 59

Saakashvili, Mikheil 7
Sarkozy, Nicolas 10
Saudi Arabia: arms exports, EU's bargaining chip 73–74; EU as diplomatic broker 34; EU's compromised relations 17, 28–29, 71–72, 73; IS, changing policy 73–74;

regime's negative policies 19; Yemen war 73, 90
Schengen Agreement 16
Skripal, Julia 59–60
Skripal, Sergei 59–60
soft power 2, 25–26
Solana, Javier 8
South China Sea dispute 50–51
South Korea, Trump policy changes 41, 47
South Ossetia 58
sovereignty: democratic partners, military action 89; equality, pragmatic actions 29–30, 78; military sovereignty, EU states 115–116
Spain: EATC participation 117; Eurocorps 119; joins NATO and EEC 140; PESCO implementation 123–124
Stoltenberg, Jens 108
strategic enablers 98–99, 107, 116–117, 122–123
Syria: Arab Spring 11, 17; civilian protection, intervention dilemmas 92–93; EU diplomatic potential 34; multi-agenda war 76–77, 80–81, 90; political alliances/opposition 18, 58; refugee crisis 12, 76; Trump's military strategy 40, 42

Taiwan 40
terrorism: anti-terrorism, military actions 86, 88–89; Brussels attacks and intelligence gaps 96–97; domestic security 24; intelligence service cooperation 29; IS and Paris attacks 94–95
Tillerson, Rex 44
Trans-Pacific Partnership (TPP) 38–39, 52–53
Trump, Donald: anti-internationalist views 35; free-trade agreements and protectionism 37–39, 47, 129; Iran nuclear deal withdrawal 34, 42, 135; NATO budget contributions 113, 114; NATO, EU interests insecure 47, 109, 141; North Korea, crisis to meeting 41; populist influence 13; relations with Putin 42; Syrian war response 40, 42, 93; unpredictable and unrationalised policies 43–46, 130; unpredictable/unrationalised policies 141; Xi meeting and Chinese relations 40; *see also* United States (US)
Trump, Ivanka 44
Tsai, Ing-Wen 40
Tunisia: Arab Spring 11, 17; EU's hesitant support 18, 76, 79–80

Turkey: EU relations 72; Greece, bilateral disputes 102; Libyan security intervention 106; selective foreign policies 74
Tusk, Donald 108–109

Ukraine and EU relations: democracy, adoption challenges 11, 15, 19, 30, 67; EU trade agreement, political mistakes 5–7; NATO deployment 103–104; non-EU disinterest 60–61; post-Crimean annexation 57–58; Russia's geopolitical opposition 5–6, 56
United Kingdom (UK): Afghanistan, NATO response 94; "Anglosphere" relations 128; anti-IS coalition 77; Brexit referendum lies 139; Brexit, strategic illusions and realities 127–130; China, post-Brexit proposal 128; EU and foreign policy, post-Brexit 134–136; EU military HQ option, blocked 105, 106, 109, 133; European cooperation, post-war 127; European joint expeditionary force agreements 133–134; European military cooperation, post-Brexit 131–134; EU strategic partnership obstacles 137; Libya, security intervention 75; national military HQ 105; NATO, post-Brexit role 130; Skripal assassination plot 59–60; 'Special relationship' with US 126–127, 128–129, 130; Syrian war responses 42, 93; UKIP and Brexit 13
United Nations (UN): EU's security commitments 91–92; Mali and Libya, security interventions 75, 88; Responsibility to Protect (R2P) principle 30; Security Council and organisational value 64; UNIFIL, EU deployment 91; Universal Declaration of Human Rights 22
United States (US): Afghanistan invasion, post 9/11 89, 94, 96; anti-IS coalition 18, 77, 88–89; EU alliance of mixed interests 46–48, 79, 109; EU reliance in NATO operations 98–99, 106, 114; EU-US alliance, operational options 109–110; Grand Strategy to Asia and Chinese relations 38–40, 49, 51, 104; Iran nuclear deal withdrawal 34, 42, 135; Iraq invasion and crisis 42, 44, 45, 96; Middle East policy, friends and foes 41–42, 45, 91; National Security Strategy (NSS) 42; NATO and Cold War policies 9–10, 102; North Korea, crisis to meeting 41; protectionism impacts 38–39; relations with Japan 53–54, 63; Russian threat

reassessed 39; Saudi arms trade 73; South Korea, policy changes 47; 'Special relationship' with UK 126–127, 128–129, 130; Syrian war responses 40, 42, 93; Trump and NATO spending 113, 114; Trump and North Korea 41; Trump-Putin relations 42; Trump's anti-free-trade agreement stance 37–38, 45, 52–53; Trump's populist nationalism 13, 139; Trump's unpredictable/unrationalised policies 43–46, 130, 141

Western European Union (WEU) 127
Wilhelm II, Emperor 43–46

Xi, Jinping: authoritarian nationalism 12–13, 52; China's military strategy 39; Trump meeting and US relations 40

Yanukovych, Viktor 6
Yemen war 73, 90

"Zwischeneuropa" states and the EU 67–70